Economic Geography

This book series serves as a broad platform for scientific contributions in the field of Economic Geography and its sub-disciplines. *Economic Geography* wants to explore theoretical approaches and new perspectives and developments in the field of contemporary economic geography. The series welcomes proposals on the geography of economic systems and spaces, geographies of transnational investments and trade, globalization, urban economic geography, development geography, climate and environmental economic geography and other forms of spatial organization and distribution of economic activities or assets.

Some topics covered by the series are:

- Geography of innovation, knowledge and learning
- Geographies of retailing and consumption spaces
- Geographies of finance and money
- Neoliberal transformation, urban poverty and labor geography
- Value chain and global production networks
- Agro-food systems and food geographies
- Globalization, crisis and regional inequalities
- Regional growth and competitiveness
- Social and human capital, regional entrepreneurship
- Local and regional economic development, practice and policy
- New service economy and changing economic structures of metropolitan city regions
- Industrial clustering and agglomeration economies in manufacturing industry
- Geography of resources and goods
- Leisure and tourism geography

Publishing a broad portfolio of peer-reviewed scientific books *Economic Geography* contains research monographs, edited volumes, advanced and undergraduate level textbooks, as well as conference proceedings. The books can range from theoretical approaches to empirical studies and contain interdisciplinary approaches, case studies and best-practice assessments. Comparative studies between regions of all spatial scales are also welcome in this series. Economic Geography appeals to scientists, practitioners and students in the field.

If you are interested in contributing to this book series, please contact the Publisher.

More information about this series at http://www.springer.com/series/15653

Yi Liu

Local Dynamics of Industrial Upgrading

The Case of the Pearl River Delta in China

 Springer

Yi Liu
School of Tourism Management
Sun Yat-sen University
Guangzhou, China

ISSN 2520-1417 ISSN 2520-1425 (electronic)
Economic Geography
ISBN 978-981-15-4299-2 ISBN 978-981-15-4297-8 (eBook)
https://doi.org/10.1007/978-981-15-4297-8

This Springer imprint is published by the registered company Springer Nature Singapore Pte Ltd.
The registered company address is: 152 Beach Road, #21-01/04 Gateway East, Singapore 189721, Singapore

To my father Liu Liqiang
and mother Zhong Huiwen

Foreword

As the world economy is moving into a new decade of the 2020s, we are experiencing major transformations and challenges in the global geopolitical economy. One of the key issues at stake is economic globalization that has been underpinned by the emergence of global production networks in all sorts of industries and national economies since the 1990s. During the past two decades, China was one of the national economies that benefited much from its deepened participation in economic globalization. Its strategic coupling with the dynamics of global production networks has led to the rapid emergence of major economic corridors and high growth regions within its vast national territory. And yet not all regions and localities in China have gained equally from such coupling with globalization dynamics.

It is in this context of massive and unequal industrial transformation in China that this book makes a major contribution to the existing debates on industrial upgrading. Liu's careful approach to conceptualizing the different coupling mechanisms and their geographical implications for understanding industrial development in a particular high-growth region of China, the Pearl River Delta (PRD), is especially welcomed. His richly grounded empirical analysis not only eschews the general input–output approach in many sweeping economic studies of global value chains, but also compels us to focus more sharply on the economic actors who actually perform such upgrading and, in doing so, hold down both benefits and perils associated with economic globalization to their specific places and regions. To illustrate his actor-specific mechanisms of strategic coupling, Liu offers very useful in-depth material on electronics, apparel, and automotive—three major industries in the PRD that have been coupled differentially with global production networks.

At a more personal level, it gives me enormous pleasure to write this foreword to Liu's new book that is based on his doctoral work at the National University of Singapore. As his main thesis supervisor, I witnessed firsthand his tireless energy in both work and leisure! So it is a great outcome to see his ideas and hard work during doctoral research being further refined and developed into this book-length publication. This book will be an enduring contribution to our understanding of the dynamics of industrial transformation in China and serving as a useful guide for researchers and policy makers contemplating the role of global production networks in economic development in many different parts of the world. I am sure like me, you will find many instructive lessons to be learnt in this work.

January 2020

Henry Wai-chung Yeung
Distinguished Professor
National University of Singapore
Singapore, Singapore

Preface

Industrial upgrading is a non-stop episode between later-comer and advanced economies in our contemporary global economy. Some regions are catching up and chasing each other, while some are left behind and perished Living in the Pearl River Delta (PRD) in China, I have been worried by the question that how late-comer local firms in China can upgrade before those foreign firms decide to leave. This question spurred me to change my major from urban planning to economic geography while pursuing the Ph.D. degree.

Now, the answer is in this book. But unfortunately, there is no easy and quick solution for latecomer regions like the PRD to upgrade. Somewhere, later-comer economies can learn from previous experiences and bypass or even overtake; somewhere they have to pave their own paths; and somewhere surely fail. The earlier movers, earlier-mover firms, surely will not be waiting for their potential competitors to grow up without doing anything. In contrast, they will keep shaping their capabilities to secure their leading position. Hence from the perspective of geography, the trajectory of industrial upgrading is bounded to be a highly geographically variegated landscape across different regions. The key is to reveal in what spatial conditions, firms can better work with their foreign counterparts and upgrade.

Drawing upon a perspective of relational economic geography, the research question of this book is further detailed into how strategic coupling between late-comer regions and the global economy affects local industrial upgrading and how institutional and spatial conditions matter during the process of local upgrading. The central argument of this book is that latecomer regions strategically couple with the global economy in different ways which lead to dynamic outcomes of local upgrading. In order to explain the dynamics, this book conceptualizes a fourfold typology of strategic coupling including: *captive, cooperative, reciprocal, and absorptive coupling*. The variety results from different configurations of knowledge gaps and power relations between local firms and foreign firms. This book further argues that these knowledge gaps and power relations are not only influenced by inter-firm governance patterns but also subject to changing capabilities of local firms and institutional–spatial contexts in which they are embedded. The more developed synergy within strategic coupling is, the more upgrading will occur.

This book empirically investigates the development of the PRD from the 1980s to the 2000s to show that the region has been upgraded from an agricultural backwater into one of the worlds' leading manufacturing hubs. Starting with captive coupling, the PRD's regional trajectory of upgrading has gradually become divergent among different industries. In the electronics industry, the captive coupling has been developed and reinforced whereby foreign-invested enterprises (FIEs) dominate the pace of upgrading and the achievement of local upgrading is limited. In the apparel industry, the captive coupling has evolved into cooperative coupling in which local private enterprises have taken over the dominant role of FIEs and achieved substantial upgrading. In the automotive industry, the reciprocal coupling has been developed in the form of joint ventures between local state-owned enterprises and global automakers under strong national intervention. Process upgrading has been significantly achieved in the joint ventures and their local suppliers. This book has yet to identify the formation of absorptive coupling in the PRD, but it would probably be developed in the apparel industry in the future. The PRD case demonstrates that the domestic market, regional supply networks, and competitive dynamics within the global production networks (GPNs) are the most important assets for fostering local upgrading. Successful cases of local upgrading largely derive from the synthesis of various assets, rather than relying on one single type of assets.

Echoing with many studies in economic geography, international political economy, and development studies, this book aims to reveal the dynamic process of upgrading embedded in the global industrial shifts between the North and the South that beyond the explanation from mainstream economics. It would contribute to both the studies of industrial upgrading and GPNs. To the former, this book delineates how diverse geographical outcomes of industrial upgrading are produced by three key actors (foreign firms, local firms, and state institutions). This process cannot be simplified into a rigid trajectory or mystified as a secret that latecomer economies cannot know. To the later, this book theorizes the causality between strategic coupling and local upgrading on the basis of the case of the PRD. It provides a geographical reinterpretation for the studies of the global value chain (GVC) and offers a typology of strategic coupling as a critical complement to the framework of the GPNs. This book reminds policy makers of seeking for niche strategies by identifying multi-scalar conditions, rather than placing their hopes in some corner-cutting strategies, mathematic models or the helps from the global lead firms.

Guangzhou, China   Yi Liu

Acknowledgements

My deepest gratitude and thanks are given to my Ph.D. supervisor, Prof. Henry Yeung, for his endless patience, warmest care, insightful critiques, and enthusiastic encouragement that educate me to complete this research. I also give my honest thanks to A/P Godfrey Yeung at the National University of Singapore and A/P Jun Zhang who is previously at the National University of Singapore and currently in the University of Toronto, for their substantial helps in the past years to this book. I am grateful for the generous financial supports from the National University of Singapore for completing my fieldwork. My sincere appreciations are also given to my former teachers and classmates at Sun Yat-sen University who have provided substantial helps for my fieldworks, as well as all the interviewees who had unreservedly shared their experiences with me. The final editing helps from my students are also appreciated, including Huang Kaixuan, Pu Xueru, Meng Lingkun, Ji Jiehan, Cao Yihan, and Gao Feifan.

Finally, I am forever indebted to my family members, my parents, and my wife Zhang Yu, for their unfailing supports which make me strong and faithful to complete this study, particularly for my father who has been unable to witness the publication of this book.

Contents

Abbreviations

ATC	Agreement on Textiles and Clothing
CEPA	Closer Economic Partnership Arrangement
CKD	Complete knock-down
CM	Contract manufacturers
DRAM	Dynamic random access memory
EIAD	Electronics Industrial Association of Dongguan
EMS	Electronics manufacturing service
EPE	Export-processing enterprise
FAW	First Auto Work
FG	Flying geese
FIE	Foreign-invested enterprises
FSBF	Front-shop-back-factory
GAC	Guangzhou Automotive Corporation
GADA	Guangdong Apparel Designer Association
GAERI	Guangzhou Automotive Engineering Research Institute
GAIA	Guangdong Apparel Industrial Association
GAIG	Guangzhou Automotive Industrial Group
GDP	Gross Domestic Product
GHARI	Guangqi Honda Automobile Research Institute
GPN	Global production network
GVC	Global value chain
IC	Integrated circuit
ICT	Information and communication technology
IPR	Intellectual property right
IRB	Institutional Reviewing Board
IVA	Industrial value added
MFA	Multi-Fiber Agreement
NIE	Newly industrialized economy
NIS	National innovation system
OBM	Original branded manufacturer

ODM	Original design manufacturer
OEM	Original equipment manufacturer
PCB	Printed circuit board
PRD	Pearl River Delta
RCA	Revealed competitive advantage
REG	Relational economic geography
SFR	Small input, fast output, and rolling development
SKD	Semi-completely knock-down
SME	Small- and medium-sized enterprise
SOE	State-owned enterprises
SPS	Single-point supply
TNC	Transnational Corporation
TVE	Township and village enterprise

List of Figures

List of Tables

Chapter 1
Introduction

1.1 Thread of Industrial Upgrading in the Pearl River Delta

Industrial upgrading has been acknowledged as one of the most critical issues for latecomer firms to improve their competitiveness and succeed when they enter the global economy. As a latecomer region, the Pearl River Delta (PRD) in the People's Republic of China (hereafter China) has been integrated into the global economy since the national 'open-door' reform[1] in 1978. From 1979 to 2009, GDP in this region increased by about 15–17% annually (GDSY 2010).[2] This record has far surpassed that of the four Asian Dragons: Hong Kong, Singapore, South Korea, and Taiwan, which grew at around 7–8% per year during their economic takeoff in the 1960s and the 1970s. The PRD has thus been considered as the fifth Dragon (Clark and Kim 1993; Sung et al. 1995; Chui et al. 1997). However, whether the region has achieved industrial upgrading is in question. Are local firms upgraded or marginalized over time? How do they get upgraded or fail to upgrade? Theoretically, why should we study industrial upgrading in such a latecomer region and what have we not known yet? A recent episode helps contextualize the importance of these questions.

In February 2011, when Barack Obama met Silicon Valley's top luminaries in a dinner party in California, each guest was asked to come with a question for the President. But when Steven Jobs of Apple spoke, President Obama interrupted and asked a question of his own: 'what would it take to make iPhones in the United States?'

---

[1]It refers to the program of economic reforms called 'Socialism with Chinese characteristics' in China that were started in December 1978, by reformists within the Communist Party of China led by Deng Xiaoping.

[2]The GDP data are at current prices adjusted according to GDP index of Guangdong Province in statistics yearbook with 1980 as the base year.

© Springer Nature Singapore Pte Ltd. 2020
Y. Liu, *Local Dynamics of Industrial Upgrading*, Economic Geography,
https://doi.org/10.1007/978-981-15-4297-8_1

Mr. Jobs replied briefly and negatively: "Those jobs would not coming back." Eleven months after the meeting, a *New York Times* report entitled *How the U.S. Lost Out on iPhone Work* detailed the answer of Mr. Jobs (Duhigg and Bradsher 2012).[3] The report showed that lower wage was no longer the key reason that Apple's products had to be made overseas. It was the speed, flexibility, supply networks and a large amount of engineers (with more than high school but not necessarily a bachelor's degree) that the US plants could not match.

In the beginning of the 2000s, Apple products were largely made within the USA. But by 2004, Apple had turned to overseas manufacturing. By 2011, almost all of the 70 million iPhones, 30 million iPads, and 59 million other products Apple sold were manufactured outside the USA. The components of these products were procured from about 160 suppliers, many of which were located in Japan, Korea, Singapore, Taiwan, and China.[4] Eventually, these components were assembled by a few contract manufacturers (CMs), particularly by two Taiwanese firms—Foxconn and Quanta in the PRD.

Cited in the *New York Times* report, a former high-ranking Apple executive commented that 'the focus of Apple's works in Asia came down to two things: factories in Asia can scale up and down faster and Asian supply chains have surpassed what's in the U.S. The result is that we can't compete at this point'. The reason was also pointed out by another former high-ranking Apple executive that the whole supply chains are in China now and the speed and flexibility of Foxconn's manufacturing capabilities are 'breathtaking'. The comments imply that the story is not all about Foxconn, but also involves the supply chains and networks supporting Foxconn in the PRD.

When Apple delivered their orders to suppliers in Asia, Apple's American suppliers were also moving to Asia as well. Corning Inc. is an American-based supplier of Apple which manufactures large panes of strengthened glass. In the past few years, Corning had continued employing more than 1000 Americans to satisfy the flood of orders for iPhones. But Corning now has decided to establish new factories in South Korea and China. Hence, Corning could get closer to the assembly plant and save production and logistic costs; and more importantly get closer to its Asian clients which are imitating Apple by using large panes of strengthened glass from Corning. But this relocation did not guarantee Corning's success (Duhigg and Bradsher 2012).

A local firm in the PRD has been upgraded and is now challenging Corning's position. Competition has arrived from the Lens One Technology Co. (LOT) collocating with Foxconn in Shenzhen. The owner of the LOT is a Chinese engineer who has been working in the glass panes industry in the PRD for about twenty years. Before serving Apple, the LOT was making panes for watches, clockers, or components used in electronic products. By learning from Foxconn, the LOT has developed an

---

[3]The *New York Times* report on January 21, 2012, available at: http://www.nytimes.com/2012/01/22/business/apple-america-and-a-squeezed-middle-class.html?_r=2&ref=general&src=me&pagewanted=all.

[4]Apple's *Report of Supplier Responsibility* in 2011, available at: http://www.apple.com/supplierresponsibility/.

integrated production system in its relatively smaller industrial parks. Meanwhile, it has heavily invested in precision technologies in strengthened glass making and cutting. These efforts have qualified the LOT's competence. When Apple was developing iPhone 4, the LOT proactively contacted Apple and eventually won over large orders of strengthened glass from Corning. By the end of 2010, the LOT had made over 40 million pieces of glass for iPhone 4. Corning's managers complained that Chinese governments did everything for firms like the LOT and even subsidized all the R&D expenditures. This comment could be exaggerated, but the worry was true.[5]

While the *New York Times* report reflects the anxiety of the American President and manufacturers over the loss of competitiveness, the PRD's media and authorities also show great anxiety over the sustainability of the region. Since the mid-1980s, the PRD has been critiqued for over-dependence on labor-intensive industries and lacking in industrial upgrading (Liang 1989, 1999; Yan et al. 2008). Shenzhen's municipal leaders have repeatedly claimed that the city is facing four challenges of sustainability: land, energy, environment and population, and thus, they must promote industrial upgrading that may not favor labor-intensive firms like Foxconn.[6] A local news report argued that the PRD was seriously losing competitiveness due to raising labor wages and living costs.[7] One important sign is that Vietnam replaced the PRD as the largest subcontracting base for Nike's products in 2010. There are also new challenges to PRD's industrial growth, such as shortages of land resources, raising labor wages, environmental degradation, and increasing raw material costs (Huang and Chen 2009). All these problems point to industrial upgrading as an ultimate solution (Yu and Zhang 2009). Pressures for industrial restructuring and upgrading also increased after the string of suicides in Foxconn's industrial town in 2010.[8]

To mitigate these pressures of restructuring and upgrading, the Guangdong government has tried since the mid-2000s to transform the PRD from a low-cost manufacturing site into a high-end manufacturing zone. In 2008, a policy named 'dual transformation' was launched specifically for promoting regional upgrading.[9] It aims to relocate low-value-added industries from the PRD to peripheral areas within Guangdong Province and to attract higher-value-added industries and talents to the PRD. This policy is informally phased as the strategy of 'emptying the cage for

---

[5]Source of LOT's information: a Chinese news analysis from *21 Century Economic Broadcast* published on September 17, 2010, at: http://www.21cbh.com/HTML/2010-7-19/4MMDAwMDE4NzM4MQ_3.html.

[6]News reports from Shenzhen's official website, available at: http://www.sznews.com/zhuanti/content/2009-04/21/content_3710541.htm.

[7]*Yangchen Evening Paper*, news report on 4 July 2011, available at: http://news.iqilu.com/china/gedi/2011/0704/500882.html.

[8]The Foxconn suicides occurred between January and November, 2010, when eighteen Foxconn employees attempted suicide with fourteen deaths. See a detailed analysis on *Financial Times* by John Gapper on September 21, 2011, at: http://www.ft.com/intl/cms/s/0/9f0fb872-d88e-11e0-8f0a-00144feabdc0.html#axzz1lhi1lwn9.

[9]It means moving low skilled labor out and attracting new talents in. See: http://www.gd.gov.cn/gdgk/gdyw/201106/t20110617_144739.htm.

new birds'.[10] For the first time, industrial upgrading has officially become a regional political imperative. Although doubting 'where the new birds are', local cadres have actively enforced this policy. It is not only for the alleged 'good sake' of regional economy, but also for the advancement of local cadres' own political careers. By March 2011, official reports had asserted that the progress of regional upgrading was 'satisfactory'. Thirty-five funded industrial parks in Guangdong have been built in the past three years which accommodated about 2000 firms relocated from the PRD. These firms produced a total industrial output of 200 billion *yuan* in 2010. A large area of land was thus vacated to create space for establishing new industries, but the actual figure was not disclosed.[11]

The above episode implies that, during the restructuring of Apple's global production network, the PRD has improved its regional manufacturing capabilities by developing certain competitive edges beyond the advantages of lower wage costs. This improvement has enabled the region to manufacture some high value-added products like iPhone, rather than processing only cheap and undifferentiated components. However, this contrasting view of the competitiveness of the PRD has opened up some critical questions. How does the PRD manage to develop such competitiveness? Are foreign firms (e.g., Foxconn) the key contributors to this accomplishment? Is local upgrading (e.g., the LOT) significant? Do regional policies play a positive or negative role during the upgrading process?

A common thread of the above story is that industrial upgrading in the PRD is not a self-contain process within a single firm, but involves firms and non-firm actors at different time–space contexts. There are *foreign firms* like Apple's subcontractors, Foxconn and Corning that have further embraced developing regions as an important part of their business. There are *local firms* like the LOT that has experienced upgrading through working for foreign firms. There are also *proactive local and regional states* that try to accelerate the pace of regional upgrading by manipulating territorialized resources, such as land and policies. The engagement of these actors becomes as a critical context in which industrial upgrading turns out to be a complex and dynamic process beyond a simple mode or trajectory can represent. Will the engagement produce a different outcome of upgrading comparing with the circumstances in developed regions? How does this difference inform us about existing theories and research in economic geography? All these questions become my primary motivation for investigating into industrial upgrading in such a latecomer region in China.

---

[10]It means releasing lands from low value-added manufacturing to accommodate more high value-added industries (see http://www.gd.gov.cn/ghgy/ywsd/201108/t20110831_148650.htm).

[11]An official news report on the progress of regional upgrading, available at: http://www.gov.cn/jrzg/2011-03/25/content_1831697.htm.

1.2   Missing Links in the Theories of Industrial Upgrading

Industrial upgrading refers to a process that firms move from processing simple items to conducting higher-value-added activities in their portfolio of operations such as manufacturing complex parts and products, constructing integrated production systems, conducting research and development activities, brand creation, or marketing. Examining the progress of latecomer (local) upgrading is a critical issue because it determines whether a latecomer firm can sustainably survive in intensified global competition. If the firm fails to upgrade, it tends be marginalized at a truncated position making undifferentiated and low-value-added products. Sooner or later, it will be replaced by other low-cost producers.

There are generally four types of upgrading: product, process, functional, and sectoral upgrading (Humphrey and Schmitz 2002). The global value-chain (GVC) literature argues that the key mechanism of local upgrading is a process of knowledge diffusion from global lead firms to their suppliers. Global lead firms have dominant governance power in their value chains. They tend to offer limited upgrading opportunities in order to prevent nurturing suppliers that may mature and be their new competitors (Humphrey and Schmitz 2001; Gereffi et al. 2005). Under this arrangement of governance power, local firms may launch collective action to increase bargaining power or to pursue indigenous innovation in order to create their own knowledge with the help of state institutions (Viotti 2003; Schmitz 2004; Giuliani et al. 2005; Hobday and Perini 2005; Lundvall 2007). Is this the necessary destiny of latecomer firms in the pursuit of upgrading? By probing into both geographical and non-geographical studies, this book has identified some important missing links in the existing literature that can shed light on an alternative understanding of latecomer upgrading (Chap. 2).

Within the discipline of economic geography, there is a wide range of studies that have already documented industrialization, regional development, industrial clustering, global industrial shifts, and the changing geographies of production (see the series reviews in Yeung 2000; Yeung 2001, 2002; Bathelt 2003; Bathelt and Glückler 2005; Bathelt 2006; Reimer 2007). However, none of these analyses take industrial upgrading as the central analytical concern, but instead tackle some related issues such as learning, innovation, and industrial restructuring. They also do not bring together intra- and extra-forces that shape regional development to examine the process of upgrading in the context of global integration.

Beyond the discipline of geography, industrial economics, economic sociology, and development studies have paid tremendous attention to revealing the typologies, mechanisms, trajectories, and politics of upgrading with both empirical and theoretical depth (Gereffi 1999; Humphrey and Schmitz 2002b; Schmitz 2004; Gereffi et al. 2005; Giuliani et al. 2005; Ozawa 2005; Gereffi and Frederick 2010). However, these studies tend to hold a either firm-centric or state-centric view toward industrial upgrading and explain it under a rigid analytical trajectory. Scholars in the GVC literature argue that local upgrading is ultimately determined by the patterns of inter-firm governance whereby global lead firms define the extent of upgrading of their suppliers. Development studies keep emphasizing the role of states in promoting indigenous innovation against the control of lead firms. But in what ways will different inter-firm or firm–state relations impact local upgrading? More importantly, these studies have yet to acknowledge the influence of geographical factors, such as local (social or cultural) contexts, regional assets (labor, nature resources, and markets), and competitive dynamics in the global economy. In other words, this book finds that the analytical driver of the geography of industrial upgrading is unclear (Chap. 2). Geography here does not mean the spatial structure of industrial upgrading, but rather refers to the ongoing process in which multi-scalar forces produce an upgrading outcome under certain economic and institutional contexts. The synthesis of two different strands of literature above identifies two missing links.

First, in the context of a globalizing region, industrial upgrading is not a purely autonomous or self-contained action of a single firm, but should be related to the collective endeavor of a group of actors which are interconnected through the process of global integration. However, we have not known much about how different patterns of integration between latecomer regions and the global economy, would affect the outcomes of local upgrading.

Second, the earlier works have found the power asymmetry between lead firms and local suppliers within value chains, but these works have yet to recognize influences from the institutional and spatial contexts in which the value chains are embedded. These institutional–spatial conditions may underpin local firms and reshape their asymmetrical power relations. The power dynamics of local upgrading remains unclear.

How can these missing links be resolved? Apparently, we need a broader analytical framework that can incorporate the spatiality of value chain. For this purpose, this book draws upon an analytical framework in geographical studies which have identified the right balance of the internal and external forces that shape regional development in globalization (Henderson et al. 2002; Coe et al. 2004; Poon et al. 2006; Pike 2007). These efforts have conceptualized the integration between latecomer regions and the global economy as a process of *strategic coupling*, referring to 'a mutually dependent and constitutive process involving shared interests and cooperation between two or more groups of actors who otherwise might not act in tandem for a common strategic objective' (Yeung 2009: 332). This strategic coupling is considered as a key mechanism to the rapid growth of latecomer regions in East Asia in which local firms and nation-states coordinate, mediate, and arbitrage regional assets to meet TNCs' demands (Coe et al. 2004; Yang 2009; Yeung 2009). This concept enables this book to analyze both economic and institutional (political or social) influences from firms or non-firm actors (state institutions) in the process of local upgrading. However, its current conceptualization is a bit fuzzy. The typology of strategic coupling remains ambiguous, and we have not known sufficiently how local upgrading occurs in strategic coupling. Situated in such an intellectual context, my book attempts to fill in a theoretical gap in the understanding of the casual relations between strategic coupling and industrial upgrading.

1.3 A Relational Perspective on Industrial Upgrading

The key research question driving this study is how strategic coupling between late-comer regions and the global economy affects local upgrading. Drawing upon the empirical case of the PRD, the research objectives of this book are threefold. First, I examine how industrial upgrading takes place in the region through the process of strategic coupling and who the key drivers might be. Second, I identify the types and evolution of strategic coupling developed through multi-scalar forces. Finally, I elucidate the outcomes of local upgrading in relation to the variety of coupling as well as the alternative pathways of local upgrading under different institutional–spatial conditions.

The analytical tool this study deploys is a relational perspective in economic geography (see Chap. 3). The relational perspective focuses on the role of networks (actors and structures), relationality, and power relations between economic actors in shaping the organization of economic activities over places (Bathelt and Glückler 2003; Boggs and Rantisi 2003; Yeung 2005; Jones 2009; Bathelt and Glückler 2011). The process of upgrading is relational because when and where a firm decides to upgrade is subject to diverse influences embedded in intra-, inter-, and extra-firm relations. On the one hand, these relations provide various channels for firms to accumulate the necessary resources for upgrading. On the other hand, implementing an upgrading action may receive support or restriction from other stakeholders that may be suppliers, customers, strategic partners, or other institutional actors (e.g. governments). These relational features are not novel in economic geography, but my effort is to synthesize the role of these relational effects on local industrial upgrading.

The relational perspective serves this study in many ways. It highlights actor specificity, relationality, and the embeddedness of economic relations in institutional–spatial contexts. Hence, it enables this study to consider extra-firm influences together with inter-firm governance conceptualized in the GVC literature. Meanwhile, the relational perspective does not treat power in an absolute or pre-determined manner, but rather views it as a relational effect subject to different conditions or contexts embedded in economic, social, or political fabrics. More specifically, it is subject to the mutual interests and possessed resources of actors. In such a way, this perspective guides my study that considers the influences from multi-scalar forces and power dynamics among different actors for pursuing respective aims of upgrading. Adopting this perspective, however, we should be aware of two potential problems. On the one hand, networks per se do not lend to causal explanation. On the other hand, students of this perspective should avoid being preoccupied by an excessively micro-scalar analysis (see a detailed critique in Sunley 2008).

The central argument of this book is that industry upgrading in a globalizing region is mainly driven by strategic coupling which in turn is constituted by the interactive effects among local firms, foreign firms, and regional institutions. The upgrading outcomes depend on the evolutionary patterns and power dynamics of strategic coupling which means that the variety of coupling patterns and power relations within the coupling are the explanatory variables. The major theoretical contribution of this book is to theorize such a variety by conceptualizing a fourfold typology of strategic coupling and explain various outcomes of industrial upgrading accordingly. The typology includes *captive coupling, cooperative coupling, reciprocal coupling,* and *absorptive coupling.* This variety of strategic coupling is derived from the different configurations of technology and market gaps between local firms and foreign firms:

- When both technology and market gaps are large, *captive coupling* tends to be developed in which foreign firms fully control local upgrading. The deeper local firms are captive to foreign partners, the faster will the upgrading be facilitated.
- When technology gap becomes small but market gap is still large, *cooperative coupling* is formed through which local firms work for foreign firms under moderate power relations. The more developed are their complementarity and mutual interests, the higher is the potential for upgrading.
- When market gap becomes small but technology gap remains large, *reciprocal coupling* can be developed. Firms couple for exchanging technology and market resources possessed exclusively by each partner. Under this nuanced situation, the more balanced are power relations, the more synergy is there for upgrading.
- When both gaps are small, *absorptive coupling* can possibly take place in which local firms work with foreign firms to absorb knowledge and implement local upgrading autonomously. The more capable are local firms of multi-tasking within GPNs, the more will upgrading occur.

The primary concern of local firms is to reduce the gaps with foreign firms so that they can move away from captive coupling and eventually achieve absorptive coupling. However, as interpreted in the last section, previous studies mainly believe that lead firms have overwhelming power in defining the pattern of governance and the gaps (Bair 2005; Gereffi et al. 2005; Pietrobelli and Rabellotti 2011). Local firms have little power to bargain with lead firms, unless they invest heavily in indigenous innovation or launch joint actions (Clark and Kim 1995; Hobday 1995; Schmitz 1999, 2004; Giuliani et al. 2005). Contrary to this over-deterministic view of governance and upgrading, this book offers an alternative understanding by examining the casual relations between coupling and upgrading.

Although the governance pattern is defined and enforced by global lead firms, local firms may mobilize resources embedded within specific institutional–spatial contexts to leverage the control of lead firms. This local initiative does not necessarily challenge the power of lead firms. In contrast, local firms may bypass the power or even foster more synergy with lead firms. Hence, lead firms may be willing to share or co-develop knowledge with local firms. Therefore, although the pattern of industrial governance does not change, local firms may be able to develop different types of strategic coupling, thus achieving various forms of industrial upgrading, particularly functional upgrading. The possibility depends on the availability of assets at different scales (local, regional, national, and global). This is the general mechanism upgrading that this book aims to exemplify.

There are two main empirical tasks for this study to accomplish: (1) to examine the formation of strategic coupling in the PRD and the correspondent outcomes of upgrading; (2) to identify the institutional–spatial conditions that enable local firms to leverage the governance power of lead firms. In doing so, this book contributes to the field of economic geography and studies of globalization by three ways (see details in Chap. 8). First, the book advances the school of relational economic geography by theorizing the typology of strategic coupling in a coherent and logical reasoning, rather than based on empirical conclusion. Second, this book offers a more realistic perspective for understanding the geography of industrial upgrading and the rise of some latecomer firms which the GVC literature cannot explain. Last but not least, this book offers alternative strategies of upgrading beyond the limited options provided in the governance literature and development studies.

1.4   Empirical Contexts of the Case

The empirical case study place of this book locates in the PRD in South China. It is the largest alluvial delta in Guangdong Province in China (see Fig. 1.1). In 1985, the PRD area was officially named as an economic-open zone with specific economic privileges, including 4 cities and 13 counties. In 1994, the PRD was extended to nine cities and six counties. The Greater-PRD (GPRD) was conceptualized later referring to the PRD plus Hong Kong and Macao. In 2003, Guangdong provincial governments proposed a concept of the 'Pan-Pearl River Delta' (PPRD) to represent a much broader economic area which includes eight provinces, one autonomous region, Hong Kong, and Macau which are connected by the drainage area of the Pearl River. In this book, the PRD only refers to its economic definition as the area of the Delta in

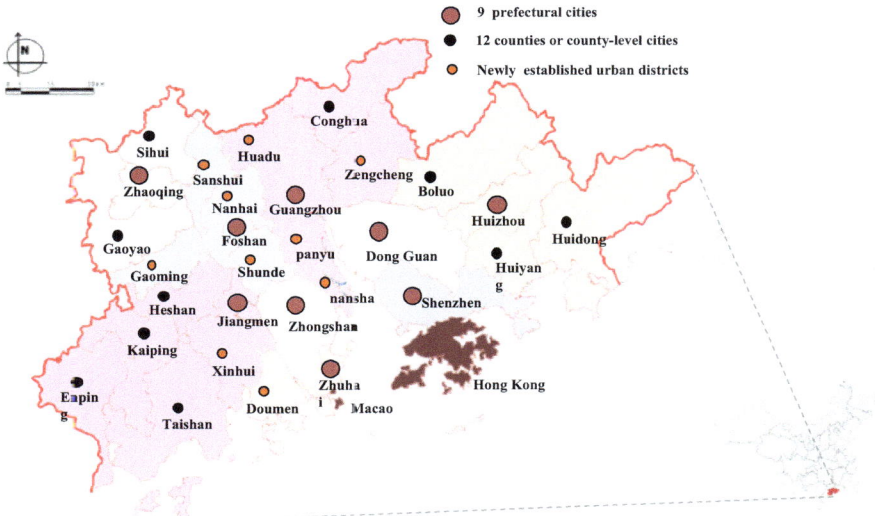

Fig. 1.1 Location of the Pearl River Delta in China

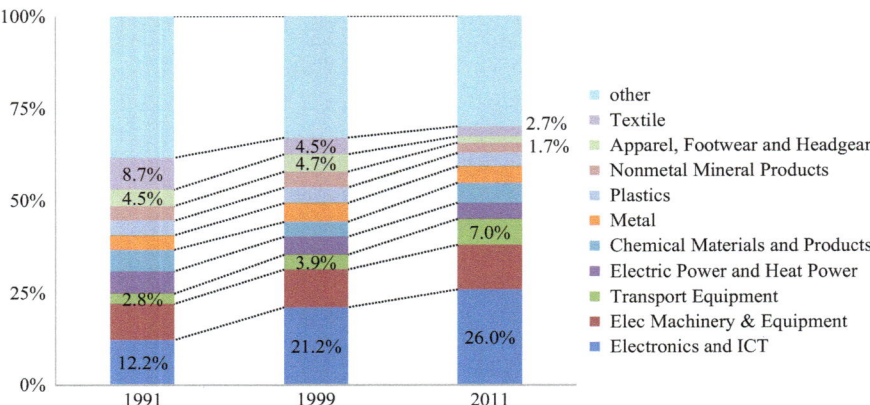

Fig. 1.2 Changing industrial structure of the PRD (1991–2009). *Note* In percentage of total industrial output (Guangdong Statistic Yearbook in 1992, 2000, and 2010)

1994. After rounds of adjusting administrative divisions, the PRD currently includes nine cities and ten counties with an area of 41,698 km^2 (see Fig. 1.2).

The PRD had a long tradition as a national window of foreign trading for hundreds years due to its geographical location: close to Southeast Asia and far from the political center of China. It was a national foreign trading port and also the origin of the Chinese diaspora widely scattered in North America, Europe, and South East Asia (Skinner 1985; Johnson and Peterson 1999; Cartier 2001; Lin 2004). However, during the period of Mao Zedong (1949–1976), the PRD was disfavored by the central government in terms of state investments and other preferential industrial policies. The main reason was because of its location at a vulnerable costal frontier with undesirable proximity to the capitalist's enclaves of Hong Kong and Macao. Moreover, this region lacked basic industrial and natural resources to support heavy industries which were selected as strategic industries in national development schemes at that time (Yang 1990). From 1949 to 1979, state-owned enterprises (SOEs) in Guangdong only received 2.2% capital investments from the central government (Sit and Yang 1997: 195). These deliberate policy actions of the central government resulted in the PRD's lack of regional assets, such as a strong industrial base, at the eve of the open-door reform in 1978.

After 1978, the central state strategically turned to reshape the PRD into a vanguard of China's national economy for export-orientated industrialization. Most of the marketization policies were implemented here first and then transferred to inner regions once the policies worked well (Enright et al. 2005; Wu 2005).

At a national scale, instead of giving financial or material supports, China's post-reform regime gave the PRD greater leeway than its peer regions to practice market forces, attract foreign direct investment (FDI), and promote exports, thus integrating with the global economy. This institutional leeway satisfied both the interests of local initiatives and global capitalists so that they could practice capitalism without

Table 1.1 'Lead One Step Ahead' policy framework (Chen and Pu 1999; Vogel 1989; Sung et al. 1995)

Category	Contents
Five-year fiscal plan	• Fixed sum of 1 billion *yuan* per year, while all the remaining revenues are kept for its own use • Self-reliant in respect of investment • A bigger share of foreign exchange earnings • Renewed annually with minor changes
Power decentralization	• Greater planning power at provincial level • Allowed to access the global economy via Hong Kong connections; greater authority to approve foreign investment projects
Special economic zones	• Shenzhen and Zhuhai • Lower taxation for foreign firms • Larger jurisdiction in policy reform
Financial system	• Allowed to set up independent provincial investment company, greater authority in commerce
Labor	• Greater power in labor management including reforming its labor system and the power to raise bonuses above the national level
Price system	• Greater power in pricing at provincial and urban levels
Corporation	• Encouraging the development of township–village enterprises

violating relevant laws about public ownership in China (Xu 1988; Chen and Pu 1999; Enright et al. 2003). This national liberalization policy was framed as the 'Lead One Step Ahead' policy and resulted in a specific form of 'Red Capitalism' in China in which market logics of capitalism were practiced in the name of market socialism (Vogel 1989; Lin 1997). As shown in Table 1.1, the liberalization policy decentralized great autonomous power to Guangdong, particularly to the PRD in a very flexible manner, such as the central-local fiscal arrangement (Sung et al. 1995).

Another reason for the PRD to be chosen for economic reform is its geographical location and underdeveloped industries base. As locating far away from the political center, which was regarded as a disadvantage before the opening reform, the PRD was considered as an appropriate place for practicing marketization within the socialist state of China. Any possible failure of the reform within this region would not generate devastating effects on the mainstay of China's economy. The region also has geographical proximity to the capitalists' enclaves of Hong Kong and Macao located in the edges of the PRD. This locational advantage makes it easier to attract foreign investments. The insignificance of the PRD's industrial base was also an advantage. Because the PRD almost had no heavy or complex industries, attracting foreign investments would not create much pressure for local economic restructuring. Moreover, to a certain degree, the PRD is not as indispensable as other regions, such as the Yangzi River Delta which was regarded as the economic center of China, the industrial heartland in Northeast China (e.g., heavy industrial base in Manchuria), and even the inland industrial base in Southwest China (Xu and Li 1990). Apart from these institutional and geographical factors, the existing overseas social connections also served as a regional asset that facilitated the industrialization of the PRD. These connections had been constrained before 1978. Encouraged by both central and local authorities, these social networks had effectively brought in foreign investments after the 1978 reform. These investments were mediated by oversea Chinese residing mainly in Hong Kong, Taiwan, Southeast Asia and North America (Sung et al. 1995; Hsing 1996; Lin 1997).

After three decades of rapid industrialization, the PRD was transformed from an agricultural backwater into one of the world's leading manufacturing hubs. Dozens of industrial clusters have been developed in various sectors, such as electronics, home appliances, telecommunication equipment, toys, automobile, watches and clocks, textile, apparel, footwear, plastics products, and ceramics (Sung et al. 1995; Enright et al. 2005).

The achievement of industrial growth is significant. Indicators in Table 1.2 show that the PRD has become a frontier of the national economy. In terms of GDP, the PRD's share in Guangdong Province increased from 48% in 1980 to 86% in 2015 and from 2.6 to 9.1% share in China. During this process, the PRD served a key platform of foreign investment and trading of the country. Most of the foreign investments of Guangdong agglomerated in the PRD: from 41% in 1980 to 90% in 2009. The tendency of export-oriented industrialization was clear. The export value of the PRD sharply increased in the past decades. By 2015, the PRD had accounted for almost the entire export (95%) of the province and some 27% of the national export value at the same time.

Along with the remarkable economic growth, the industrial structure of the PRD has been changed in favor of industries with higher value added, such as information and communication technology, electronic machinery and equipment, electronics and transportation equipment (see Fig. 1.2). During the 1980s, the PRD mainly relied on light and traditional manufacturing industries to kick-start industrialization such as the textile, apparel, footwear, toy, or electronics industries. Since 1990s, three key industries showed the tendency of regional restructuring and sectoral upgrading. As the cornerstone of the regional economy, the electronics industry (including electronics product, ICT, and electronic machinery) became more dominant over time. Its regional share grew continuously from 22% in 1991 to 38% in 2009. Meanwhile, the influence of traditional industries (textile and apparel) was reducing. Their regional shares of industrial output decreased from 13% in 1991 to 5% in 2009. In contrast to this decline, the transport equipment industry achieved the most significant growth from 2.8% in 1991 to 7% in 2009. The growth of this industry was mainly contributed by the rise of the automotive industry through specific national support (see details in Chap. 7). Apart from these three major industries, some new- or high-tech industries were emerging in the region as well, such as aerospace, biomedical, nuclear power equipment, green energy (solar energy photovoltaic and wind power), and environmental protection. The total industrial output of these industries reached 400 billion *yuan* in 2008 (GDEIC 2010).

The above aggregate empirical data point to industrial upgrading in the PRD. Previous studies have offered some reasons for industrial growth, such as the importance role of foreign investments, economic decentralization from the central government,

Table 1.2 Economic profile of the PRD in China (Guangdong Statistic Yearbook in 2010, 2001, and 1995; the Pearl River Delta and the Yangzi River Delta Statistic Yearbook 2010; National Statistic Yearbook of China in 2009, 2001, 2011, and 2016)

Items	PRD	Percentage of GD (%)	Percentage of China (%)
Land area (km^2)	54,733	30	0.57
GDP (billion, yuan)			
1980	12	48	2.6
1990	101	65	5.4
2000	842	78	8.5
2010	3740	82	9.1
2015	6227	86	9.1
Utilized foreign investments (billion, USD)			
1980	0.1	46	4.8
1990	1.3	61	12
2000	10.4	72	17
2010	18.3	51.8	17.3
2015	25.7	47.9	20.3
Export value (billion, USD)			
1980	0.6	28	3.4
1990	18	80	29
2000	85	92	34
2010	431.8	95.3	27.4
2015	608	94.5	26.8
Total population (million, persons)			
1990	23.7	40	2.1
2000	42.9	57	3.3
2010	56.1	53.7	4.2
2015	58.7	54.1	4.3
Total employed labor (million, persons)			
2000	19.1	48	2.6
Total retail sales of consumer (billions, yuan)			
2010	1297.8	74.5	8.3
2015	2252	71.9	7.5

and the land reform policy (Sit and Yang 1997; Shen et al. 2000; Yeh et al. 2006; Lin 2009). But these studies have not really considered the issue of industrial upgrading.

According to Yeung (2009: 328), 'East Asian experiences in regional development should be understood in its historical and geographical contexts, primarily because of the simultaneous presence of three key ingredients—local firms (public or private), developmental state institutions (often at the national level), and lead firms in GPNs.'

These three ingredients (actors) are not unique, but they occur in different historical moments in developed regions in Western Europe and North America. To this point, the standard analytical toolkit in the previous literature of economic geography is insufficient to explain the dynamics in the PRD. The PRD does not own promising regional/relational assets which have sustained industrial upgrading and growth in developed regions, such as thick institutional networks (Amin and Thrift 1994), abundant associational economies (Cooke and Morgan 1998), strong untraded interdependencies (Storper 1997), regional innovation systems (Cooke et al. 1997; Scott 1998), or regional learning networks (Morgan 1997; Hudson 1999; Hassink 2005).

What then are the regional assets that the PRD's firms deploy in their pursuit of upgrading? What would the local upgrading trajectories be? Compared with Asian NIEs which went through rapid industrialization in an earlier stage (White 1988; Beeson 2004), will the PRD case offer a different story or new theoretical insights in terms of upgrading studies? Bearing these questions in mind, this book considers the PRD as an appropriate case. The region deserves more scrutiny of its dynamics of industrial upgrading.

1.5 Book Structure

The book is organized into nine chapters. This chapter has provided an overview of the research questions, objectives, and the intellectual contexts of the book. The empirical field has also been introduced. Chapter 2 critically reviews the multi-disciplinary base of literature on industrial upgrading, including economic geography, economic sociology, industrial economics, development studies, and business studies. This effort shows why studying upgrading through an economic geographical perspective is necessary.

Chapter 3 proceeds with a new theoretical framework drawing upon the GPN studies derived from relational economic geography. I elaborate on the formation, typology and power dynamics of strategic coupling and how the variety of coupling produces the dynamics outcomes of upgrading.

As the first empirical chapter, Chap. 4 examines the extent of industrial upgrading and the formation and transformation of strategic coupling in the PRD. This work shows how huge knowledge gaps and highly asymmetrical power relations form captive coupling in the 1980s. Since 1980s, the PRD has started to move away from captive coupling. This tendency is illustrated by the divergent performances of key actors, changing trading partners, the fading role of Hong Kong firms and emerging new regional assets in the PRD.

The main empirical analysis of this book is developed in Chaps. 6–8 which delineate different scenarios of strategic coupling and the correspondent outcomes of upgrading. These empirical chapters examine three key industries that represent regional industrial change: electronics, apparel, and automotive (see Sect. 1.4). The constellation of these industries demonstrates upgrading through different industrial specificities in terms of knowledge complexity (from low to high), industrial organizations (from simple to sophisticated), and governance types (from relational to modular).

Chapter 5 is about the electronics industry in which local firms and TNCs constitute to the main story. The chapter begins with a discussion of the global industrial tendency and the features of modular governance in the electronic industry. The central analysis rests in the formation and retention of captive coupling in this industry. This phenomenon is explained by the knowledge gaps, strategies, and power relations between foreign firms and local firms under the modular governance. By demonstrating three case studies, this chapter shows various local upgrading strategies in captive coupling and the potential formation of cooperative coupling.

While captive coupling is reinforced in the electronics industry, Chap. 6 delineates an impressive scenario of local upgrading in the apparel industry. The analytical focus is placed on how local firms manage to move away from captive coupling toward cooperative coupling. Two industrialized towns and two local firms are used to illustrate this upgrading trajectory. It further explains why changing power relations and synergy within cooperative coupling is the key to understand local upgrading trajectories that constitute the 'changing rules of the game'.

Different with previous two chapters, Chap. 7 tackles the automotive industry where firm–state relationships are the primary determinant of industrial upgrading. These firm–state relationships are essential to the formation of reciprocal coupling. By interpreting the current debate, this chapter examines the role of state power and corporate power in the automotive industry. It shows how reciprocal coupling is formed in the automotive industry in the PRD based on the interplay among strong interventions from Chinese central state, proactive SOEs and global lead firms (automakers). Drawing upon a comparative study between two joint ventures, this chapter demonstrates how synergy is better developed within a balanced power relation and how it influences local upgrading within the joint ventures and their regional supply networks.

As a conclusion, Chap. 8 provides a heuristic summary of key findings, academic contributions, and policy implications of this study. It then points out the main accomplishments and limitations of this study. Finally, a research agendum is discussed for future investigation.

References

Amin, A., & Thrift, N. (1994). Globalization and regional development. *Ponte, 50*(7-8), 67–81.

Bair, J. (2005). Global capitalism and commodity chains: Looking back. *Going Forward. Competition and Change, 9*(2), 153–180.

Bathelt, H. (2003). Geographies of production: Growth regions in spatial perspective I-innovation, institutions and social systems. *Progress in Human Geography, 27,* 763–778.

Bathelt, H. (2006). Geogrpahies of production: Growth regimes in spatial perspective III-toward a relaticnal view of economic action and policy. *Progress in Human Geography, 30*(2), 223–236.

Bathelt, H., & Glückler, J. (2003). Toward a relational economic geography. *Journal of Economic Geography, 3*(2), 117–144.

Bathelt, H., & Glückler, J. (2005). Resources in economic geography: from substantive concepts towards a relational perspective. *Environment and Planning A, 37*(1), 1545–1563. https://doi.org/10.1068/a37109.

Bathelt, H., & Glückler, J. (2011). *The relational economy: Geographies of knowing and learning.* New York: Oxford University Press.

Beeson, M. (2004). The rise and fall (van Diermen) of the developmental state: The vicissitudes and implications of East Asian interventionism. In L. Low (Block). *Developmental states: relevancy, redundancy or reconfiguration?* (pp. 29–40). New York: Nova Science Publishers.

Boggs, J. S., & Rantisi, N. M. (2003). The 'relational turn' in economic geography. *Journal of Economic Geography, 3*(2), 109–116.

Cartier, C. (2001). *Globalizing South China.* Oxford: Blackwell.

Chen, J., & Pu, X. (Eds.). (1999). *'The fifty years of Guangdong'—Official statistics report of Guangdong Provincial Government (in Chinese).* Beijing: China Statistics Press.

Chui, S. W.-K., Ho, K.-C., & Lui, T.-L. (1997). *City-states in the global economy: Industrial restructuring in Hong Kong and Singapore.* Boulder: Westview Press.

Clark, G. L., & Kim, W. B. (1993). Industrial restructuring and regional adjustment in the Asian NIEs. *Environment and Planning A, 25*(1), 1–4.

Clark, G. L., & Kim, W. B. (1995). *Asian NIEs and the global economy: Industrial restructuring and corporate strategy in the 1990s.* The Johns Hopkins University Press.

Coe, N., Hess, M., Yeung, H. W.-C., Dicken, P., & Henderson, J. (2004). 'Globalizing' regional development: a global production networks perspective. *Transactions of the Institute of British Geographers, 29*(4), 468–484.

Cooke, P., Gomez Uranga, M., & Etxebarria, G. (1997). Regional innovation systems: Institutional and organisational dimensions. *Research Policy, 26*(4-5), 475–491.

Cooke, P., & Morgan, K. (1998). *The associational economy. Firms, regions, and innovation.* Oxford: Oxford University Press.

Duhigg, C., & Keith, B. (2012). "How the U.S. Lost Out on iPhone Work". In New York Times. New York.

Enright, M. J., Chang, K. M., Scott, E. E., & Zhu, W. (2003). Hong Kong and the Pearl River Delta: The economic Interaction. Hong Kong: The 2022 Foundation.

Enright, M. J., Scott, E. E., & Chang, K. M. (2005). *Regional powerhouse: The Greater Pearl River Delta and the rise of China.* Singpore: Wiley.

GDEIC. (2010). *Twelve five-year plan development planning of the strategic and new industries in Guangdong (in Chinese).* Guangzhou: Guangdong Economic and Informatization Commission.

GDSY. (1995). *Guangdong statistical yearbook 1995 (in Chinese).* Beijing: Guangdong Provincial Burenu of Statistics.

GDSY. (2001). *Guangdong statistic yearbook (in Chinese).* Beijing: Guangdong Provincial Burenu of Statistics.

GDSY. (2010). *Guangdong statistic yearbook (in Chinese).* Beijing: Guangdong Provincial Burenu of Statistics.

Gereffi, G. (1999). International trade and industrial upgrading in the apparel commodity chain. *Journal of International Economics, 48*(1), 37–70.

Gereffi, G., & Frederick, S. (2010). The global apparel value chain, trade and the crisis: Challenges and opportunities for developing countries. In O. Cattaneo, G. Gereffi, & C. Staritz (Eds.), *Global value chains in a postcrisis world.* Washington, DC: Worldbank.

Gereffi, G., Humphrey, J., & Sturgeon, T. (2005). The governance of global value chains. *Review of International Political Economy, 12*(1), 78–104. https://doi.org/10.1080/09692290500049805.

Giuliani, E., Pietrobelli, C., & Rabellotti, R. (2005). Upgrading in global value chains: Lessons from Latin American clusters. *World Development, 26*(2), 549–573. https://doi.org/10.1016/j.worlddev.2005.01.002.

Hassink, R. (2005). How to unlock regional economies from path dependency? From learning region to learning cluster. *European Planning Studies, 13*(4), 521–535. https://doi.org/10.1080/09654310500407134.

Henderson, J., Dicken, P., Hess, M., Coe, N., & Yeung, H. W.-C. (2002). Global production networks and the analysis of economic development. *Review of International Political Economy, 9*(3), 436–464. https://doi.org/10.1080/09692290210150842.

Hobday, M. (1995). East-Asian latecomer firms—Learning the technology of electronics. *World Development, 23*(1), 1171–1193.

Hobday, M., & de Barros Perini, F. A. (2005). *Latecomer entrepreneurship: A policy perspective* (pp. 17–19). Paper presented at the IPD Task Force Meeting, Rio de Janeiro, Brazil.

Hsing, Y.-T. (1996). Blood, thicker than water: interpersonal relations and Taiwanese investment in southern China. *Environment and Planning A, 28*(12), 2241–2261.

Huang, Y., & Chen, S. (2009). Crisis of industrialization in the Pearl River Delta. *EAI Background Brief No. 444*. Singapore: East Asia Institute.

Hudson, R. (1999). The learning economy, the learning firm and the learning region: A sympathetic critique of the limits to learning. *European Urban and Regional Studies, 6*(1), 59–72.

Humphrey, J., & Schmitz, H. (2001). Governance in global value chains. *Ids Bulletin-Institute of Development Studies, 32*(3), 19–36.

Humphrey, J., & Schmitz, H. (2002). How does insertion in global value chains affect upgrading in industrial clusters? *Regional Studies, 36*(1), 1017–1027. https://doi.org/10.1080/0034340022000022198.

Johnson, G. E., & Peterson, G. G. (1999). *Historical dictionary of Guangzhou (Canton) and Guangdong*. Lanham, Md: Scarecrow Press.

Jones, M. (2009). Phase space: Geography, relational thinking, and beyond. *Progress in Human Geography, 33*(4), 487–506.

Liang, J. Q. (1989). Industrial upgrading: An emergent but difficult issue (in Chinese). *Special Zone Economy (Te Qu Jing Ji), 5*(15), 1–16.

Liang, G. L. (1999). Development of integrated circut industry in china (in Chinese). *Electronic Chemicals, 10*, 6–9.

Lin, G. C. S. (1997). *The red capitalism in South China: Growth and development of the Pearl River Delta*. Vancouver: UBC Press.

Lin, G. C. S. (2004). Toward a post-socialist city? Economic tertiarization and urban reformation in the Guangzhou metropolis, China. *Eurasian Geography and Economics, 45*(1), 18–44.

Lin, G. C. S. (2009). *Developing China: Land, politics, and social conditions*. London: Routledge.

Lundvall, B. Å. (2007). National innovation systems—Analytical concept and development tool. *Industry and Innovation, 14*(1), 95–119.

Morgan, K. (1997). The learning region: Institutions, innovation and regional renewal. *Regional Studies 31*(5), 491–503.

Ozawa, T. (2005). *Institutions, industrial upgrading, and economic performance in Japan—the 'Flying-Geese' paradigm of catch-up growth*. Northampton, Massachusetts: Edward Elgar.

Pietrobelli, C., & Rabellotti, R. (2011). Global value chains meet innovation systems: Are there learning opportunities for developing countries? *World Development, 39*(1), 1261–1269.

Pike, A. (2007). Editorial: Whither regional studies? *Regional Studies, 41* 1), 1143–1148.

Poon, J. P. H., Hsu, J.-Y., & Jeongwook, S. (2006). The geography of learning and knowledge acquisition among Asian latecomers. *Journal of Economic Geography 6*(4), 541–559. https://doi.org/10.1093/jeg/lbi021.

Reimer, S. (2007). Geographies of production I. *Progress in Human Geography, 31*(2), 245–255. https://doi.org/10.1177/0309132507075373.

Schmitz, H. (1999). Collective efficiency and increasing returns. *Cambridge Journal of Economics, 23*(4), 465–483.

Schmitz, H. (2004). *Local enterprises in the global economy*. UK: Edward Elgar.

Scott, A. J. (1998). From silicon valley to hollywood: Growth and development of the multimedia industry in California. In H. J. Braczyk, P. Cooke, & M. Heidenreich (Eds.), *Regional innovation systems: The role of governances in a globalized world* (pp. 136–162). New York: UCL Press.

Shen, J. F., Wong, K.-Y., Chu, K.-Y., & Feng, Z. Q. (2000). The spatial dynamics of foreign investment in the Pearl River Delta, south China. *The Geographical Journal, 166*(4), 312–322.

Sit, V. F.-S., & Yang, C. (1997). Foreign-investment-induced exo-urbanisation in the Pearl River Delta, China. *Urban Studies, 34*(4), 647–677.

Skinner, G. W. (1985). Presidential address: The structure of Chinese history. *Journal of Asian Studies, 44,* 271–292.

Storper, M. (1997). *The regional world: Territorial development in a global economy.* London and New York: Guilford Press.

Sung, Y. W., Wong, R. Y.-C., & Lau, P. W. (1995). *The fifth dragon: The emergence of the pearl river delta.* Singapore: Longman.

Sunley, P. (2008). Relational economic geography: A partial understanding or a new paradigm? *Economic Geography, 84*(1), 1–26.

Viotti, E. B. (2003). National learning systems: A new approach on technological change in late industrializing economies and evidences from the cases of Brazil and South Korea. *Technological Forecasting and Social Change, 69*(1), 653–680.

Vogel, E. (1989). *One step ahead in China: Guangdong under reform.* Cambridge, MA: Harvard University Press.

White, G. (Block). (1988). *Developmental states in East Asia.* New York: St. Martin's Press.

Wu, J.-L. (2005). *Understanding and interpreting Chinese economic reform.* Singapore: Thomson/South-Western.

Xu, X. Q. (1988). Accelaration of urbanization in the Pearl River Delta through the opening reform (in Chinese). *Journal of Geography, 43*(3), 201–210.

Xu, X. Q., & Li, S. M. (1990). China's open door policy and urbanization in the Pearl River Delta region. *International Journal of Urban and Regional Research, 14*(1), 49–69.

Yan, X. P., Lin, G., J., P., & Zhou, R. B. (2008). Industrial upgrading and international competitiveness of the Greater Pearl River Delta (in Chinese). *Journal of Economic Geography in China (Jing Ji Di Li), 27*(1), 927–978.

Yang, D. (1990). Patterns of China's regional development strategy. *The China Quarterly, 122*(1), 230–257. https://doi.org/10.1017/s0305741000008778.

Yang, C. (2009). Strategic coupling of regional development in global production networks: Redistribution of taiwanese personal computer investment from the pearl River Delta to the Yangtze River Delta, China. *Regional Studies, 43*(3), 385–407.

Yeh, A. G. A., Sit, V. F. S., Chen, G., & Zhou, Y. (Eds.). (2006). *Developing a competitive Pearl River Delta in South China under one country-two systems.* Hong Kong: Hong Kong University Press.

Yeung, H. W.-C. (2000). Organizing 'the firm' in industrial geography I: Networks, institutions and regional development. *Progress in Human Geography, 24*(2), 301–315.

Yeung, H. W.-C. (2001). Regulating 'the firm' and sociocultural practices in industrial geography II. *Progress in Human Geography, 25*(2), 293–302.

Yeung, H. W.-C. (2002). Industrial geography III: Industrial restructuring and labour markets. *Progress in Human Geography, 26*(3), 367–379.

Yeung, H. W. (2005). Rethinking relational economic geography. *Transactions of the Institute of British Geographers, 30*(1), 37–51.

Yeung, H. W.-C. (2009). Regional development and the competitive dynamics of global production networks: An East Asian perspective. *Regional Studies, 43*(3), 325–351.

Yu, H., & Zhang, Y. (2009). New initiatives for industrial upgrading in the Pearl River Delta. *EAI Background Brief* (p. 16).

Chapter 2
Unpacking the Geography of Industrial Upgrading

> *There is a gap [in the studies of industrial upgrading] as many of us have seen. But in what ways and to what extent does geography matter? We are still not clear about it* (Timothy Sturgeon, (Currently as a senior research affiliate in the Industrial Performance Center of the Massachusetts Institute of Technology, Timothy Sturgeon is one of the leading scholars in the studies of industrial upgrading. This comment was made during the workshop on *Value Chains, Production Networks, and the Geographies of Development* in Singapore, December 2011.) on 1 Dec 2011).

2.1 Questions in Industrial Upgrading

Since decades ago, mainstream economic geographers have devoted tremendous efforts to investigate regional development in relation to industrialization, global industrial shift, agglomeration and production organization, as well as recent research foci such as institutional influences, clustering, innovation, and networked regional economies. However, these studies have yet to place the issue of industrial upgrading as the central analytical concern. To a large extent, industrial upgrading is treated as equal to a process of industrial growth or development without its distinct economic–geographical features.

In the era of globalization, to a latecomer, attracting foreign investments or export-oriented industrialization has become a well-known pathway of promoting regional economic development. Particularly in East Asia, these strategies have been adopted and significantly boosted regional industrial growth since the second half of the twentieth century (Webber 1994; Clark and Kim 1995; Gereffi 1999; Hobday 2001). However, when a latecomer region has achieved substantial industrial growth, whether industrial upgrading is accompanied is in question. On the one hand, the prosperity of regional economy as a whole does not guarantee benefits for all stakeholders. Local firms may not be able to catch up with transnational corporations (TNCs) and hence can only earn marginal profits. TNCs capture and distribute most of the value

© Springer Nature Singapore Pte Ltd. 2020
Y. Liu, *Local Dynamics of Industrial Upgrading*, Economic Geography
https://doi.org/10.1007/978-981-15-4297-8_2

created within the region. Under this shallow forms of industrial growth and global integration, local firms in latecomer regions may be stuck in low-value-added and undifferentiated manufacturing works (see critiques in Steinfeld 2004; Dicken 2007). If the firm fails to upgrade, it will be technologically and organizationally marginalized at a truncated position within GPNs. Sooner or later, it will be replaced by other low-cost producers. In this sense, examining the progress of latecomers (local) upgrading is a critical issue. How does industrial upgrading, particularly local (firm) upgrading, happen? What are the geographical conditions that may facilitate or hinder the process of local upgrading? Economic geographers have yet to answer these questions.

This chapter provides a critical assessment of the contemporary literature on industrial upgrading. It covers a multi-disciplinary base, including economic geography, economic sociology, industrial economics, and development studies. The assessment is organized into two sections according to geographical and non-geographical studies. The next section reviews geographical studies. It shows how geographers have implicitly tackled different dimensions of industrial upgrading and the missing links. The third section focuses on non-geographical studies including two main strands of literature: (1) the GVC approach; (2) latecomer economies in development studies. These studies have been the mainstream of contemporary upgrading research for almost two decades. A thematic summary of these two sections is showed in Table 2.1. Critical assessments are developed for each of the two sections in which important missing links are identified. This chapter ends with a discussion of the ways in which synthesis of both geography and other discipline can shed light on the study of industrial upgrading.

2.2 Industrial Change and Regional Development

In the geographical literature, the issue of industrial upgrading is normally subsumed in a wide range of work related to global industrial restructuring and the changing geographies of production (see a series of reviews in Yeung 2000, 2001, 2002; Bathelt 2003, 2005, 2006; Reimer 2007). This section reviews this strand of literature including the new spatial division of labor, global industrial relocation, capitalist imperatives, debates about flexibility, the new regionalism, clustering economy, and learning/innovation in production networks. Industrial upgrading is implicitly addressed in these studies, such as adopting new organization forms or production modes; developing new technologies or products; as well as functional restructuring in the forms of vertical integration or specialization.

Table 2.1 Research themes and insights in studies of industrial upgrading

Research themes	Key authors	Analytical focus	Insights for upgrading studies
Industrial restructuring	• Allan Scott • Ash Amin • Doreen Massey • Eric Schoenberger • Gorden Clark • Meric Gertler • Michael Storper • Ray Hudson • Richard Walker	• Imperatives of capitalism • Spatial fixes and accumulation • Industrial reallocation • Spatial division of labor • New industrial space, Neo-Marshallian nodes • Flexible/Lean/Post-Fordism production system • Industrial restructuring cost • Internationalization of firms	• Incentives of capitalists • Structural forces of upgrading • Patterns of global shifts • Industrialization as a form of upgrading
New regionalism and cluster	• Allan Scott • Anders Malmberg • Ash Amin • Nigel Thrift • Michael Storper • Phil Cooke • Peter Dicken • Peter Maskell • Richard Florida • Ron Boschma • Ron Morgan	• Embeddedness • Proactive states and associational economies • Relational assents • Institutional thickness • Learning regions and collective learning • Regional innovation system • Untraded interdependency • Economies of agglomeration and clustering • Horizontal production networks	• Supportive or challenging institutional environment • The embeddedness of firms • Synthesis of cluster • Mechanisms of collective learning
Learning and innovation in global production network	• AnnaLeeSaxenian • HaraldBathelt • Henry Yeung • NebahatTokatli • Neil Coe • Peter Dicken • Philips Kelly • Ron Boschma	• Formation and dynamics of global production networks • Strategic coupling • Network and scale of innovation • Proactive states and transnational corporations • Home-based advantages of local firms the global economy	• Global integration of regional economies • Upgrading as a form of network restructuring • Reposition through upgrading • Channels of knowledge diffusion
National strategy and latecomer economy	• Alice Amsden • Bengt-ÅkeLundvall • Chalmers Johnson • Christopher Freeman • Gordon White • KanameAkamatsu • Shigehisa Kasahara • Terutomo, Ozawa	• Flying geese paradigm • Sequences of domestic industrial upgrading • Export-oriented industrialization • Roles of developmental states • Firm–state relations • National innovation system	• Bargaining power of states • National strategies of upgrading • Networks and systems of learning and innovation
Industrial governance	• Gary Gereffi • Hubert Schmitz • Jennifer Bair • John Humphrey • Khalid Nadvi • Peter Gibbon • RaphealKaplinsky • Stafano Ponte • Timothy Sturgeon	• Commodity chain/global value chain • Value-chain governance • industrial standard governance • Asymmetrical power relations in value chains • Collective efficiency and joint action • Supply chain management • Competitiveness management	• Incentives, strategies and typologies of upgrading • General mechanisms of upgrading • Upgrading as a governance issue • Global governance and knowledge transfer
Local practices of upgrading	• Carlo Pietrobelli • Dieter Ernst • Elisa Giuliani • Hubert Schmitz • John Humphrey • Michael Hobday • Michael Porter • Roberta Rabellotti	• Industrial specificity of upgrading • Local resistance to governance • Latecomer strategies • Catching-up politics for developing economies • Industrial policy and regional politics • Competitiveness of clustering	• Global governance and local resistance • Protectionism for domestic upgrading • Local strategies for upgrading

2.2.1 Industrial Change and Capitalist Imperatives

Earlier works on industrial change in regional development were focusing on dein-dustrialization in developed regions. Capitalists' imperatives and capital–labor relations were considered as driving forces in shaping the spatial reorganization of production in which firms exploited maximum usage of their labor with lower costs among various regions (Massey 1979; Harvey 1982; Hudson 1988; Massey 1995).

By investigating the spatial restructuring of British regional economies in the 1960s, Massey (1979, 1995) argued that this relocation did not result from regional industrial policies, but from the locational behaviors of capitalists. The behaviors changed as a response to geographical inequality in different conditions of production. Rounds of industrial changes constructed an uneven economic landscape so as to sustain industrial growth. This view was considered as a Marxist view in contrast to the neo-classical industrial location theory. It explained the new spatial division of labor by three conditions (Dicken 1976; Frobel et al. 1980; Hudson 1988). First, inexhaustible disposable labor became available in South/East Europe and other developing countries. Second, the standardization of technologies enabled production disintegration in which less sophisticated segments were separated from the core manufacturing activities. Third, the available of modern transport and communication technologies enabled the dispersion of production segments among distant places at a global scale. In Harvey (1982)'s account, this process was driven by the imperative of accumulation (e.g., decreasing profits) through two forms of spatial fixes: new investments in the built environment (temporal deferral) and new investments in new production sites (spatial displacement). In these studies, industrial growth was related to the changing capitalists' imperatives as a renewal process of accumulation regimes. These production regimes were no longer constrained within an isolated place with endowed technical, organizational, and cost factors, but evolved into a networked spatial organization operating in different regions.

Storper and Walker (1989) also attributed the underlying forces of industrial transformation to the capitalist's imperatives and the rise of new industries, new products, or new production skills. Radical technological upgrading served as breaking points which led to a series of periodic industrial shifts in the centers of industrial growth, such as the shift from UK to the USA, from West Europe to East and South Europe, or the shift from the Northeast to the Southwest of the USA. These industrial changes embodied a sense of upgrading referring to the improvement of 'capacity to control the pattern of economic events but that these events represent opportunities to restructure the inherited system of production' (Clark and Kim 1993: 1).

In general, studies of industrial changes in economic geography shared a common understanding that the capitalist imperatives played a dominant role at a global scale. Considered as a Marxist view, the imperatives of industrial change were mainly tied to organizational skills for the control of labor and the profit-seeking nature of capitalists. This view was revisited in recent studies about Thailand's economic recovery (Glassman 2001, 2007). In the case of Thailand, the renewal of spatial fixes (industrial restructuring and asset reinvestments) was driven by the capitalist logic of accumulation based on a combination of home-country and host-country contexts.

Although the Marxist approach has articulated the capitalist imperative in driving industrial change, it tended to hold an essentialist view on the fundamental conflict of capitalism and focused more on global or structural forces without recognizing forces at other geographical scales (Jessop et al. 2008). As Storper (2001: 158) argued, '[t]he strong point of Marxism is that it considers capitalism as a system…But this has also become its greatest limitation: it has never been able to go beyond large-scale descriptions to cause-and-effect analyses of the detailed internal dynamics and processes of capitalism…[and never] being able to analyze the real margins of variation which are possible within the system.'

2.2.2 Adopting New Production Organizations: The 'Flexibility' Debate

Along with the ebb tide of Marxist geography in the late 1980s and the early 1990s, economic geographers gradually turned to focus on diverse industrial shifts and the changing organization of production at the global scale. New patterns of production organization emerged, such as the 'flexible production' or the lean production system, to replace mass production hitherto known as 'Fordism' in the contemporary world economy (Gertler 1988; Schoenberger 1988; Scott 1988a, b; Walker 1988; Amin and Thrift 1992). Proponents in this strand of literature emphasized the improvement of efficiency by upgrading production systems in a more flexible manner. But the opponents argued that this type of systematic upgrading would have negative impacts to the stability of production and labor management, thus reducing efficiency (Gertler 1988). The shared understanding in this debate was that networked forms of production organization were becoming prevalent and replaced the traditional production modes of Fordism and Taylorism. This shift can be considered as process upgrading in Schmitz's (2002b) account.

One of the well-known studies was the case of 'Third Italy' where a large group of small- and medium-sized enterprises (SMEs) agglomerated and developed dense horizontal production relations in the pursuit of flexile specialization (Piore and Sabel 1984). The prosperity of Third Italy was considered as the 'second industrial divide' that represented an episodic upgrading of industrial system from mass production to flexible specialization, in contrast to the previous 'first' industrial divide that referred to the shift from craft production to mass production since the 1900s. Based on the study of Silicon Valley, Scott (1988b) added further weight to the heated debate on flexible production as new industrial spaces in which high-tech enterprises agglomerated and specialized in certain component production for lower transaction costs and better interactive learning. Firms in the information and communication technology (ICT) industries were the main forces in constructing this kind of new industrial spaces. The automotive industry was also revealed as another representative industry adopting this change (Schoenberger 1987; Hudson 1994, 1997). Many automotive manufacturers in North America and Eastern/Western Europe upgraded their production systems by adopting the 'just-in-time' production or the 'lean' production system which was derived from Japanese automotive assemblers such that Toyota and Honda.

During adopting the flexible production system, firms also improved their managerial skills to cope with new systems (Gertler 1993). Experiences from industries in EU regions showed that new investments were put into automated production technologies and research and development (R&D) for reducing employment and improving efficiency in processing materials (Rainnie 1993; Hudson 1997). Meanwhile, various rounds of corporate merger and acquisition activities were conducted so that firms could concentrate their governance power to control globally decentralized production sites. Scholars also documented this change in traditional industries such as the apparel industry (Park 1994; Essletzbichler and Rigby 2001; Essletzbichler 2003). Instead of following this shift toward flexible production systems, latecomer firms in East Asia mainly relocated mass production to places with lower production cost, such as from Japan to South Korea, Hong Kong, Taiwan, and then China. Rather than using labor-saving technologies, these East Asian firms tended to adopt different employment strategies such as hiring illegal foreign workers, recruiting part-time workers, training highly skilled employees, and substituting labor with automation (Kim 1993; Leung 1993; Tsay 1993; Hsu and Chiang 2001).

In explaining the mechanism of this organizational upgrading, geographers argued that the motivation for adopting the 'flexible' production system came from the internal limits of Fordism due to its fixed-purpose and dedicated machinery system. It also resulted from the increasing demands for a quicker response to changing market conditions (Schoenberger 1988, 1989). However, being flexible was not the universal solution for all firms and was only suitable in certain industries and regions. In the case of the chemical industry in Teesside, North England, Chapman (2005) pointed out flexible specialization was not be a proper strategy for the technological improvement of local firms, because they suffered from the heave burden of sunk costs through investing in new production lines. Consequent critiques also pointed out that successful cases of adopting flexibility actually covered just a small range of places, such as South Italy, Silicon Valley and East Europe. Moreover, the flexible production model was mainly related to small firms in infant industries (Schoenberger 1989; Glasmeier 1994; Storper 1995).

Although adopting flexible production has its own limits, geographers have recognized the significance of this emerging network form of production organization at both regional and global scales. Region was conceptualized as a crucial platform for a new round of vertical or horizontal integration among firms with tighter inter-firm relationships and greater demands of proximity and trust (Amin and Robins 1990; Harrison 1992). Moreover, different regions were seen as interconnected, thus generating neo-Marshallian nodes of production spaces (Amin and Thrift 1992). The flexibility debate has indeed shed important light on the geography of industrial restructuring by articulating a process of regionalization when firms and regions adopt new production system.

2.2.3 Intra-regional Foundations of Industrial Growth: An Institutional Perspective

Since the mid-1990s, geographers' interests gradually moved from the 'new industrial space' to institutional factors that facilitated regional development, such as relational assents, institutional thickness, associational economies, learning networks, regional innovation system, and the untraded interdependency of firms (Amin and Thrift 1994; Saxenian 1994; Florida 1995; Cooke et al. 1997; Morgan 1997; Storper 1997; Cooke and Morgan 1998). This strand of literature was termed *new regionalism* in Lovering (1999). The proliferation of these studies showed a distinctive shift from the earlier concern with input–output relations and transaction costs to non-cost-based factors within a region, such as institutional environment/arrangement, inter- or extra-firm networks and state institutions. These factors influenced the strategies and behaviors of economic actors due to the 'embeddedness' of economic actions in political/social/cultural contexts (Granovetter 1985; Dicken and Thrift 1992; Park 1996). These institutional factors did not directly increase profits or reduce production costs for in situ enterprises, while played an important role in facilitating learning and innovation, fostering collaboration and cultivating mutual trust. In the era of globalization, these factors were considered as new assets to sustain regional competitiveness (Storper 1995; Amin 1999; Barnes and Gertler 1999; Maskell and Malmberg 1999a; Boschma 2004).

There was a wide range of studies recognizing the importance of regionalized inter-firm collaboration, networking policies and associational economies since the early 1990s. They were concerned with various ties of proximity, mutual interaction, and associational economies as the positive channels and facilitators of knowledge sharing, spillover and learning (Amin 1999; Boschma and Lambooy 1999; Martin 2000). In their investigation of some developed regions, such as Baden-Württemberg in Germany and Emilia-Romagna in Italy, Cooke and Morgan (1993) revealed the network relations between firms and public or quasi-public intermediary agencies had contributed to substantial regional economic growth. Cooke and Morgan (1998) further explained that proactive associational economies were the key actors in cultivating inter-firm cooperation, public–private networks, and public welfare (e.g., education or infrastructures) which contributed to regional prosperity. Based on the cases of regional development in EU and Wales, scholars pointed to the important role of proactive regional institutions in transferring micro-level innovation into meso-level innovation, underpinning the so called 'learning regions' (Florida 1995; Hudson 1997; Morgan 1997; Hudson 1999; Hassink 2005).

In contrast to looking at specific institutional arrangements, another group of studies conceptualized the importance of the 'untraded interdependencies' (Storper 1995, 1997b; Scott and Storper 2003). This concept served as a critique of the previous flexibility debate that focused only on trade-based relations and transaction costs. Examining regions in Emilia-Romagna, Tuscany, Veneto, and Marches in Italy; Silicon Valley, Orange County, and Hollywood in the USA, Storper (1997) argued that regions have become a nexus of untraded interdependencies in global capitalism. In those regions, conventions of production were developed to reduce uncertainty, to facilitate technological upgrading and to foster innovation. The case of British Motorsport Valley provided a vivid example of the benefits of untraded interdependency existing among hundreds of small firms within a radius of 50 miles area (Henry et al. 1996; Pinch and Henry 1999).

Geographers further focused on clusters and innovation since the late 1990s. In these studies, cognitive and cultural approaches were applied to unpack the pattern of learning, knowledge diffusion, and innovation within regions (Malmberg and Maskell 1999, 2002, 2006; Maskell and Malmberg 1999b, 2007; Maskell 2001; Todtling and Trippl 2004; Scott 2006). The analytical origin of these studies derived from an evolutionary approach and a resource-based view of firms in institutional economics (Nelson and Winter 1982; Barney 1991; Nelson 1994). According to these studies, 'sustainable competitiveness of firms and regions is built on specialized learning capabilities and continuous upgrading of an existing knowledge base' (Maskell and Malmberg 1999b: 181).

Examining industrial clusters in the fifty largest metropolitan regions in North America, Florida (2002) demonstrated a positive relation between the spatial clustering of diverse industries and the outputs of innovation. The cases of Silicon Valley and Hollywood in the USA illustrated how successful clusters were sustained by intensive interactive learning activities within localized business networks (Scott 1998, 2005). Trippl and Otto (2009) investigated the restructuring process of old clusters in Styria and Saarland and pointed out that knowledge-intensive-oriented adjustment was one of the most effective ways to vitalize clusters. In Cambridge's biotechnology cluster, firm–university relations became vital because they fostered technological upgrading and commercialization within the cluster (Casper and Karamanos 2003). In Italian textiles and clothing clusters, Dunford (2006) identified a 'magic circle' of mutual learning and innovation. The circle was formed by a large group of interdependent clusters surrounding Milan as the center where knowledge about technologies and managerial skills were highly circulated. Channels of knowledge diffusion could be frequent staff turnover, shared suppliers, informal collaboration (e.g., collective discussion), industrial gossip, and trackside observation.

In sum, the analytical focus of cluster studies rested in the articulation of various types of learning mechanisms, such as interactive innovation, diffusion of tacit knowledge, face-to-face communication, and knowledge spillover derived from the economies of agglomeration and the localization of learning activities (Scott 1998; Hudson 1999; Scott and Storper 2003; Boschma 2004; Maskell et al. 2006; Maskell and Malmberg 2007). A basic typology of knowledge channels is summarized according to formal/traded and informal/untraded relations (see Table 2.2). Indeed, the 'new regionalism' approach has demonstrated a solid account of intra-regional factors that sustain regional industrial growth. But this approach has two fundamental limits. On the one hand, it tends to be inward-looking and treats region as an analytical entity, thus neglecting exogenous forces beyond regions (see detail critiques in Lovering 1999; MacKinnon et al. 2002). On the other hand, the causality between institutional influences and regional growth is still unclear. Dense institutional environment

Table 2.2 Types of linkages to external sources of knowledge and partners (Fig. 2 in Trippl et al. 2009: 448)

	Static (knowledge transfer)	Dynamic (collective learning)
Formal/traded relation	*Market relations* • Contract research • Consulting • Licenses • Buying intermediate goods	*Formal networks* • R&D collaborations • Shared use of R&D facilities
Informal/untraded relation	*Spillovers* • Recruiting specialists • Monitoring competitors • Participating in fairs, conferences • Reading scientific literature, patent specifications	*Informal networks* • Informal contacts

does not necessarily lead to better performance of firms. Over-institutionalized environment may produce lock-in effects to reduce the competitiveness of firms over time (Grabher 1993).

2.2.4 (Global) Networks of Production and Innovation

While the institutional approach holds a more intra-regional perspective, some geographers have highlighted the role of exogenous forces in shaping regional industrial development and upgrading. In line with development studies, geographers have devoted substantial efforts to documenting the rise of many latecomer regions that have benefited from their integration into the global economy (Clark and Kim 1993, 1995; Huchet 1997; Sit and Yang 1997; Young and Lan 1997; Yeung 2001). Since the 2000s, drawing upon a network approach, economic geographers have further refined their analytical focuses on the mechanisms of global integration in terms of global–local relations, network structure, and the embeddedness of firm networks (Bunnell and Coe 2001; Dicken et al. 2001; Henderson et al. 2002; Bathelt et al. 2004; Todtling and Trippl 2005; Boschma and Wal 2007; Coe et al. 2008b; Hsu et al. 2008). Scholars in this vein have argued for two propositions. First, the global economy is contributed by TNCs embedded in GPNs which integrate different regions at a global scale. Hence, plugging into GPNs is a necessary step for a region to achieve continuous and substantial industrial growth (Coe et al. 2004). Knowledge diffuses within production networks, rather than circulates within a region. Second, local factors (e.g., economic, social, or political) can play a significant role in facilitating the integration process, while stronger regional capacities would benefit more from the integration (Amin and Cohendet 1999; Fan 2011).

The propositions above have been partly verified based on the experiences in East Asian regional development. In the case of Hsinchu Science-based Industrial

Park in Taiwan, it kept upgrading with technological edges based on the efforts of an international technological community. Comprising Taiwanese business elites and overseas returnees, this technological community has provided a flexible and responsive channel for long-distance knowledge transfer between Taiwan and Silicon Valley (Saxenian and Hsu 2001; Saxenian 2002; Hsu 2004; Hsu et al. 2008). In other industrial parks in Taiwan, Tainan, and Taichung industrial parks, significant industrial upgrading was sustained by intensive technological transfer from Japanese electronics lead firms to Taiwanese partners/manufacturers within the same GPNs in the LCD and machinery industries (Yang et al. 2009).

A nuance contribution was made by Coe et al. (2004) which conceptualized the integration between latecomer regions and the global economy as a process of *strategic coupling*. Drawing upon the automobile industry in Thailand, the authors illustrated how local firms achieved substantial growth and upgrading by plugging with the GPN coordinated by BMW in German. Yeung (2009a) provided a heuristic account toward different approaches of strategic coupling among East Asian latecomer regions including: the Yangzi River Delta and the PRD in China; Seoul and Gyeonggi-do areas in South Korea; Taipei-Hsinchu area in Taiwan; Penang, Selangor, and Johor regions in Malaysia; Bangkok and Eastern region in Thailand. Through the process of strategic coupling, local firms in these regions gained access to advanced technology and market resources embedded in various GPNs. Some local firms in these regions even upgraded into new lead firms (Yeung 2007a). In China, similar cases studies were also conducted in such diverse industries (the automotive, ICT, and textile industries) among different cities, such as Beijing, Shanghai, Wenzhou, Suzhou, and Dongguan (Depner and Bathelt 2005; Liu and Dicken 2006; Wei et al. 2007, 2009a; Yang 2007).

Although local firms received significant growth among these latecomer regions, geographers also critically pointed out the potential of shallow upgrading, because the channels of knowledge diffusion were mainly controlled by global lead firms. They tended to develop certain technological enclaves (Wang and Lee 2007; Wang and Lin 2008) or exclusively transferred technologies through backward linkages which connected with their home countries, rather than the host countries (Yang and Liao 2009; Xiao and He 2010). To overcome these problems, strong local initiatives and home-based advantages were suggested as a complement, such as state efforts, low R&D costs, or local cultural and social advantages (Wei 2002, 2010; Zhou and Tong 2003; Yeung 2007a; Zhou 2008a, b). In Turkey's apparel industry, geographers identified another strategies specific to industrial upgrading: plugging into different GPNs and exploiting less regulated markets by trading 'imperfect products' (Tokatli 2003, 2007, 2008; Tokatli and Kizilgun 2004). This strategy enabled Turkish firms to earn sufficient profits and critical time for knowledge accumulation. They therefore managed to upgrade from full-package into brand-name manufacturing and marketing.

2.2.5 Critical Assessments: Where Is the Geography of Industrial Upgrading?

This section has so far reviewed sequentially four strands of literature that are considered as relevant studies of industrial upgrading. Although they have different limitations, their common problem is that the geography of industrial upgrading is unclear or implicit. As stated in Chap. 1, geography here does not mean the spatial structure of industrial upgrading, but refers to the ongoing process in which actors strategize and implement industrial upgrading in a locality with specific economic, institutional, and spatial contexts. On the one hand, industrial upgrading has not been well studied yet in mainstream economic geography. By and large, industrial upgrading is treated synonymous as industrial growth, learning, or innovation, while some of its distinctive features, such as conducting high-value-added activities or diversifying corporate functions through organizational learning, are neglected. On the other hand, the analytical perspectives of earlier studies tend to rest at a single spatial scale, either global or regional, while lacks a multi-scalar perspective for investigating how actors from different scales implement the strategies of upgrading in a latecomer region.

In a globalization era, industrial upgrading has become an increasingly critical issue, particularly for latecomer regions and firms. However, the prosperity of a latecomer region does not guarantee benefits for all stakeholders. Although a latecomer region can achieve substantial industrial growth through export-oriented industrialization, this major growth may be contributed by TNCs at the same time when local firms are further marginalized. Even though local firms manage to experience significant industrial growth, the overall achievement may still be shallow. Local firms may focus narrowly in low-value-added segments that produce undifferentiated products based on labor-intensive modes of production. In other words, though local firms actively participate in value creation, they may be excluded from much of the value distribution and capture. Even worse, firms may be technologically and organizationally locked into a peripheral position within a particular GPN. In this circumstance, local firms are highly uncompetitive and powerless. They will be easily replaced by the subsequent relocation of TNCs, the discrimination of policy makers, or the rise of other low-cost producers. Therefore, industrial upgrading can serve as a useful lens for investigating the detail mechanisms of regional development and the evolutionary dynamics of the global economy. However, situated in such a context of globalizing regional development, the analytical insights and toolkits in the existing geographical literature are insufficient to explain the dynamics of industrial upgrading.

The literature on capitalist industrial change and the flexibility debate renders a sense of systematic imperatives to industrial growth in terms of profit-seeking accumulation regime and production efficiency. Whenever a region is losing competitiveness, the solution would be either relocation or adopting flexible production. But these interpretations are too narrow for explaining the varieties of industrial development in today's global economy. In the literature, on new regionalism and industrial clusters, scholars either praise positive institutional factors or attribute the failure of regional economic growth to institutional lock-in. These intra-regional factors are related to learning or innovation and have not examined upgrading activities per se. Moreover, many of these East Asian regions do not develop similar kinds of institutional thickness, associational economies, strong untraded interdependencies, and regional innovation systems. In those regions, there is a relative absence of substantial relational assets and learning regions capable of generating indigenous technologies and innovation (Yeung 2009a). Therefore, the distinctive contexts of Asian regions further legitimize the necessity of studying industrial upgrading.

In the past decades, the analytical focus on regional industrial change has gradually shifted from a global level to a meso level (regional, industrial), from the societal structure to the local institutional conditions of networked economies. But these studies tended to explain industrial change through the imperatives of capitalists and the need of adopting new production organization. Many other influential factors were absent in their analyses, such as proactive state institutions and institutional environment. In the literature on new regionalism, scholars tended to focus on the meso-level analysis in which most of their attentions were rested in many institutional factors in terms institutional environment and arrangement. An actorless view tended to be developed in which some basic features and practices of firms were omitted, such as strategies and performance. This actorless view also overlooks the dark sides of networking which may generate conflict, tension, misinterpretation, or distrust in an over-socialized region (Grabher 2006; Lowe 2009).

As a complement to previous studies and premised on a network approach, the GPN studies develop a more balanced analytical framework which recognizes multiscalar force in shaping regional development. One key contribution of this approach is the conceptualization of strategic coupling as a crucial mechanism to explain the globalizing process of latecomer regions. The GPN framework captures the changing pattern of global integration and shows the value of actor specificity in conducting economic geographical research. However, this approach has yet to place the topic of industrial upgrading as their central analytical focus. A latecomer region can achieve substantial industrial growth by taking industrial opportunities provided by lead firms within GPNs. But how and why will local upgrading happen? Will different types of coupling produce a different outcome of upgrading? What are the geographical conditions that may facilitate or hinder the process of local upgrading? Economic geographers have yet to provide answers to these questions. Particularly, at a micro-level analysis, the typology of upgrading and the strategies of local firms in upgrading have not been well examined (More details of the critique and conceptualization of strategic coupling is in Chap. 3).

In sum, the issue of industrial upgrading is seldom examined directly in the existing geographical studies. While the geography of industrial upgrading remains unclear, scholars outside geography have devoted remarkable efforts in revealing the mechanisms of industrial upgrading.

2.3   The Latecomer Economy: Mechanisms, Governance, and Politics in Studies of Economic Development

In non-geographical studies, there are plenty of sound works about industrial upgrading among the disciplines of economic sociology, institutional economics, and other development studies (see Table 2.1). The first part of this section reviews main theories tackling the divers of latecomer economy pertinent to upgrading, including the 'flying geese' (PDFGD) paradigm, the developmental state literature, and the national innovation system (NIS) literature. These three theories are considered as state-centric approaches. I then present a firm-centric approach in the GVC literature. It is probably the most influential field in the contemporary studies of upgrading. While the first two sections illustrate the role of more powerful actors (nation-states and global lead firms), the penultimate part of this section reviews the upgrading of less powerful actors (local firms or suppliers). Overall, these studies articulate the mechanisms of upgrading in terms of incentives, strategies, driven forces, typologies, trajectories, barriers, governance, and politics.

2.3.1   The Drivers of National Upgrading: The State-Centric Approaches

The upgrading of global lead firms is mainly related to the literature of innovation. My specific attention of this book is on the upgrading of latecomer economy, rather the global economy as a whole. The common thread of the FG, developmental state, and NIS literature is that nation-states can be proactive actors in stimulating domestic industrial upgrading through direct intervention or providing institutional supports. The key is to facilitate knowledge sharing, diffusion, and reproduction. However, they over emphasize the effectiveness of state capacity, and regard states as the key actors while not firms in private section during the process of upgrading.

As many latecomer regions have acquired unprecedented degree of openness and growth, such as the ones in East Asia, firms and states in those regions find themselves are competing in a common platform but under unequal terms. The latecomer economy thus bears a special meaning in the era of globalization not as just simple as economic development (Storper et al. 1998). Plenty of studies have been devoted to identify nation-states as a key driver to industrial upgrading in East Asia. The FG paradigm was a much earlier influential work developed in the 1930s and popularized in the 1960s (Akamatsu 1961; Ozawa 2002, 2005; Kasahara 2004;). The first generation of FG paradigm concerned the state-led industrial development as a process of moving from import substitution to export orientation. The second generation of FG paradigm proposed an industrial sequence of upgrading on the basis of shifting comparative advantages under strong state intervention.

Akamatsu's (1961) FG paradigm was considered as the third version of FG that identified the international division of labor in East Asia as an unbalanced growth

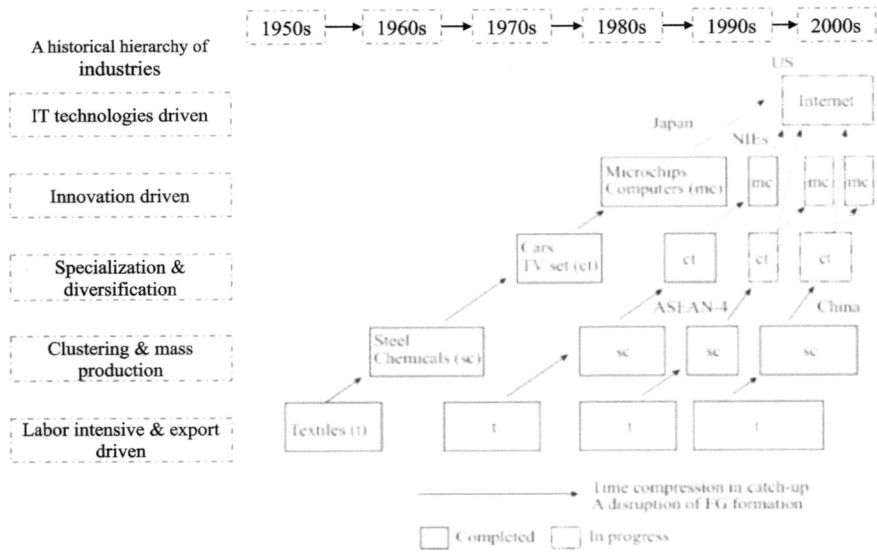

Fig. 2.1 Sequences of industrial upgrading in East Asian NIEs (Adapted from Fig. 7.1 in Ozawa 2005: 141)

model. This model was 'aligned successively behind the advanced industrial nations according to their different stages of growth' (Ozawa 2005). The postulated logic was that the production of commoditized goods would continuously move from the more advanced countries to the less advanced ones. Ozawa (2002, 2005) updated the FG model into an industrial-specific sequential development in the forms of various spatial clustering among Asian countries (see Fig. 2.1). In Ozawa's account (2005: 28), the latecomer upgrading was an outcome of 'incessant learning which has been made possible in terms of crafting economic policies and pre-arranging the requisite institutions designed to make the best use of the prevailing politico-economic conditions both at home and overseas at each stage of catch-up.' However, the FG paradigm tended to hold an over-optimistic view to the upgrading of the East Asian late comers. It predicted that Japan would continuously be the leading economic power in East Asia dominating the sequence of industrial upgrading in other Asian countries. It neglected influences from other forces, such as various regionalized forces based on class-divided systems (Hart-Landsberg and Burkett 1998). Moreover, the mechanism of technological transfer in the FG paradigm was oversimplified as a process of reverse engineering and learning by doing (Kasahara 2004).

Sharing many similarities with the FG paradigm, scholars developed another strand of literature termed as a 'developmental state' mode of capitalism for explaining the rise of East Asia in the late twenty century (Johnson 1982; White 1988; Amsden 1989, 1997; Wade 1990; Huff 1999; Bagchi 2000). The main characteristics of a developmental state were: being a 'rational planed' state, autonomous bureaucracy, close firm–state relationships, and strategic preferential industrial poli-cies. These characteristics were considered as effective institutional infrastructures for developmental state institution to achieve domestic upgrading against competi-tive pressure and the external control of TNCs in market-led countries, such as the USA. A key prerequisite for fulfilling this upgrading process was the existence of a 'pilot agency' (Douglass 1994; Kohli 1994; Huff 1999; Chu 2002). In Japan's con-text, it was the celebrated Ministry of International Trade and Industry (MITI) the main focus in Johnson (1982) and Ozawa (2005). In their explanations, the success-ful upgrading of Japan highly depended on the consistency of industrial planning in which the MITI played the role as both a protector and a promoter. However, the key problem with the developmental state approach was that it over-emphasized the significance of state capacity and close firm–state relations. In fact, these institu-tional infrastructures might go wrong and cause serious negative impacts to domestic economies. Moreover, state supports might be limited. They were effective in boost-ing technological imitation, transfer, or diffusion, but did not necessarily do better than the private sector in stimulating innovation (Beeson 2004; Ozawa 2005).

More recent studies extended analytical scopes from nation-states to a national innovation system since the late 1980s and the early 1990s. The NIS literature implied the issue of upgrading by articulating interactions and synergy within national pro-duction systems, industrial complexes, and inter-firm networks that shape domestic technological innovation and diffusion (Lundvall 1985, 1992, 2007). This concept was widely diffused through the study on the NISs of Japan and South Korea (Free-man 1987, 1994, 1995). Scholars in this vein proposed that state institutions should focus on constructing knowledge infrastructures (universities and research institutes) and wider institutional settings including the national education systems, labor mar-kets, financial markets, intellectual property rights, market regulations, and welfare regimes. These factors are deemed as determinant factors to the innovation/upgrading capability of states (Lundvall 2007). Nevertheless, there were insufficient empirical evidence to support and legitimate the NIS framework as a system. As Ernst (2007) has argued, a NIS is hardly considered as nationally bounded system, while it is per-meated with each other through the international linkages of knowledge diffusion, particularly upon GPNs.

2.3.2 A Firm-Centric Approach in Studies of Global Value Chain

In contrast to the state-centric approaches, the GVC approach in economic sociology and development studies rests its analytical focus on corporate actors in value-chain governance. It has become the most influential work in the contemporary studies of industrial upgrading. The GVC approach derives from the commodity chain research. A commodity chain was originally defined as a network of labor and production process whose end result was a finished commodity (Gereffi and Korzeniewicz 1994a, b). It was then conceptualized as a GVC (Gereffi 1999; Kessler 1999; Gibbon 2001). Based on empirical studies from developing countries, the GVC proponents shared similar understandings as below (Gereffi 1999; Bair and Gereffi 2001; Humphrey and Schmitz 2002b; Schmitz 2004; Gereffi et al. 2005; Pomerleano and Shaw 2005; Dunn et al. 2006; Staritz et al. 2011; Sturgeon and Kawakami 2011).

Upgrading is a general nature of firms to secure survival and competitiveness through innovation, learning, or acquisitions. There are generally four types of firm-level upgrading (Humphrey and Schmitz 2000, 2002a, b; Schmitz 2004):

(1) *Process upgrading*: transforming inputs into outputs more efficiently by reorganizing production systems or introducing superior technologies, e.g., installing new processing lines or improving processing skills;

(2) *Product upgrading*: moving into more sophisticated product lines in terms of increased unit values, e.g., making better products, adopting new design, adding new component into the products;

(3) *Functional upgrading*: acquiring new, high value added, or superior functions, such as from simple processing into full package production, from OEM to ODM/OBM,[1] or adding other functions like design, marketing, management, branding and retailing;

(4) *Sectoral (chain) upgrading*: applying the competence acquired in a particular function to move to a new sector which is more skilled, complicated or higher value added, so as to reap the economies of scopes.

Lead firms, suppliers, and the patterns of value-chain governance constitute the scenario of upgrading in which lead firms play a determinant role with strong bargaining power over their suppliers. The bargaining power of lead firms originates from their market and technological advantages. Suppliers tend to be less powerful because they are substitutable. Suppliers can initiate local joint actions or increase the capability of integrated production in order to increase their bargaining power, but these efforts cannot fundamentally reshape the asymmetrical power relation.

To maintain production stability and industrial standards, lead firms would help local suppliers in product and process upgrading, but they tend deliberately to block functional upgrading because this upgrading will challenge their market positions. In other words, lead firms define the content and extent of local upgrading. Hence, by inserting into value chains, producers in developing countries can experience fast product and process upgrading. But they will make little progress in functional upgrading, while developed country producers engage less difficulty in these two kinds of upgrading.

By investigating into how USA lead firms shaped their offshore production networks and fostered upgrading in East Asia, studies found a dichotomy pattern of governance known as *buyer-driven* and *producer-driven* value chains (Gereffi 1996, 1999). In the apparel industry in East Asia, which represented the buyer-driven mode

---

[1] OEM: original equipment manufacturer; ODM: original design manufacturer; OBM: original brand manufacturer.

of governance, lead firms were the gate keepers of upgrading opportunities. Whether East Asian suppliers/subcontractors could upgrade was determined by their abilities to establish close linkages with a diverse array of lead firms from the USA and West Europe. Empirical studies of Japan, South Korea, Hong Kong, Taiwan, and Singapore supported this argument that lead firms were the primary sources of material inputs, capital, technologies, and managerial knowledge in those chains. The dichotomy between the buyer-driven and producer-driven mode of governance was consequently critiqued to be oversimplified in understanding the global economy (Gereffi 2001a; Humphrey and Schmitz 2001). As a response, Gereffi et al. (2005) developed a fivefold governance framework based on three variables: complexity of information and knowledge transfer, extent of knowledge codification, and supplier capabilities (see Fig. 2.2). The various configurations of these variables reflect different extent of transaction costs that determine the pattern of governance in value-chain governance.

Based on this topology, the GVC approach highlights the strength of governance power in explaining the possibility of upgrading in respective types of chains. In traditional industries where technologies are simple and increasingly become standardized and matured, like the bicycle, toy, bag, textile, and apparel industries, the governance pattern tends to be *captive*, while is changing *into relational* governance more recently (Gereffi 1999, 2001b; Bair and Gereffi 2001, 2003; Galvin and Morkel 2001; Gereffi et al. 2005; Frederick and Gereffi 2011; Morris et al. 2011). Lead firms subcontract most of the manufacturing works and become global buyers which local

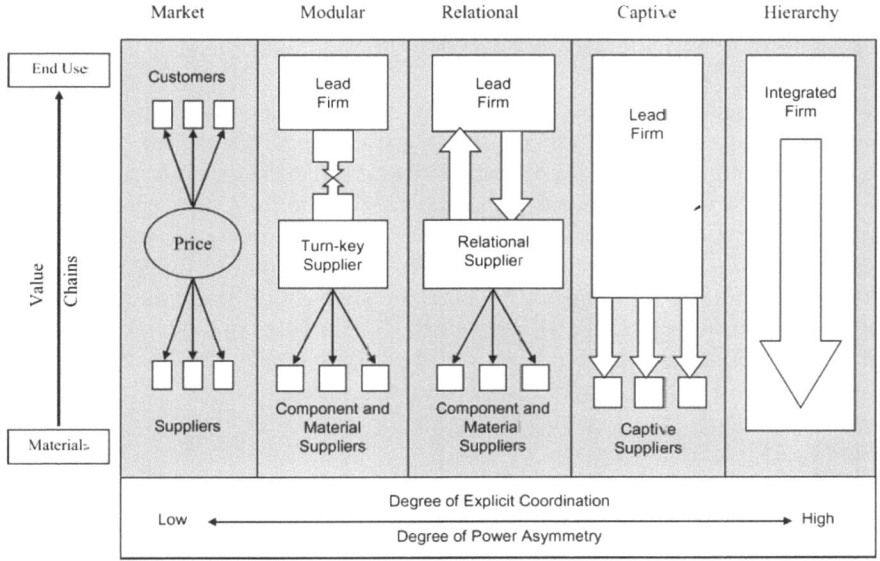

Fig. 2.2 Five types of global value-chain governance (Adapted from Fig. 1 in Gerreffi et al. 2005: 89)

suppliers or subcontractors are captive to. This is because the most important competitive edges in those industries are no longer production technologies, but design, marketing, and distribution capabilities. Latecomer upgrading in these industries tends to be achieved through learning by doing, organizational acquisition, and technological assistance from global buyers. The captive governance would be changed into relational governance when local suppliers manage to develop strong capabilities of integrated production. In this case, local suppliers reduce dependency on a single lead firm, but are still under global industrial governance. Global buyers reinforce the parameters set within value chains and extend the parameters as industrial standards for suppliers to follow at a global scale (Nadvi and Wältring 2004; Nadvi 2008).

Among industries with highly sophisticated and rapidly changing technologies, such as the electronics and other high-tech industries, the governance pattern tends to be *modular*. Due to high technological and capital entry barriers, firms in these industries progressively prefer technological modularization and standardization that integrates a customer's needs for direct monitoring and control. Hence, lead firms may concentrate on maintaining their technological cutting edges by adopting industrial specialization and outsourcing strategies simultaneously in fierce market competition (Principe and Honday 2003; Nadvi and Halder 2005; Gibbon and Ponte 2008; Cattaneo et al. 2010; Sturgeon and Kawakami 2011). Suppliers tend to develop strong technological competences and become quick followers of global lead firms. Otherwise, they would be marginalized into manufacturing peripheral parts or products with trivial profits. The recent emergence of platform developers diversifies the modular governance at a global scale which provides more upgrading opportunities to suppliers, while also increases the risk of technological lock-in (Chesbrough and Kusunoki 2001; Sturgeon and Kawakami 2011). I will further explain this dynamics in Sect. 5.2 in Chap. 5.

In some industries with sophisticated technologies and complex production networks such as the automotive industry, upgrading opportunities for suppliers are fewer under the captive and modular governance. As GVC scholars have argued, this is because technologies are too complicated to be fully codified; meanwhile, transaction costs and asset specificity are also high due to the consolidation of global lead firms (Freyssenet and Lung 2000; Gereffi 2001b; Kaplinsky 2004; Gereffi et al. 2005; Sturgeon and Biesebroeck 2011). A small group of global auto assemblers plays a dominant role in supervising their production bases in different clusters at a global scale. Even their key suppliers, which have strong technological cutting edges in certain components, are subject to this governance mode.

2.3.3 Local Upgrading in the Global Economy

The above two sections review the important role of global lead firms and nation-states in the process of local upgrading. In contrast to them, there is a growing body of literature investigating how local firms (or suppliers) struggle for upgrading through various means. Three groups of studies are presented.

The first group of studies comes from Hobday's works on the trajectories of latecomer upgrading in Japan, South Korea, Taiwan, Hong Kong, Singapore, and other East Asian NIEs (Hobday 1995, 1998, 2001, 2008; Hobday and de Barros Perini 2005; Hobday and Rush 2007). Lessons from East Asian NIEs show some common characteristics. Most of the successful cases of upgrading came from the firms which served as 'quick followers' of their lead firm counterparts. This view resonated with the GVC literature. Local suppliers did not heavily rely on indigenous innovation, but learned and acquired advanced technologies through various forms of cooperation with lead firms, such as joint ventures, technological licensing, subcontracting, and strategic alliance. A general trajectory was summarized in Fig. 2.3. Latecomers firms are narrowed to occupying simple production segments at the earlier stage. Product upgrading was driven by lead firms. Process upgrading tended to come later than product upgrading and often brought significant improvement in productivity. The

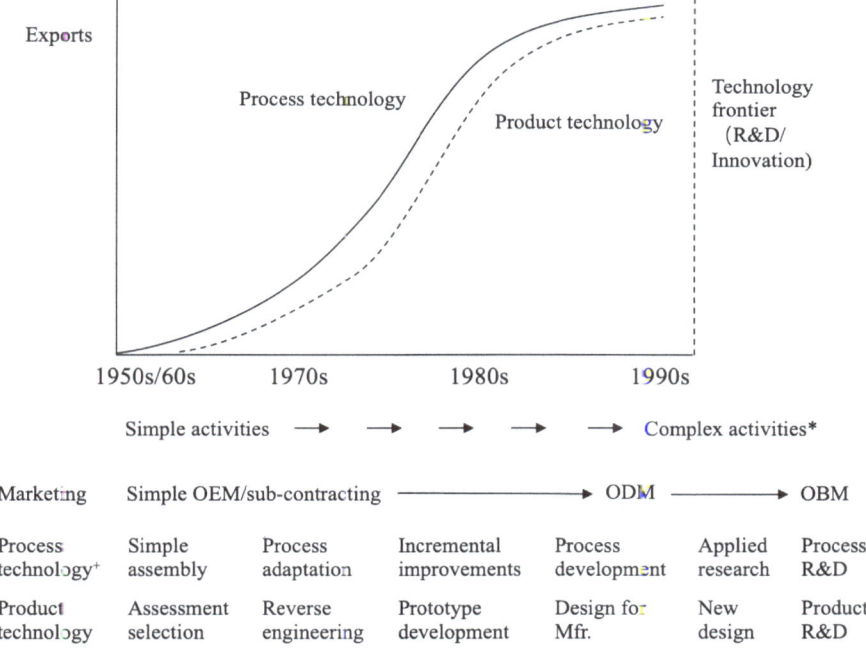

Marketing	Simple OEM/sub-contracting			→ ODM		→ OBM
Process technology[+]	Simple assembly	Process adaptation	Incremental improvements	Process development	Applied research	Process R&D
Product technology	Assessment selection	Reverse engineering	Prototype development	Design for Mfr.	New design	Product R&D

*No stages or linearity, but a general tendency to catch up cumulatively, through time with capabilities building systematically upon each other.
[+]Although it is useful to distinguish between process and product technology for analytical purposes, in practice the two are often inextricably entwined.

Fig. 2.3   Trajectories of industrial upgrading in East Asian NIEs (Fig. 1 in Hobday 1995: 1184)

latecomer firms experienced less functional upgrading unless national states provided substantial investments, such as the cases in the automotive and electronics industries in South Korea and Taiwan.

The second group of studies focuses on upgrading in clusters located in Latin American countries in which sectoral specificity and knowledge diffusion mechanisms were the analytical foci (Pietrobelli and Olarte 2002; Pietrobelli and Rabellotti 2004, 2011; Giuliani 2005; Giuliani et al. 2005; Pietrobelli and Saliola 2008). Examining twelve industrial clusters and forty firms in seven countries, including Brazil, Chile, Colombia, Peru, Mexico, and Costa Rica, Giuliani et al. (2005) identified that sectoral specificity had significant influence on the content and extent of upgrading (see Table 2.3). Pietrobelli and Rabellotti (2011) examined the learning opportunities diffused from GVC to domestic markets and how national innovation systems reacted to facilitate this process. Collective action among local firms was revealed as an important ways of facilitating local upgrading.

The third group of studies focuses on local response as a resistance to the governance imperatives of lead firms (Humphrey and Schmitz 2002a; Schmitz 2004). The governance power of lead firms is endowed by their capabilities in production-parameter setting in their value chains. The purpose of enforcing parameter setting

Table 2.3 Sectoral specificity of industrial upgrading (Adapted from Giuliani et al. 2005)

Industries	Types of upgrading	Rationale
Traditional manufacturing	Active product and process upgrading; rare functional upgrading	Knowledge circulation within clusters, vertical joint actions among suppliers and buyers and multilateral horizontal cooperation
Natural resources-based industries	Process and product upgrading, rare functional upgrading	Intensive application of advanced technologies, public research institutes, and the horizontal joint actions of local associations; rare functional upgrading because of the strict control of industrial standards on food production
Complex product industries	Few cases of upgrading	Little interaction between leader firms and local suppliers
Specialized supplier industries	Active product, process upgrading, and functional upgrading	Thick horizontal cooperative relations and active associational economies, collective initiatives, such as joint R&D activities and joint participation to trade fairs

is to maintain product definition[2] and avoid the risk of supplier failure[3] (Humphrey and Schmitz 2002b). A fundamental imperative of chain governance was identified based on industrial clusters in Mexico, Brazil, Italy, Spain, German, Taiwan, Pakistan, India, and other developing regions (Schmitz 1999; Schmitz and Knorringa 2000; Humphrey and Schmitz 2001, 2002a, 2008; Humphrey 2003; Schmitz 2004). Global lead firms would help local firms to upgrade in order to serve them better. However, these lead firms would impede upgrading whenever they felt competitive pressures from their local suppliers. As a response, local firms launched joint actions to bargain with lead firms. For instance, in the blue Jeans clusters in North America (e.g., Paso and Torreon in Mexico), local manufacturers were seriously confined to translating buyer's specifications into practical knowledge even though that knowledge was necessary for production (Bair and Gereffi 2001, 2003; Bazan and Navas-Alemán 2004; Navas-Aleman and Bazan 2005). In the literature on competitiveness and corporate restructuring, scholars suggested that probably the most valuable strategy for local firms to leverage the governance power of lead firms was to agglomerate together and plug into multiple value chains (Porter 1990, Porter 2000, 2003; Hoskisson et al. 1994; Porter 1996, 1998; Kaplinsky 2000). For instance, investigating into the local automobile industry in Brazil and India, Quadros (2004) demonstrated that local firms developed certain tolerance to strict governance by inserting into multiple value chains which connected to North America and Europe.

2.3.4 Critical Assessments: Whether the Geography of Industrial Upgrading?

This section has shown how non-geographers have articulated the mechanisms of upgrading in the global economy. These studies have informed our understandings of how latecomers pursue industrial upgrading through various means. The state-centric approaches, represented by the studies of FG paradigm, developmental state, and NIS, have demonstrated the important role of nation-states in upgrading in terms of planning preferential industrial policies, forming specific institutions and cultivating indigenous innovative environment. Premised on a firm-centric approach, the GVC literature has revealed dynamics between inter-firm organizations and upgrading in relation to transaction costs and the power of corporate governance. This strand of literature makes significant contributions by leading us to appreciate the importance of value-chain governance that brings upgrading opportunities for latecomers. As a complement, studies of latecomer economies show us the trajectory, industrial specificity, and local resistance in upgrading. These studies have reaffirmed my concern that industrial upgrading is a crucial issue that constitutes the ongoing dynamics

---

[2]It means that lead firms tend to provide precise product specification to suppliers and monitor them.

[3]It means the situation that suppliers fail to follow product definition and make their buyers become vulnerable.

of the global economy. According to these studies, the upgrading process apparently cannot be simplified into a trade-based process of development. It involves changes of technological capacities and corporate functions. It is also more than a process of innovation, as latecomer firms may upgrade through a deliberate strategy of learning that focuses on the mastering and improving of the absorbed technologies from their partners (Viotti 2003). More importantly, the dynamics of strategic actions and power relations are involved during the process of upgrading. With respect to these contributions, I offer two critiques from a geographical perspective.

First of all, these studies have yet to articulate the spatiality of industrial upgrading and thus do not help us appreciate the influences of geographical factors, such as local contexts, regional assets, and resources embedded in GPNs.

In the state-centric approaches, scholars adopted the 'nation-states' as an analytical unit, while neglecting the geographical heterogeneity at subnational scales (regional and local). In other words, these studies are embedded in methodological nationalism. These scholars tended to treat domestic economic environment as homogenous territories and considered the environment as a nationally bounded system. Hence, they argued for the 'national stages of development' as a reproducible model. But this assumption would be highly problematic when applied to a large territorial country, like China, India. and the USA (Chan 1993). As Bernard and Ravenhill (1995: 171) argued, 'rather than Japan's development trajectory being replicated in country after country, industrial diffusion [in East Asia] has been characterized by shifting hierarchical networks of production and partial diffusion into diverse politic-economic contexts at differing historical junctures.' In studies of NIS, scholars critiqued that the 'national systems' were seldom nationally bounded, but were interwoven by the transnational production networks composed by TNCs and suppliers (Ernst 2002, 2005; Ernst and Kim 2002). Empirical studies from East Asian regions also affirmed that the diverse trajectories of regional development were produced by regionalizing production networks arching over the globe rather than by nationalized production systems (Kim 1993; Lüthje 2004; Yeung 2007a, 2009a).

The GVC approach is also insufficient in explaining latecomer upgrading because of its vague spatial ontology. The value chain is conceptualized as a global–local dichotomy of linear structure without contexts. The rationale of the GVC approach lies on sectorally and organizationally specific realities which are the distinctive features of the *chain* metaphor. Hence it overlooks a critical issue which is the embeddedness of value chains. It neglects a fact that the strategy of firms is not fully autonomous, but embedded in spatial contexts in terms of institutional conditions and territorialized assets (Hess 2004). To this point, Bair (2005: 153) argued that 'closer attention to the larger institutional and structural environments in which commodity chains are embedded is needed.' (see more detail critiques in Coe et al. 2008a). Moreover, the GVC approach premises on the determinant power of global lead firms and tends to hold a view that local upgrading, particularly functional upgrading, will necessarily challenge the power of lead firms. Although scholars in the GVC approach have pointed out the efforts of clustering and joint actions from local firms to increase their bargaining power, the global–local nexus still gives no place for analyzing regional and national influences. I argue that incorporating regional and national forces into upgrading studies is important, because these forces may enable local firms either to leverage the power of global lead firms or to nurture more mutual interests with them. In doing so, local upgrading may not necessarily create tension within the value chain. Even more synergy can be identified once local firms develop certain competitive advantages by utilizing institutional assets embedded at regional and national scales. This critical potential has been identified in recent works adopting the GPN approach and I will detail the potential of power dynamics in the next chapter.

Second, these studies of upgrading prefer to be either state-centric or firm-centric in investigating upgrading. This mono-actor perspective has failed to appreciate the synergy among all stakeholders.

The state-centric approaches largely focus on the roles of national institutions and pay insufficient attention to the actual process of technological transfer and absorption at a firm-level analysis. As I have pointed out in Sect. 2.3.1, most of their analyses are quite partial because of their methodological nationalism, while the actual performances of firms are often neglected. These studies often take upgrading for granted because they consider knowledge spillover would happen alone with the prosperity of foreign investment and international trade, but few of empirical surveys are provided to verify this mechanism (Kasahara 2004). To this point, geographers have shown some evidence pointing to the disappointed outcomes of knowledge spillover from foreign investments (Young and Lan 1997; Wang and Lee 2007; Wang and Lin 2008). The GVC approach explicitly articulates the performance of firms in upgrading, while it is premised on a firm-centric approach as I have critiqued in Sect. 2.3.2. Institutional–spatial influences are absent in the value chain analyses. How can the problem of mono-actor perspectives be overcome? I would argue that a broader analytical framework is needed to incorporate both approaches. This work can lead us to appreciate the synergy among all key actors, such as global lead firms, platform developers, CMs, local suppliers and various state institutions, and so on.

2.4   Whither the Geography of Industrial Upgrading?

This chapter provides a critical review of the contemporary studies of industrial upgrading in both geographical and non-geographical literature. The review helps me position the entire book upon a solid ground for answering two basic questions: why studying industrial upgrading is needed; and what we have not known yet. I have summarized the main content of this chapter in Fig. 2.4.

In relation to the geographical literature, I post a 'where' question in the sense that the issue of upgrading is hardly found in mainstream economic geography. It tends to be subsumed into various relevant topics. Based on my assessment, I argue that studying upgrading is valuable, because it leads us to examine regional development in a more critical manner by looking at the catching-up process of local firms. Economic geographers indeed have tackled relevant issues about upgrading which provide some insights for this study, such as global and regional forces of industrial

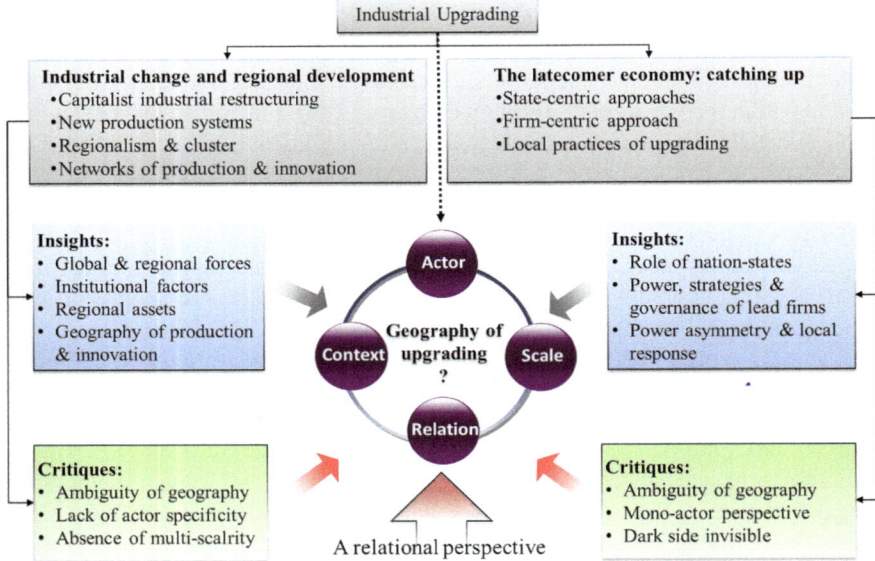

Fig. 2.4 Summary of the literature review and research positioning (drawn by author)

changes, institutional factors in shaping new regional economies, regional assets that underpin region competitiveness, as well as the geography of production and innovation in the era of globalization. These insights guide me to situate this study in a context of globalizing regional development and to pay specific attention to the interaction between firms and state institutions. But these studies have yet to appreciate the variety of upgrading and the power dynamics within value chains/production networks in the process of upgrading. I thus suggest geographers should focus more on actor's behaviors in the process of upgrading, such as incentives, strategies, and practices, which could be considered as a micro-level analysis to a certain degree.

When looking for insights outside geography, I propose a 'whether' question. Non-geographical studies have unpacked the mechanisms of upgrading in three different approaches: state influence, lead firm governance, and local practices. But the geography of these studies is ambiguous. These studies guide me to appreciate the power dynamics and upgrading strategies within various types of value chains. But is industrial upgrading replicable among developed and developing regions? What are the geographical conditions that facilitate or hinder the process of upgrading? How will different institutional–spatial contexts reshape the power, as well as the strategies of upgrading?

By recognizing both insights and limitations of the precedent studies above, I propose a 'whither' question of how a geographical investigation can shed light on the study of industrial upgrading. According to the synthesis of intellectual insights in Fig. 2.4, this study identifies two critical missing links pertinent to the geography of upgrading.

First of all, in the context of a globalizing region, latecomer upgrading is not a purely autonomous or self-contain action of a single firm, but is produced by lead firms, local firms, and state institutions through the process of global integration. The earlier works have informed us the features of global forces and regional forces, respectively. But we have not known much about how different patterns of integration between latecomer regions and the global economy would affect the outcomes of local upgrading.

Second, coming from different scales, these actors are not just rooted in various value chains, but are also embedded in respective institutional–spatial relations. Due to such institutional–spatial embeddedness, the process of local upgrading is neither a purely autonomous process of indigenous learning, nor a predetermined outcome under different governance patterns. Instead, local upgrading is also subject various institutional–spatial conditions. The earlier works have informed the powerful role of global lead firms and the problems of the external dependence of local firms. But we have not known much about how those institutional–spatial conditions would enable local firms to leverage the power of lead firms. In other words, the power dynamics of local upgrading is unclear.

In order to fill in these gaps, a broader analytical tool is needed that can incorporate both firms and non-firm actors from different scales, and then involve economic, institutional, and spatial relations within one single analytical framework. I argue that the relational perspective in economic geography can serve this purpose. Derived from relational thinking in regional development in the 1980s, this perspective focuses on revealing the 'complex nexus of relations among actors and structures that effect dynamic changes in the spatial organization of economic activities' (Yeung 2005: 37). The preoccupation of the next chapter is to develop my analytical framework, conceptualization, and propositions based on this relational perspective.

References

Akamatsu, K. (1961). A theory of unbalanced growth in the world economy. *Weltwirtschaftliches Archiv, 82*(2), 196–215.

Amin, A. (1999). An institutionalist perspective on regional economic development. *International Journal of Urban and Regional Research, 23*(2), 365–378.

Amin, A., & Cohendet, P. (1999). Learning and adaptation in decentralised business networks. *Environment and Planning D-Society & Space, 17*, 87–104.

Amin, A., & Robins, K. (1990). The re-emergence of regional economies? The mythical geography of flexible accumulation. *Environment and Planning D-Society & Space, 8*(7–34).

Amin, A., & Thrift, N. (1992). Neo-Marshallian nodes in global networks. *International Journal of Urban and Regional Research, 16*(4), 571–587.

Amin, A., & Thrift, N. (1994). Globalization and regional development. *Ponte, 50*(7–8), 67–81.

Amsden, A. H. (1989). *Asia's next giant: South Korea and Late Industrialization*. New York: Oxford University Press.

Amsden, A. H. (1997). Bringing production back in—Understanding government's economic role in late industrialization. *World Development, 25*(4), 469–480.

Bagchi, A. K. (2000). The past and the future of the developmental state. *Journal of World-Systems Research, 6,* 398–442.

Bair, J. (2005). Global capitalism and commodity chains: Looking back, going forward. *Competition and Change, 9*(2), 153–180.

Bair, J., & Gereffi, G. (2001). Local clusters in global chains: The causes and consequences of export dynamism in Torreon's blue jeans industry. *World Development, 29*(11), 1885–1903.

Bair, J., & Gereffi, G. (2003). Upgrading, uneven development, and jobs in the North American apparel industry. *Global Networks—A Journal of Transnational Affairs, 3*(2), 143–169.

Barnes, T. J., & Gertler, M. S. (Eds.). (1999). *The new industrial geography: regions, regulation and institutions.* London, New York: Routledge.

Barney, J. (1991). Firm resources and sustained competitive advantage. *Journal of Management, 17*(1), 99–120.

Bathelt, H. (2003). Geographies of production: Growth regions in spatial perspective I-innovation, institutions and social systems. *Progress in Human Geography, 27,* 763–778.

Bathelt, H. (2005). Geographies of production: growth regimes in spatial perspective (II)—Knowledge creation and growth in clusters. *Progress in Human Geography, 29*(2), 204–216. https://doi.org/10.1191/0309132505ph539pr.

Bathelt, H. (2006). Geographies of production: Growth regimes in spatial perspective III—toward a relational view of economic action and policy. *Progress in Human Geography, 30*(2), 223–236.

Bathelt, H., Malmberg, A., & Maskell, P. (2004). Clusters and knowledge: Local buzz, global pipelines and the process of knowledge creation. *Progress in Human Geography, 28,* 31–56.

Bazan, L., & Navas-Alemán, L. (2004). The underground revolution in the Sinos Valley: A comparison of upgrading in global and national value chains. In H. Schmitz (Block), *Local enterprises in the global economy* (pp. 110–139). UK: Edward Elgar.

Beeson, M. (2004). The rise and fall (van Diermen) of the developmental state: The vicissitudes and implications of East Asian interventionism. In L. Low (Block), *Developmental states: Relevancy, redundancy or reconfiguration?* (pp. 29–40). New York: Nova Science Publishers.

Bernard, M., & Ravenhill, J. (1995). Beyond product cycles and flying geese: regionalization, hierarchy, and the industrialization of east asia. *World Politics, 47*(2), 171–209, https://doi.org/10.1017/s0043887100016075.

Boschma, R. A. (2004). Competitiveness of regions from an evolutionary perspective. *Regional Studies, 38*(1), 1001–1014.

Boschma, R. A., & Lambooy, J. G. (1999). Evolutionary economics and economic geography. *Journal of Evolutionary Economics, 9*(2), 411–429.

Boschma, R. A., & Wal., A. L. J. (2007). Knowledge networks and innovative performance in an industrial district: The case of a footwear district in the South of Italy. *Industry and Innovation, 14*(2), 177–199.

Bunnell, T. G., & Coe, N. M. (2001). Spaces and scales of innovation. *Progress in Human Geography, 25*(1), 569–589.

Casper, S., & Karamanos, A. (2003). Commercializing science in Europe: The Cambridge biotechnology cluster. [Article]. *European Planning Studies, 11*(1), 805–822. https://doi.org/10.1080/0965431032000121355.

Cattaneo, O., Gereffi, G., & Staritz, C. (Eds.). (2010). *Global value chains in a postcrisis world.* Washington, DC.: World Bank.

Chan, S. (1993). *East Asian dynamism: Growth, order and security in the pacific region.* Boulder: Westview Press.

Chapman, K. (2005). From 'growth centre' to 'cluster': Restructuring, regional development, and the Teesside Chemical Industry. *Environment and Planning A, 37*(4), 597–615.

Chesbrough, H., & Kusunoki, K. (2001). The modularity trap: Innovation, technology phase shifts, and the resulting limits of virtual organizations. In L. Nonaka, & D. J. Teece (Eds.), *Managing industrial knowledge* (pp. 202–230). London: Sage Press.

Chu, Y. H. (2002). Re-engineering the developmental state in an age of globalization: Taiwan in defiance of Neo-liberalism. *China Review, 2*, 29–59.

Clark, G. L., & Kim, W. B. (1993). Industrial restructuring and regional adjustment in the Asian NIEs. *Environment and Planning A, 25*, 1–4.

Clark, G. L., & Kim, W. B. (1995). *Asian NIEs and the global economy: Industrial restructuring and corporate strategy in the 1990s*. The Johns Hopkins University Press.

Coe, N. M., Dicken, P., & Hess, M. (2008a). Global production networks: realizing the potential. *Journal of Economic Geography, 8*(3), 271–295. https://doi.org/10.1093/jeg/lbn002.

Coe, N. M., Dicken, P., & Hess, M. (2008b). Global production networks—Debates and challenges. *Journal of Economic Geography, 8*(3), 267–269. https://doi.org/10.1093/jeg/lbn006.

Coe, N., Hess, M., Yeung, H. W.-C., Dicken, P., & Henderson, J. (2004). 'Globalizing' regional development: A global production networks perspective. *Transactions of the Institute of British Geographers, 29*(4), 468–484.

Cooke, F., Gomez Uranga, M., & Etxebarria, G. (1997). Regional innovation systems: Institutional and organisational dimensions. *Research Policy, 26*(4–5), 475–491.

Cooke, F., & Morgan, K. (1993). The network paradigm: New departures in corporate and regional development. *Environment and Planning D-Society & Space, 11*(5), 543–564.

Cooke, P., & Morgan, K. (1998). *The associational economy. Firms, regions, and innovation*. Oxford: Oxford University Press.

Depner, H., & Bathelt, H. (2005). Exporting the German model: the establishment of a new automobile industry cluster in Shanghai. *Economic Geography, 81*, 53–81.

Dicken, P. (2007). *Global shift: Mapping the changing contours of the world economy* (5th ed.). London: Sage.

Dicken, P., Kelly, P., Olds, K., & Yeung, H. W.-C. (2001). Chains and networks, territories and scales: toward a relational framework for analyzing the global economy. *Global Network, 1*(2), 89–112.

Dicken, P., & Thrift, N. (1992). The organization of production and the production of organization— Why business enterprises matter in the study of geographical industrialization. *Transactions of the Institute of British Geographers, 17*(3), 279–291.

Douglass, M. (1994). The 'developmental state' and the newly industrialised economies of Asia. *Environment and Planning A, 26*(4), 543–566.

Dunford M. (2006). Industrial districts, magic circles, and the restructuring of the Italian textiles and clothing chain. *Economic Geography, 82*, 27–59.

Dunn, E., Sebstad, J., Batzdorff, L., & Parsons, H. (2006). Lessons learned on MSE upgrading in value chains—A synthesis paper. *AMAP BDS knowledge and practice microREPORT #71, USAID/G/EGAT/MD*. Washington, DC: ACDI/VOCA.

Ernst, D. (2002). Global production networks and the changing geography of innovation systems: Implication for developing countries. *Economics of Innovation and New Technology, 11*, 497–523.

Ernst, D. (2005). Pathways to innovation in Asia's leading electronics-exporting countries—A framework for exploring drivers and policy implications. *International Journal of Technology Management, 29*(1–2), 6–20.

Ernst, D. (2007). Beyond the 'global factory' model: Innovative capabilities for upgrading China's IT industry. *International Journal of Technology and Globalisation, 3*(4), 437–459.

Ernst, D., & Kim, L. (2002). Global production networks, knowledge diffusion, and local capability formation. *Research Policy, 31*(8–9), 1417–1429.

Essletzbichler, J. (2003). From mass production to flexible specialization: The sectoral and geographical extent of contract work in US manufacturing, 1963–1997. *Regional Studies, 37*(8), 753–771.

Essletzbichler, J., & Rigby, D. L. (2001). Industrial and regional restructuring in the US women's dress industry, 1963–92. *Environment and Planning A, 33*(8), 1385–1410.

Fan, P. (2011). Innovation, globalization, and catch-up of latecomers: cases of Chinese telecom firms. *Environment and Planning A, 43*(4), 830–849.

Florida, R. (1995). Towards the learning region. *Futures, 27*, 527–536.

Florida, R. (2002). The economic geography of talent. *Annals of the Association of American Geographers, 92*(4), 743–755.

Frederick, S., & Gereffi, G. (2011). Upgrading and restructuring in the global apparel value chain: Why China and Asia are outperforming Mexico and Central America. *International Journal of Technological Learning, Innovation and Development, 4*(1/2/3), 67–95.

Freeman, C. (1987). *Technology policy and economic performance: Lessons from Japan*. London: Pinter.

Freeman, C. (1994). The economics of technical change. *Cambridge Journal of Economics, 18*, 463–514.

Freeman, C. (1995). The national innovation systems in historical perspective. *Cambridge Journal of Economics, 19*, 5–24.

Freyssenet, M., & Lung, Y. (2000). Between globalization and regionalization: What is the future of the automobile industry? In J. Humphrey, Y. Lecler, & M. Salerno (Eds.), *Global strategies and local realities: The auto industry in emerging markets*. GERPISA: Macmillan.

Frobel, F., Heinrichs, F., & Kreye, O. (1980). *The new international division of labour*. Cambridge: Cambridge University Press.

Galvin, P., & Morkel, A. (2001). The effect of product modularity on industry structure: The case of the world bicycle industry. *Industry and Innovation, 8*, 31–47.

Gereffi, G. (1996). Commodity chains and regional division of labor in East Asia. *Journal Asian Business, 12*, 75–112.

Gereffi, G. (1999). International trade and industrial upgrading in the apparel commodity chain. *Journal of International Economics, 48*, 37–70.

Gereffi, G. (2001a). Beyond the producer-driven/buyer-driven dichotomy—The evolution of global value chains in the Internet era. *Ids Bulletin-Institute of Development Studies, 32*(3), 30–40.

Gereffi, G. (2001b). Shifting governance structures in global commodity chains, with special reference to the internet. *American Behavioral Scientist, 44*(10), 1616–1637.

Gereffi, G., Humphrey, J., & Sturgeon, T. (2005). The governance of global value chains. *Review of International Political Economy, 12*, 78–104. https://doi.org/10.1080/09692290500049805.

Gereffi, G., & Korzeniewicz, M. (Eds.). (1994). *Commodity chains and global capitalism*. Westport: Greenwood Press.

Gereffi, G., & Korzeniewicz, M. (1994b). *Commodity chains and global capitalism*. USA: Greenwood.

Gertler, M. S. (1988). The limits to flexibility—Comments on the Post-Fordist vision of production and its geography. *Transactions of the Institute of British Geographers, 13*(4), 419–432.

Gertler, M. S. (1993). Implementing advanced manufacturing technologies in mature industrial regions: Towards a social model of technology production. *Regional Studies, 27*, 665–680.

Gibbon, P. (2001). Upgrading primary products: A global value chain approach. *World Development, 29*(2), 345–363.

Gibbon, P., & Ponte, S. (2008). Global value chains: From governance to governmentality? *Economy and Society, 37*(3), 365–392. https://doi.org/10.1080/03085140802172680.

Giuliani, E. (2005). Cluster absorptive capacity: Why do some clusters forge ahead and others lag behind? *European Urban and Regional Studies, 12*(3), 269–290.

Giuliani, E., Pietrobelli, C., & Rabellotti, R. (2005). Upgrading in global value chains: Lessons from Latin American clusters. *World Development, 26*(2), 549–573. https://doi.org/10.1016/j.worlddev.2005.01.002.

Glasmeier, A. (1994). Flexible districts, flexible regions? The institutional and cultural limits to districts in an era of globalization and technological paradigm shifts. In A. Amin & N. Thrift (Eds.), *Globalization, institutions, and regional development in Europe* (pp. 118–146). Oxford: Oxford University Press.

Glassman, J. (2001). Economic crisis in Asia: The case of Thailand. *Economic Geography, 77*(2), 122–147.

Glassman, J. (2007). Recovering from crisis: The case of Thailand's spatial fix. *Economic Geography, 83*(4), 349–369.

Grabher, G. (1993). The weakness of strong ties: the lock-in of regional development in the Ruhr area. In G. Grabher (Block), *The embedded firm: On the socioeconomics of industrial networks* (pp. 255–277). London: Routledge.

Grabher, G. (2006). Trading routes, bypasses, and risky intersections: mapping the travels of 'networks' between economic sociology and economic geography. *Progress in Human Geography, 30*(2), 163–189. https://doi.org/10.1191/0309132506ph600oa.

Granovetter, M. (1985). Economic action and social structure—the problem of embeddedness. *American Journal of Sociology, 91*(3), 481–510.

Harrison, B. (1992). Industrial districts-old wine in new bottles. *Regional Studies, 26*(5), 469–483.

Hart-Landsberg, M., & Burkett, P. (1998). Contradictions of capitalist industrialization in East Asia: A critique of "flying geese" theories of development. *Economic Geography, 74*(2), 87–110.

Harvey, D. (1982). *The limits to capital*. Oxford: Blackwell.

Hassink, R. (2005). How to unlock regional economies from path dependency? From learning region to learning cluster. *European Planning Studies, 13*(4), 521–535. https://doi.org/10.1080/09654310500407134.

Henderson, J., Dicken, P., Hess, M., Coe, N., & Yeung, H. W.-C. (2002). Global production networks and the analysis of economic development. *Review of International Political Economy, 9*(3), 436–464. https://doi.org/10.1080/09692290210150842.

Henry, N., Pinch, S., & Russell, S. (1996). In pole position? Untraded interdependencies, new industrial spaces and the British motor sport industry. *Area, 28*, 25–36.

Hess, M. (2004). 'Spatial' relationships? Towards a reconceptualization of embeddedness. *Progress in Human Geography, 28*(2), 165–186. https://doi.org/10.1191/0309132504ph479oa.

Hobday, M. (1995). East-Asian latecomer firms—Learning the technology of electronics. *World Development, 23*, 1171–1193.

Hobday, M. (1998). Product complexity, innovation and industrial organization. *Research Policy, 26*, 689–710.

Hobday, M. (2001). The electronics industries of the Asia-Pacific: Exploiting international production networks for economic development. *Asian-Pacific Economic Literature, 15*, 13–29.

Hobday, M. (2008). *East vs South East Asian innovation systems*. Paper presented at the Presentation to Regional Integration and Deep Integration Conference, CARIS Annual Conference, Sussex University, 22–23 May 2008.

Hobday, M., & de Barros Perini, F. A. (2005). *Latecomer entrepreneurship: A policy perspective*. Paper presented at the IPD Task Force Meeting, Rio de Janeiro, Brazil, 17–19, 2005.

Hobday, M., & Rush, H. (2007). Upgrading the technological capabilities of foreign transnational subsidiaries in developing countries: The case of electronics in Thailand. *Research Policy, 36*, 1335–1356.

Hoskisson, R. E., Johnson, R. A., & Moesel, D. D. (1994). Corporate divestiture intensity in restructuring firms-effects of governance, strategy and performance. *Academy of Management Journal, 37*(5), 1207–1251.

Hsu, J. Y. (2004). The evolving institutional embeddedness of a late-industrial district in Taiwan. *Tijdschrift Voor Economische En Sociale Geografie, 95*, 218–232.

Hsu, C. W., & Chiang, H. C. (2001). The government strategy for the upgrading of industrial technology in Taiwan. *Technovation, 21*(2), 123–132.

Hsu, J. Y., Poon, J. P., & Yeung, H. W. C. (2008). External leveraging and technological upgrading among East Asian firms in the US. *European Planning Studies, 16*, 99–118. https://doi.org/10.1080/09654310701747993.

Huchet, J.-F. (1997). The China circle and technological development in the Chinese electronics industry. In B. Naughton (Block), *The China circle: Economics and electronics in the PRC, Taiwan and Hong Kong* (pp. 254–289). Washington, D.C: Brokking Institution Press.

Hudson, R. (1988). Uneven development in capitalist societies: Changing spatial divisions of labour, forms of spatial organization of production and service provision, and their impacts on localities. *Transactions of the Institute of British Geographers, 13*(4), 484–496.

Hudson, R. (1994). New production concepts, new production geographies? Reflections on changes in the automobile industry. *Transactions of the Institute of British Geographers, 19*(3), 331–345.

Hudson, R. (1997). Regional futures: Industrial restructuring, new high volume production concepts and spatial development strategies in the new Europe. *Regional Studies, 31*(5), 467–478.

Hudson, R. (1999). 'The learning economy, the learning firm and the learning region': A sympathetic critique of the limits to learning. *European Urban and Regional Studies, 6*, 59–72.

Huff, W. G. (1999). Turning the corner in Singapore's developmental state. *Asian Survey, 39*(2), 214–222.

Humphrey, J. (2003). Globalization and supply chain networks: The auto industry in Brazil and India. *Global Networks, 3*(2), 121–141.

Humphrey, J., & Schmitz, H. (2000). Governance and upgrading: Linking industrial cluster and global value chain research. Brighton: IDS Working Paper, 120, Institute of Development Studies, University of Sussex.

Humphrey, J., & Schmitz, H. (2001). Governance in global value chains. *Ids Bulletin-Institute of Development Studies, 32*(3), 19–36.

Humphrey, J., & Schmitz, H. (2002a). Developing country firms in the world economy: Governance and upgrading in global value chains. *INEF Report, 61, University of Duisburg*. Duisburg.

Humphrey, J., & Schmitz, H. (2002b). How does insertion in global value chains affect upgrading in industrial clusters? *Regional Studies, 36*, 1017–1027. https://doi.org/10.1080/0034340022000022198.

Humphrey, J., & Schmitz, H. (2008). Inter-firm relationships in global value chains: Trends in chain governance and their policy implications. *International Journal of Technological Learning, Innovation, and Development, 1*(3), 258–282.

Jessop, B., Brenner, N., & Jones, M. (2008). Theorizing sociospatial relations. *Environment and Planning D-Society & Space, 26*(3), 389–401. https://doi.org/10.1068/d9107.

Johnson, C. (1982). *MITI and the Japanese miracle: The growth of industrial policy, 1925–1975*. Stanford: Stanford University Press.

Kaplinsky, R. (2000). Globalisation and unequalisation: What can be learned from value chain analysis? *The Journal of Development Studies, 37*(2), 117–147.

Kaplinsky, R. (2004). Spreading the gains from globalization—What can be learned from value-chain analysis? *Problems of Economic Transition, 47*(2), 74–115.

Kasahara, S. (2004). *The flying geese paradigm: A critical study of its application to east Asian regional development*. Paper presented at the United Nations Conference on Trade and Development,

Kessler, J. A. (1999). The North American free trade agreement, emerging apparel production networks and industrial upgrading: The southern California/Mexico connection. *Review of International Political Economy, 6*(4), 565–608.

Kim, W. B. (1993). Industrial restructuring and regional adjustment in Asian NIEs. *Environment and Planning A, 25,* 27–46.

Kohli, A. (1994). Where do high growth political economies come from? The Japanese lineage of Korea's "developmental state". *World Development, 22*, 1269–1293.

Leung, C. K. (1993). Personal contacts, subcontracting linkages and development in the Hong-Kong-Zhujiang Delta Region. *Annals of the Association of American Geographers, 83*(2), 272–302.

Liu, W. D., & Dicken, P. (2006). Transnational corporations and 'obligated embeddedness': foreign direct investment in China's automobile industry. *Environment and Planning A, 38*, 1229–1247. https://doi.org/10.1068/a37206.

Lovering, J. (1999). Theory led by policy: the inadequacies of the 'new regionalism' (illustrated from the case of Wales). *International Journal of Urban and Regional Research, 23*(2), 379–395.

Lowe, N. J. (2009). Challenging tradition: Unlocking new paths to regional industrial upgrading. *Environment and Planning A, 41*, 128–145. https://doi.org/10.1068/a40111.

Lundvall, B. Å. (1985). *Product innovation and user—Producer interaction*. Aalborg: Aalborg University Press.

Lundvall, B. Å. (2007). National innovation systems—Analytical concept and development tool. *Industry and Innovation, 14*, 95–119.

Lundvall, B. Å. (Block). (1992). *National systems of innovation: Towards a theory of innovation and interactive learning*. London: Pinter.

Lüthje, B. (2004). Global production network and industrial upgrading in China: The case of electronics contract manufacturing.

MacKinnon, D., Cumbers, A., & Chapman, K. (2002). Learning, innovation and regional development: A critical appraisal of recent debates. *Progress in Human Geography, 26*(3), 293–311.

Malmberg, A., & Maskell, P. (1999). Localized learning and regional economic development. *European Urban and Regional Studies, 6*, 5–8.

Malmberg, A., & Maskell, P. (2002). The elusive concept of localization economies: Towards a knowledge-based theory of spatial clustering. *Environment and Planning A, 34*(3), 429–449. https://doi.org/10.1068/a3457.

Malmberg, A., & Maskell, P. (2006). Localized learning revisited. *Growth and Change, 37*, 1–18.

Martin, R. (2000). Institutional approaches in economic geography. In E. Sheppard, & T. Barnes, J. (Eds.), *A companion to economic geography* (pp. 77–94). MA: Blackwell.

Maskell, P. (2001). The firm in economic geography. *Economic Geography, 77*(4), 329–344.

Maskell, P., Bathelt, H., & Malmberg, A. (2006). Building global knowledge pipelines: The role of temporary clusters. *European Planning Studies, 14*(8), 997–1013. https://doi.org/10.1080/09654310600852332.

Maskell, P., & Malmberg, A. (1999a). The competitiveness of firms and regions—'Ubiquitification' and the importance of localized learning. *European Urban and Regional Studies, 6*, 9–25.

Maskell, P., & Malmberg, A. (1999b). Localised learning and industrial competitiveness. *Cambridge Journal of Economics, 23*(2), 167–185.

Maskell, P., & Malmberg, A. (2007). Myopia, knowledge development and cluster evolution. *Journal of Economic Geography, 7*(5), 603–618. https://doi.org/10.1093/jeg/lbm020.

Massey, D. (1979). In what sense a regional problem? *Regional Studies, 13*(2), 233–243.

Massey, D. (1995). *Spatial divisions of labor: Social structures and the geography of production* (2nd ed.). Basinstoke: Macmillan.

Morgan, K. (1997). The learning region: Institutions, innovation and regional renewal. *Regional Studies, 31*(5), 491–503.

Morris, M., Staritz, C., & Barnes, J. (2011). Value chain dynamics, local embeddedness, and upgrading in the clothing sectors of Lesotho and Swaziland. *International Journal of Technological Learning, Innovation and Development, 4*(1/2/3), 96–119.

Nadvi, K. (2008). Global standards, global governance and the organization of global value chains. *Journal of Economic Geography, 8*(3), 323–343. https://doi.org/10.1093/jeg/lbn003.

Nadvi, K., & Halder, G. (2005). Local clusters in global value chains: Exploring dynamic linkages between Germany and Pakistan. *Entrepreneurship and Regional Development, 17*(5), 339–363. https://doi.org/10.1080/08985620500247785.

Nadvi, K., & Wältring, F. (2004). Making sense of global standards. In H. Schmitz (Block), *Local enterprises in the global economy: Issues of governance and upgrading*. Cheltenman: Edward Elgar.

Navas-Aleman, L., & Bazan, L. (2005). Making value chain governance work for the implementation of quality, labour and environmental standards: Upgrading challenges in the footwear. In E. Giulliani, R. Rabellotti, & M. P. van Dijk (Eds.), *Clusters facing competition: The importance of external linkages*. Hamshire: Ashgate.

Nelson, R. (1994). The co-evolution of technology, industrial structure, and supporting institutions. *Industrial and Corporate Change, 3*, 47–63.

Nelson, R., & Winter, G. S. (1982). *An evolutionary theory of economic change*. USA: Harvard University Press.

Ozawa, T. (2002). The 'hidden' side of the 'flying-geese' catch-up model: Japan's dirigiste institutional setup and a deepening financial morass. *Journal of Asian Economics, 12*(4), 471–491.

Ozawa, T. (2005). *Institutions, industrial upgrading, and economic performance in Japan—The 'Flying-geese' paradigm of catch-up growth*. Northampton, Massachusetts: Edward Elgar.

Park, S. O. (1994). Industrial restructuring in the Seoul metropolitan region: major triggers and consequences. *Environment and Planning A, 26*(4), 527–541.

Park, S. O. (1996). Networks and embeddedness in the dynamic types of new industrial districts. *Progress in Human Geography, 20*(4), 476–493.

Pietrobelli, C., & Olarte, B. T. (2002). Enterprise clusters and industrial districts in Colombia's fashion Sector. *European Planning Studies, 10*(5), 541–562.

Pietrobelli, C., & Rabellotti, R. (2004). *Upgrading in clusters and value chains in Latin America: The role of policies. Sustainable development department best practices series*. Washington, D. C.: Inter-American Development Bank.

Pietrobelli, C., & Rabellotti, R. (2011). Global value chains meet innovation systems: Are there learning opportunities for developing countries? *World Development, 39*, 1261–1269.

Pietrobelli, C., & Saliola, F. (2008). Power relationships along the value chain: multinational firms, global buyers and performance of local suppliers. *Cambridge Journal of Economics, 32*, 947–962. https://doi.org/10.1093/cje/ben016.

Pinch, S., & Henry, N. (1999). Paul Krugman's geographical economics, industrial clustering and the British motor sport industry. *Regional Studies, 33*, 815–827.

Piore, M. J., & Sabel, C. F. (1984). *The second industrial divide: Possibilities for prosperity*. New York: Basic Books.

Pomerleano, M., & Shaw, W. (Eds.). (2005). *Corporate restructuring: Lessons from Experience*. Washington, D.C.: The World Bank.

Porter, M. E. (1990). *The competitive advantage of nations*. London: Macmillan.

Porter, M. E. (1996). What is strategy. *Harvard Business Review*, 61–79.

Porter, M. E. (1998). Clusters and competition: Newagendas for companies, governments, and institutions. In M. Porter (Block), *On competition* (pp. 197–287). Boston: Harvard Business School Press.

Porter, M. E. (2000). Location, competition, and economic development: Local clusters in a global economy. *Economic Development Quarterly, 14*, 15–34.

Porter, M. E. (2003). The economic performance of regions. *Regional Studies, 37*(6&7), 549–578.

Principe, A., A., & Honday, M. (Eds.). (2003). *The business of system integration*. UK: Oxford.

Quadros, R. (2004). Global quality standards and technological upgrading in the Brazilian auto-components industry. In H. Schmitz (Block), *Local enterprises in the global economy* (pp. 110–139). UK: Edward Elgar.

Rainnie, A. (1993). The reorganization of large firm subcontracting. *Capital and Class, 49*, 53–76.

Reimer, S. (2007). Geographies of production I. *Progress in Human Geography, 31*(2), 245–255. https://doi.org/10.1177/0309132507075373.

Saxenian, A. L. (1994). *Regional advantage: culture and competition in Silicon Valley and Route 128*. Cambridge, MA: Harvard University Press.

Saxenian, A. (2002). Silicon valley's new immigrant high-growth entrepreneurs. [Article]. *Economic Development Quarterly, 16*, 20–31.

Saxenian, A., & Hsu, J.-Y. (2001). The Silicon Valley-Hsinchu connection: Technical communities and industrial upgrading. *Industrial and Corporate Change, 10*(4), 893–920.

Schmitz, H. (1999). Collective efficiency and increasing returns. *Cambridge Journal of Economics, 23*(4), 465–483.

Schmitz, H. (2004). *Local enterprises in the global economy*. UK: Edward Elgar.

Schmitz, H., & Knorringa, P. (2000). Learning from global buyers. *Journal of Development Studies - London, 37*(2), 177–206.

Schoenberger, E. (1987). Technological and organizational change in automobile production-spatial implications. *Regional Studies, 21*(3), 199–214.

Schoenberger, E. (1988). From Fordism to flexible accumulation-technology, competitive strategies, and international location. *Environment and Planning D-Society & Space, 6*(3), 245–262.

Schoenberger, E. (1989). Thinking about flexibility—A response. *Transactions of the Institute of British Geographers, 14*, 98–108.

Scott, A. J. (1988a). Flexible production system and regional development—The rise of new industrial spaces in North-America and Western-Europe. *International Journal of Urban and Regional Research, 12*(2), 171–186.

Scott, A. J. (1988b). *New industrial spaces: Flexible production, organisation and regional development in North America and Western Europe*. London: Pion.

Scott, A. J. (1998). From silicon valley to hollywood: Growth and development of the multimedia industry in California. In H. J. Braczyk, P. Cooke, & M. Heidenreich (Eds.), *Regional innovation systems: The role of governances in a globalized world* (pp. 136–162) New York: UCL Press.

Scott, A J. (2005). *On hollywood: The place, the industry*. Princeton and Oxford: Princeton University Press.

Scott, A. J. (2006). Entrepreneurship, innovation and industrial development: Geography and the creative field revisited. *Small Business Economics, 26*, 1–24.

Scott, A. J., & Storper, M. (2003). Regions, globalization, development. *Regional Studies, 37*(6–7), 579–593. https://doi.org/10.1080/0034340032000108697.

Sit, V. F.-S., & Yang, C. (1997). Foreign-investment-induced exo-urbanisation in the Pearl River Delta, China. *Urban Studies, 34*(4), 647–677.

Staritz, C., Gereffi, G., & Cattaneo, O. (2011). Shifting end market and upgrading prospects in global value chains: Editorial. *International Journal of Technological Learning, Innovation and Development, 4*(1/2/3), 1–13.

Steinfeld, E. S. (2004). China's shallow integration: Networked production and the new challenges for late industrialization. *World Development, 32*(11), 1971–1987. https://doi.org/10.1016/j.worlddev.2004.04.003.

Storper, M. (1995). The resurgence of regional economies, ten years later. *Eurasian Urban and Regional Studies, 2*(3), 191–221.

Storper, M. (1997). *The regional world: Territorial development in a global economy*. London and New York: Guilford Press.

Storper, M. (2001). The poverty of radical theory today: From the false promises of Marxism to the mirage of the cultural turn. *International Journal of Urban and Regional Research, 25*, 155–180.

Storper, M., Thomadakis, S., & Tsipouri, L. (Eds.). (1998). *Latecomers in the global economy*. London: Routledge.

Storper, M., & Walker, R. (1989). *The capitalist imperative: Territory, technology and industrial growth*. New York: Basil Blackwell.

Sturgeon, T., & Biesebroeck, J. V. (2011). Global value chains in the automotive industry: An enhanced role for developing countries? *International Journal of Technological Learning, Innovation and Development, 4*(1/2/3), 118–205.

Sturgeon, T., & Kawakami, M. (2011). Global value chains in the electronics industry: Characteristics, crisis, and upgrading opportunities for firms from developing countries. *International Journal of Technological Learning, Innovation and Development, 4*(1/2/3), 120–147.

Todtling F., & Trippl, M. (2004). Like phoenix from the ashes? The renewal of clusters in old industrial areas. *Urban Studies, 41*(5–6), 1175–1195. https://doi.org/10.1080/00420980410001675788.

Todtling F., & Trippl, M. (2005). One size fits all? Towards a differentiated regional innovation policy approach. *Research Policy, 34*, 1203–1219.

Tokatli, N. (2003). Globalization and the changing clothing industry in Turkey. *Environment and Planning A, 35*, 1877–1894.

Tokatli, N. (2007). Asymmetrical power relations and upgrading among suppliers of global clothing brands: Hugo Boss in Turkey. *Journal of Economic Geography, 7*, 67–92.

Tokatli, N. (2008). Global sourcing: Insights from the global clothing industry—the case of Zara, a fast fashion retailer. *Journal of Economic Geography, 8*, 21–38.

Tokatli, N., & Kizilgun, O. (2004). Upgrading in the global clothing industry: Mavi jeans and the transformation of a Turkish firm from full-package to brand-name manufacturing and retailing. *Economic Geography, 80*(3), 221–240.

Trippl, M., & Otto, A. (2009). How to turn the fate of old industrial areas: A comparison of cluster-based renewal processes in Styria and the Saarland. *Environment and Planning A, 41*(5), 1217–1233.

Trippl, M., Todtling, F., & Lengauer, L. (2009). Knowledge sourcing beyond buzz and pipelines: Evidence from the Vienna software sector. *Economic Geography, 85*(4), 443–463.

Tsay, C. L. (1993). Industrial restructuring and international competition in Taiwan. *Environment and Planning A, 25*, 111–120.

Viotti, E. B. (2003). National learning systems: A new approach on technological change in late industrializing economies and evidences from the cases of Brazil and South Korea. *Technological Forecasting and Social Change, 69*, 653–680.

Wade, R. (1990). *Governing the market: Economic theory and the role of government in east Asian industrialization.* Princeton: Princeton University Press.

Walker, R. (1988). The geographical organization of production systems. *Environment and Planning D-Society & Space, 6*(4), 377–408.

Wang, J.-H., & Lee, C.-K. (2007). Global production networks and local institution building: the development of the information-technology industry in Suzhou, China. *Environment and Planning A, 39*(8), 1873–1888. https://doi.org/10.1068/a38428.

Wang, C., & Lin, G. C. S. (2008). The growth and spatial distribution of China's ICT Industry: New geography of clustering and innovation. *Issues and Studies, 44*(2), 145–192.

Webber, M. (1994). Enter the dragon: Lessons for Australia from Northeast Asia? *Environment and Planning A, 26*, 71–94.

Wei, Y. H. D. (2002). Beyond the Sunan model: Trajectory and underlying factors of development in Kunshan, China. *Environment and Planning A, 34*(10), 1725–1747.

Wei, D. Y. H. (2010). Beyond new regionalism, beyond global production networks: Remaking the Sunan Model, China. *Environment and Planning C: Government and Policy, 28*, 72–96.

Wei, D., Y. H., Li, W., & Wang, C. (2007). Restructuring industrial districts, scaling up regional development: A study of the Wenzhou model, China. *Economic Geography, 83*(4), 421–444.

Wei, Y. H. D., Liu, Y. Q., & Chen, W. (2009). Globalizing regional development in Sunan, China: Does Suzhou Industrial Park fit a neo-Marshallian district model? *Regional Studies, 43*(3), 409–427.

White, G. (Block). (1988). *Developmental states in East Asia.* New York: St. Martin's Press.

Xiao, Z. X., & He, J. S. (2010). Industrial upgrading in electronic information product manufacturing in Pearl River Delta—Case in Dongguang Qingxi Town (in Chinese). *Special Zone Economy, 27*(3), 33–37.

Yang, C. (2007). Divergent hybrid capitalisms in China: Hong kong and Taiwanese electronics clusters in Dongguan. *Economic Geography, 83*(4), 395–420.

Yang, Y.-R., Hsu, J.-Y., & Ching, C.-H. (2009). Revisiting the silicon Island? The geographically varied 'strategic coupling' in the development of high-technology parks in Taiwan. *Regional Studies, 43*(3), 369–384.

Yang, C., & Liao, H. (2009). Backward linkages of cross-border production networks of Taiwanese PC investment in the Pearl River Delta, China. *Tijdschrift Voor Economische En Sociale Geografie, 101*(2), 199–217.

Yeung, H. W.-C. (2000). Organizing 'the firm' in industrial geography I: networks, institutions and regional development. *Progress in Human Geography, 24*(2), 301–315.

Yeung, G. (2001). *Foreign investment and socio-economic development in China: The case of Dongguan.* Palgrave: Basingstoke.

Yeung, H. W.-C. (2002). Industrial geography III: Industrial restructuring and labour markets. *Progress in Human Geography, 26*(3), 367–379.

Yeung, H. W. (2005). Rethinking relational economic geography. *Transactions of the Institute of British Geographers, 30*, 37–51.

Yeung, H. W. (2007a). From followers to market leaders: Asian electronics firms in the global economy. *Asia Pacific Viewpoint, 48*, 1–25. https://doi.org/10.1111/j.1467-8373.2007.00326.x.

Yeung, H. W.-C. (2009). Regional development and the competitive dynamics of global production networks: An East Asian perspective. *Regional Studies, 43*(3), 325–351.

Young, S , & Lan, P. (1997). Technology transfer to China through foreign direct investment. *Regional Studies, 31,* 669–679.

Zhou, Y. (2008a). *The Inside Story of China' High-Tech Industry: Making Silicon Valley in Beijing.* Lanham, MD: Rowman & Littlefield Publishers.

Zhou, Y. (2008b). Synchronizing export orientation with import substitution: Creating competitive indigenous high-tech companies in China. *World Development, 36*(11), 2353–2370.

Zhou, Y., & Tong, X. (2003). An innovative region in China: Interaction between multinational corporations and local firms in a high-tech cluster in Beijing. *Economic Geography, 79*(2), 129–152.

Chapter 3
The Interaction Between Strategic Coupling and Industrial Upgrading: A Framework

3.1 Upgrading in the Contemporary Global Economy

In an era of globalization, the territorial ensembles of economic development, such as places, cities, and regions, are interconnected into complex production networks (Amin 1998, 2002). What makes globalization different from earlier stages is that the global shift of production networks breaks up a commodity chain into many segments which are geographically separated among different while interconnected sites. By plugging into these overarching production networks, firms in latecomer regions can receive the opportunities of upgrading to learn from TNCs. To many latecomer economies presently, attracting foreign investment or export-oriented industrialization has become a well-known tool for promoting economic growth. However, whether latecomer firms are able to catch up with foreign firms and achieve industrial upgrading is in question. Without upgrading, local firms are not competitive and highly substitutable.

In order to upgrade, the GVC literature suggests latecomer firms to insert into value chains as the quick followers of global lead firms. Latecomer firms have a chance to climb up the value-added ladder step by step, if they fulfill all requirements set by lead firms (Schmitz 2004; Sturgeon and Lester 2004b; Gereffi et al. 2005). But the problem is that the local upgrading is limited because the content and extent are defined by the governance patterns of TNCs. As a response, development studies suggest that national forces (e.g., state intervention) can be a key ingredient for promoting domestic industrial upgrading against the control of TNCs. Economic geographers contribute to the debate by pointing out various regional and local factors that shed light on the regional pathways of industrial upgrading. The common thread of development studies and economic geography is the belief that institutional factors, such as states and associational economies, can be proactive actors in facilitating the process of industrial upgrading.

How can these two strands of literature be reconciled? One emphasizes the dominant role of lead firms and the other highlights institutional influences. According to

© Springer Nature Singapore Pte Ltd. 2020
Y. Liu, *Local Dynamics of Industrial Upgrading*, Economic Geography,
https://doi.org/10.1007/978-981-15-4297-8_3

my critical review in Chap. 2, a broader theoretical framework is needed to incorporate three key actors (global lead firms, state institutions, and local firms) and their contexts into analyses (see Fig. 2.4). This chapter provides a means of doing this. Instead of focusing on corporate power or state power alone, this study considers that the interaction among actors is the key for explaining the dynamics of local upgrading. This attempt is built on the concept of *strategic coupling*. In the context of globalizing regional development, it represents to the pattern of integration between latecomer regions and the global economy. The central research question driving this study is how different patterns of strategic coupling affect local industrial upgrading. This research question is resonated with Hubert Schmitz who has argued that the pattern of global integration is the focus of latecomer development:

> A key concern in industrial policy [for developing countries] is how to configure the relationship with the global economy…the choice open to them [developing countries] is not therefore whether to integrate into the global economy, but how: fast or slowly, comprehensively or selectively, taking the low or the high road (Schmitz 2007: 417).

My question includes three aspects: (1) how does industrial upgrade happen within the process of strategic coupling and who are the key drivers; (2) how does strategic coupling evolve and lead to upgrading; (3) in what ways can geographical factors, such as the institutional–spatial contexts of firms, reshape power relations, and local strategies within the coupling relationships, thus facilitating or hindering upgrading. Through examining these issues, I argue that industry upgrading in a globalizing region is mainly driven by the strategic coupling which in turn is constituted by the interactive effects among local firms, TNCs, and regional institutions. This central argument helps readers understand the ongoing dynamics of upgrading in latecomer economies, rather than deem it as a pre-determined trajectory based on stylized governance patterns or a necessary outcome of industrial promotions assisted by state institutions.

To legitimize my central argument, this chapter is organized into five sections. The next section elaborates on my epistemological selection of the relational perspective in economic geography. It articulates how the relational perspective leads us to reinterpret industrial upgrading. The third section develops a relational framework for conceptualizing casual relations between strategic coupling and industrial upgrading in the context of globalizing regional development. Actors' strategies, relations, power, and knowledge gaps are key factors that shape the formation of strategic coupling. The penultimate section theorizes four types of strategic coupling that produce local upgrading in different ways. Four propositions are developed for empirical examination. In conclusion, I discuss how my analytical framework and conceptualization contributes to the literature.

3.2 A Relational Perspective on Industrial Upgrading

To unpack the interaction between actors within global production network, the debate about relational economic geography serves as the central building blocks of this theorization. Such a relational fabric of upgrading rests on the basis of the previous conceptualization of industrial upgrading related to the literature of industrial governance and strategic management.

3.2.1 A Debate on Relational Economic Geography

The original idea of relational economic geography (REG) can be dated back to the late 1970s according to the relational thinking and the discussions of extra-regional processes in understanding regional development (Dicken 1976; Massey 1979). These works were gradually developed into a new strand of conceptual work known as the 'relational turn' in economic geography (Yeung 1994; Amin 1998; Ettlinger 2001; Bathelt and Glückler 2003; Boggs and Rantisi 2003; Yeung 2005; Jones 2009). Since the 2000s, this perspective has been deployed by geographers to articulate the formation of the network forms of production and innovation in the process of globalization, such as the GPN literature (see Chap. 2). The analytical focus of the relational perspective is the 'complex nexus of relations among actors and structures that effect dynamic changes in the spatial organization of economic activities' (Yeung 2005: 37). A debate about this perspective has recently emerged with two distinctive views.

From a proponent's sympathetic critique, contemporary works in REG are not 'relational enough.' Most of the works are only conducted in a '*thematic* sense, focusing on various themes of socio-spatial relations without theorizing sufficiently the nature of relationality and its manifestation through power relations and actor-specific practice' (Yeung 2005: 37). Bathelt and Glucker (2003: 125) located the essence of REG in analyzing 'intensions and strategies of economic actors and ensembles of actors and the patterns of how they behave.' Yeung (2005) argued that in order to operationalize a 'relational thinking,' geographers needed to move from focusing on relations per se to unraveling the fabrics of relations. For instance, further efforts are suggested to examine relationality and different types of emergent power in a relation.

From an opponent's view, the REG approach is going to be too 'relational' and too abstract so that it has a risk of losing much of its content and analytical capability (Sunley 2008). The general critique is that REG focuses on relations per se and does not identify causal mechanisms. It thus becomes 'immune' to empirical evaluation. The REG approach is also characterized as preferring a loose analytical framework and privileging a network-centric view. Therefore, REG may lack a coherent research agenda and tends to restrict on a micro-level analysis that acts like a post-essentialist or post-scale approach based on a flat spatial ontology.

This book does not read these two views as hostile, but as complimentary. Both the opponents and proponents have recognized the weaknesses of the REG approach in identifying causal mechanisms, whereas their prescriptions for overcoming this limit are different. Yeung (2005: 48) argued to 'unpack relational geometries[1] imbued with causal power capable of producing spatial change,' whereas Sunley (2008: 19) suggested to recognize the durability of economic habits and routines which rendered the patterns of economic relations as the 'reproduction and transformation of sets of rules and conventions.' By recognizing the pros and cons, this study stays in line with REG.

Sunley's (2008) suggestion points to an evolutionary approach in economic geography which focuses on revealing differentiated spatial systems that cause the evolution of economic actors (Boschma and Lambooy 1999; Boschma and Frenken 2006; Martin and Sunley 2006). The evolutionary approach has difficulty in explaining economic behaviors within a shorter time span. So far, it still has difficulties in operationalizing empirically key concepts, such as routines, path dependency, and lock-in (see the debates in a special issue lead by Boschma and Frenken 2009). To this point, the REG approach provides a more realistic and feasible epistemological toolkit for examining upgrading in a latecomer region. The merits of the relational perspective are that it does not privilege any forces and actors at different scales; it highlights various relational factors, but not solely looks at network forms of organization per se. Hence, the REG approach can incorporate both firms and non-firm actors from different scales; and then involve economic, institutional, and spatial relations within one single analytical framework. More importantly, adopting the relational perspective enables this study to bridge REG with the GVC literature, because network/chain analysis is a common thread in these two strands of literature. In doing so, this study is capable of analyzing value-chain governance, inter-firm networks, and the embeddedness (institutional–spatial contexts) of these networks within a single analytical framework.

3.2.2 Conceptualizing Industrial Upgrading: In What Sense Is It Relational?

The above discussion presents the REG approach as an appropriate analytical tool for examining industrial upgrading. Through this epistemological lens, the phenomenon of industrial upgrading is reinterpreted as a group of interconnected firms and non-firm actors which cooperate and compete with each other for their own upgrading strategies in a specific spatial context. The question is in what sense industrial upgrading is relational.

---

[1]This refers to the spatial configurations of heterogeneous relations among actors and structures through which power and identities are played out and become efficacious (Massey 1979; Yeung 2005: 38).

In a simplest way, industrial upgrading is 'to make better products, make them more efficiently, or move into more skilled activities' (Schmitz 2004: 1). More specifically, industrial upgrading is 'a process of improving the ability of a firm or an economy to move to more profitable and/or technologically sophisticated capital and skill-intensive economic niches' (Gereffi 1999). There are four general types of firm-level upgrading including process, product, functional, and channel upgrading (see Sect. 2.3 in Chap. 2). At an aggregated level, such as a regional scale, industrial upgrading would have two forms (Gereffi 1999; Boschma 2004). First is the improvement of regional competitiveness through the development of vertical integration and the intra-regional division of labor. Second is the renewal of regional economies through establishing new industries. The second type of regional upgrading could be shallow because new industries can be directly transplanted from elsewhere through the relocation of multi-plant firms and/or TNCs. During such a process, the firm may not upgrade at all. This study uses the term of *local upgrading* to refer the upgrading of local firms at either the firm level or the regional level so as to distinguish it from regional upgrading contributed by TNCs.

The process of upgrading involves relational features. The decision and implementation of upgrading are subject to diverse influences from intra-, inter- and, extra-firm relations. These relations provide various channels for firms to accumulate necessary resources for upgrading. Meanwhile, when a firm implements an upgrading action, it may receive supports or resistances from other stakeholders which can be suppliers, strategic partners, customers, or other in situ institutional actors (e.g., governments). These relational features are not novel in contemporary studies. The GVC literature has articulated various inter-firm relations within value chains and how these relations influence upgrading (Gereffi 1999; Gereffi et al. 2005; Staritz et al. 2011). Development studies have revealed firm–state relations which channel state supports and assistance to domestic firms for upgrading (Evans 1995; Beeson 2004; Meyer-Stamer et al. 2004; Cammett 2007). Geographers have also revealed various inter-organizational relations that construct regional innovation and learning networks (Morgan 1997; MacKinnon et al. 2002; Trippl et al. 2009). These relations, linkages or external connects are important because these channels not only circulate resources for firms to upgrading, but also serve as a platform where power relations and interactions affect the outcomes of upgrading.

3.3 An Analytical Framework

The aim of this section is to operationalize the relational perspective in the investigation of industrial upgrading. It first introduces the GPN framework and the conceptualization of strategic coupling. Based on these elaborations, a triangular analytical framework is developed where the mechanisms of industrial upgrading enact.

3.3.1 Global Production Networks and Strategic Coupling

A GPN is defined as a globally organized nexus of interconnected functions and operations by firms and non-firm institutions through which goods and services are produced and distributed (Henderson et al. 2002; Coe et al. 2004). The framework of GPN 'aims to reveal the multi-actor and multi-scalar characteristics of transnational production systems through intersecting notions of power, value, and embeddedness' (Coe et al. 2008a: 267). The GPN framework moves beyond the GVC approach in three ways. First, it is more realistic in its analytical commitment to the network form, not linear structure. Second, the GPN analysis involves non-firm actors, institutional arrangements and institutional environment. It is not limited to cost-based transactions, while open to other non-cost-based interactions, such as untraded interdependency, dedicated commitment, complementarity, or the social mechanisms of network governance (Jones et al. 1997; Storper 1997b; Yeung 2005). Third, the GVC approach tends to assume a pre-determined asymmetrical power relation that leads firms to have dominant power over local firms. In contrast, the GPN framework has a more flexible understanding of power which treats power in as a relational effect. The practices of power are not pre-determined, but subject to the specific relationality and the contexts of actors (Henderson et al. 2002; Yeung 2005; Hess and Yeung 2006; Hess 2008). Although lead firms are powerful in their owned value chains, local firms may find a way to leverage their power by utilizing resources resting in their institutional and spatial contexts.

Since the 1970s, geographers have witnessed an intensified articulation of latecomer economies in the Asia–Pacific region into GPNs in various industries, such as the dramatic rise of Japan, the rapid industrialization of the four East Asian 'tigers' economies and the recent ascendance of an emerging giant, China (Hoskisson and Johnson 1992; Gereffi 1994; Clark and Kim 1995; Sit and Yang 1997; Cho et al. 1998; Ozawa 2005; Dicken 2007). This integration is mainly associated with a process conceptualized as *strategic coupling* (see Fig. 3.1). The term 'strategic' implies that this integration is not just a simple process of industrial relocation in which TNCs are attracted by the growing gap of production costs between developing regions and developed regions. 'It is the interactive effects between these two fields [regions] that contribute to regional development, not just either inherent regional advantages or the industrial structure of global industries' (Coe and Hess 2011: 131). Strategic coupling occurs when regional asset structures meet the demands of firms within GPNs. Regional institutional actors, such as policy makers, play as a critical mediator in optimizing regional assets to seek for a better connection with GPNs so that local firms may take up a more promising position.

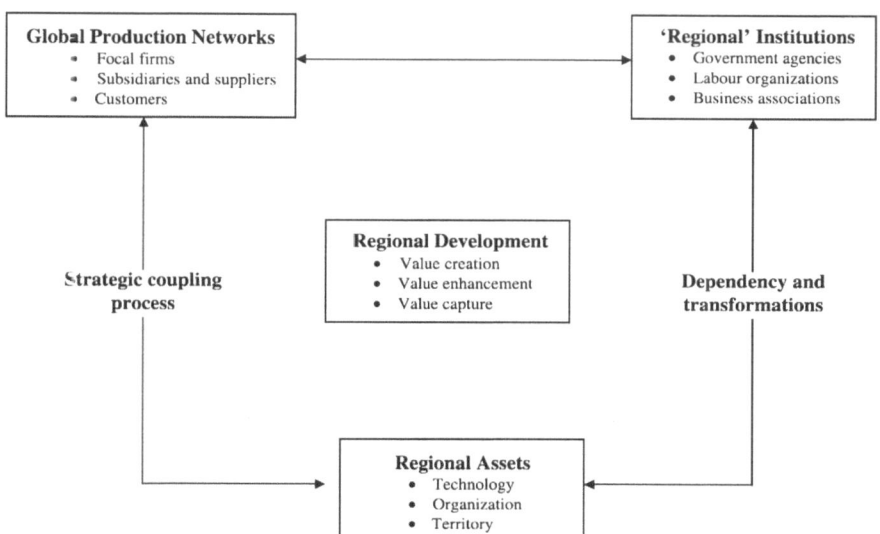

Fig. 3.1 Strategic coupling in globalizing regional development (Fig. 3.1 in Coe et al. (2004: 470))

3.3.2 Actors, Knowledge Gaps, and Tension

As shown in Fig. 3.1, the process of strategic coupling constitutes relations and power among key actors which subsequently determines the ways of value creation, enhancement, and capture. Based on Fig. 3.1, this study develops a specific framework for understanding better globalizing regional development and the dynamics of industrial upgrading (see Fig. 3.2). In Fig. 3.2, industrial upgrading takes place in a latecomer region based on strategic coupling between TNCs in GPNs and local firms in the region through which the advantages of regions interact with the strategic needs of the TNCs. Meanwhile, both TNCs and local firms indirectly couple with regional institutions through the process of institutional matching. Three key actors are identified in this relational framework: transnational corporations, local firms, and regional institutions.

Transnational corporations (TNCs) refer to firms that have the power to coordinate and control operations in more than one country, even if they do not own them. During the process of globalization, TNCs are primary players orchestrating their GPNs at a global scale. Some of them are global lead firms (branded-name firms presenting in end markets) which rest in the core positions of GPNs with superior technological and market power. Some of them grow into key suppliers or contract manufacturers for lead firms, following lead firms' steps during global industrial relocation (Humphrey 2003). Some of them pursue industrial specialization and become platform developers or specialized-product providers (Sturgeon 2002). TNCs will be attracted to locate at different regions due to their interests to take advantages of geographical differences in production or distribution factors. The advantages can

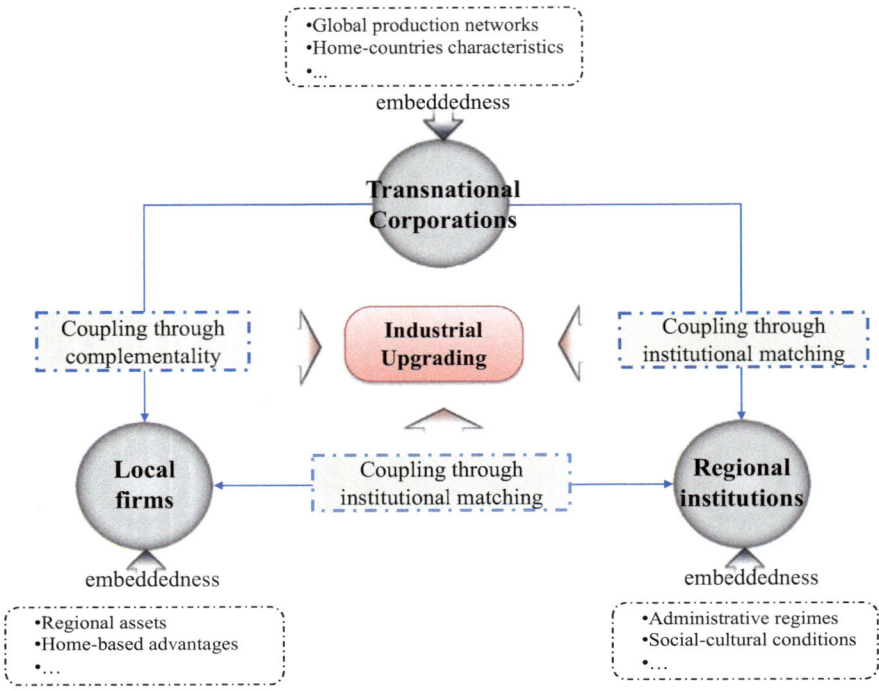

Fig. 3.2 An analytical framework of industrial upgrading in globalizing regions (compiled by author)

be ownership, locational, or internationalization advantages in Dunning's account (Dunning 1979, 1988, 1995, 2000); the capabilities in the supply-based (Gereffi et al. 2005); special natural resources, lower labor wages, or specific state policies in terms of fiscal incentives, industrial policies, trade barriers, subsidies, and so on.

Local firms (the same as latecomer firms in this book) are the firms originating within a region. Conceptually, they are similar to local suppliers in the terminology of the GVC literature. Except for earning a profit, the initiative of local firms is to catch up with TNCs to prevent being discarded or marginalized by them. To reap time-cost efficiency during the process of catching up, most of the local firms would like to develop external linkages for sourcing knowledge and seeking additional assistance in territories, networks, and society where they are embedded (Hess 2004). This is the fundamental incentive for local firms to develop strategic coupling with TNCs and regional institutions.

Regional institutions in Fig. 3.2 are represented by regional formal organizations, regionally specific institutions, local arms of national/supranational bodies, and extra-local institutions that affect activities within regions without co-present necessity (Coe et al. 2004). Governmental agencies are the most important representatives that exert power based on a political-administrative system of governance dominated by

Table 3.1   Knowledge gaps between latecomers' firms and TNCs [Adapted from Fig. 3.2 in Hobday (1995) and Schmitz (2007: 422)]

Industrial and market configuration	Technology gap	Market gap
Matured industries: standard technologies with slow change	Low	High
New industries: specific technologies with rapid change	High	Moderate
Foreign market: high demanding of design and quality, highly competitive	High	High
Domestic market: matured products with lower technological requirement and price competition	Low	Non-existent

national/regional/local states. Associational economies exist as networked forms of industrial organizations which mean for fostering inter-organizational cooperation and communication, the alleged 'collective social order' (Cooke and Morgan 1998). Regional institutions serve as a critical mediator in optimizing regional assets and providing business-friendly and supportive institutional environment. In doing so, regional benefits from attracting good-performance TNCs to locate in and generate a knowledge-spillover effect among in situ firms through various means (Trippl et al. 2009).

When strategic coupling happens in a latecomer region, three key actors engage each other and form different power relations. The opportunities of industrial upgrading result from knowledge diffusion and reproduction among the coupled actors. There are basically two main obstacles for local firms to catch up with TNCs: dislocation from the main international sources of technology and from the main international markets they seek to enter (Hobday 1995). Schmitz (2007) reinterpreted these obstacles a s technology and market gaps. Extending their ideas, I term these gaps as knowledge gaps shaped by the specific knowledge structures and prior knowledge of respective actors. Table 3.1 lists the main features of technology and market gaps that vary among different industries and market conditions.

To latecomer firms in GPNs, technology gap is a result of isolation from original sources of technologies, such as R&D centers, or the feedback loop between users and producers that spurs innovation; the difficulty of accessing proprietary technology; and weak indigenous innovation capability. Market gap originates from the difficulty for them to understand and respond to rapidly changing consumer demands when it is disconnected from the final market. Core market knowledge can be seasonal and heterogeneous market demands as well as tastes or fashion trends, skills of marketing, branding and distribution, the expertise of supply chain management, and so on (Barney 1991; Van den Bulte and Moenaert 1998; Schmitz 2004).

When strategic coupling is developed, the central concern of key actors is how to develop a better relationship that can meet partners' demands and yet fulfill their own business goals simultaneously. However, there is a fundamental tension in relation to knowledge gaps and diffusion.

The primary concern of latecomer firms is to bridge the knowledge gap between the expectations of TNCs and their in-house capabilities, and even create their own lead. In contrast, the primary issue for TNCs is to maintain these gaps at a moderate distance. They tend to define the content of local upgrading so that local suppliers can produce qualified products and will not grow up to become a new competitor toward TNCs themselves. In doing so, TNCs can reinforce their leading positions in GPNs as an industrial 'gatekeeper' (Humphrey and Schmitz 2002b; Schmitz 2004, 2007). This is the critical dilemma that TNCs encounter within strategic coupling. But latecomer firms also encounter a dilemma. The quicker latecomer firms would like to catch up, the more they need to be dependent on TNC so as to maximize learning opportunities. But this dependency may produce heavy sunk costs and cause technological and organizational lock-in. Latecomer firms, therefore, lose more bargaining power due to a high degree of asset specificity.

Between regional institutions and firms, there is a potential tension in institutional mismatching. While regional policy networks are meant to satisfy the demands of local and foreign firms, they do not necessarily produce benefits for all participants in a regional economy. In some occasions, regional polices may even pose challenges to firms' own interests (Schmitz 2007; Coe and Hess 2011). This is because regional institutions are not profit-seeking actors and may have many other value orientations, such as social welfare or political objectives. The firm–state relationship is critical. The dilemma of regional institutions in promoting upgrading is summarized in four paradoxes (Meyer-Stamer et al. 2004; Cammett 2007):

1. (1) Upgrading-life-cycle paradox: pursuing active local policy is crucial in the early stage of upgrading but effective local policy networks are likely to be available at a late stage;
2. Integrationist paradox: local policy networks which seek to achieve close relationships between local producers and global producers will be marginalized if they have successfully upgraded;
3. Location paradox: firms are increasingly demanding when it comes to locational quality but show a decreasing propensity to invest in local policy network;
4. Cost-efficiency paradox: assisting the upgrading of local firms is an ultimate way of improving regional competitiveness, but it is more time-consuming and costly in comparing with attracting the location of TNCs.

3.3.3   Power Dynamics and the Strategies of Local Firms

The above two types of tension imply that interactions and power dynamics within strategic coupling can never be static and pre-determined. In contrast, the interactions are contingent on mutual interest and power strength of each party. Due to the existence of tension, local upgrading is possible but tends to be limited. According to the GVC literature, latecomer firms hardly have a chance to avoid this destiny because of global lead firms' dominant governance power. But as I have critiqued in Chap. 2, this assertion is over deterministic and neglects the potential of power dynamics within strategic coupling.

In REG, power refers to the relational effects of a capacity to influence and the exercise of this capacity through actor-specific practices (Allen 2003; Yeung 2005; Hess 2008). This book follows Allen's (2003) conceptualization that power is anchored in institutional space. It is positional and also practical through social actions. It becomes emergent when it is practiced, while power is not inherently possessed, and is not everywhere.

To TNCs, their power is derived from two specificities: (1) their capabilities to orchestrate GPNs so that they can take advantages of geographical differences in the distribution of factors of production; (2) their capability in setting parameters and standards in industries (Gereffi 2001a; Gibbon 2001; Gereffi et al. 2005; Hess and Coe 2006; Sturgeon et al. 2009). This power of domination is organizationally embedded in GPNs and geographically embedded in their home countries/regions which serve as the sources of R&D activities, innovation, and primary strategic decisions (Coe et al. 2008a, b). TNCs control the developmental pace of their branch plants, subcontractors, and other low-tier suppliers. Meanwhile, they also bargain with regional institutions for lower production costs, better fiscal incentives, and more supportive institutional environment.

To local firms, their power comes from their technological capabilities and other competitive advantages, such as producing products and other home-based advantages. Normally, local firms are less powerful because they are substitutable, unless they possess a unique resource or develop certain technological edges, or find out a specific niche market.

To regional institutions, their power is the state-legitimated administrative power that refers to the capacity of a state to regulate behaviors and enforce order within its territory. In globalization, this power is highly localized and represented by the control of market entry and regulatory regime designed for accommodating firms. As Dicken (2007) has summarized, there are a great deal of resources and components that can shape a bargaining relationship between TNCs and host countries (see Fig. 3.3).

Why are the power relations dynamic rather than pre-determined? Within strategic coupling, the relative bargaining power of actors largely depends on the extent to which one party possesses assets sought by the other party; and the extent to which either party can control that access (Lecraw 1984; Appleyard 1996; Liu and Dicken 2006). In this sense, capability in controlling access to specific assets is a major source of bargaining strength. Where such assets are available in a number of location or organization, the power strength will be lower; or even non-existent when the asset is universal. But where a particular asset is highly localized (either geographically or organizationally), the actor who controls access to that asset will have the greatest bargaining power. Situating local upgrading in such an analytical context, there are many alternatives for latecomer firms to reshape power relations with TNCs. Local firms may increase bargaining power if they possess certain scarce resources or receive additional supports from state institutions. Local firms also can bypass the governance power if they identify alternative sources of knowledge, such as multi-tasking by inserting various value chains within the same GPN. Furthermore, local firms can directly lower tension and even develop new synergy, when they identify

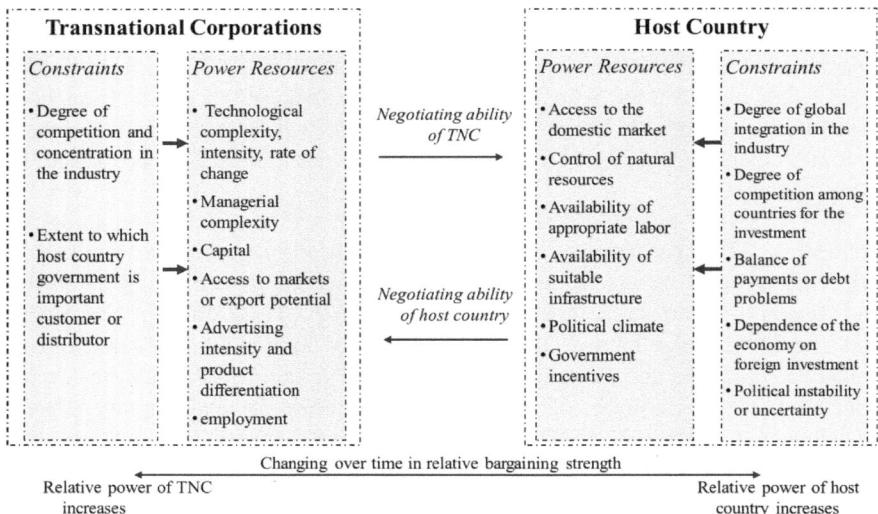

Changing over time in relative bargaining strength

Relative power of TNC
increases

Relative power of host
country increases

Fig. 3.3 Components of the bargaining relationship between TNCs and host countries. *Source* Adapted from Fig. 7.5 in Dicken (2007: 241)

more mutual interests with TNCs. Recognizing these alternatives, there are three important institutional–spatial conditions that underpin local firms to leverage power relations with TNCs.

The first condition is the *diversity of knowledge channels* that emphasizes the available networks of knowledge diffusion rather than one-way diffusion from TNCs to local firms. Trippl et al. (2009) have provided a sound summary of these linkages (see Table 2.2). By plugging into a GPN, firms would have many potential ways of knowledge accumulation, such as formal transactions, informal communication, technology transfer, organizational succession, learning by doing, learning by inter-action, benchmarking, and collective learning. These channels help local firms to reduce dependence on TNCs.

The second condition is *the availability of regional assets* which are more at regional (national) scale. The concept refers to the 'holy trinity' of technology—orga-nization—territories defined by Storper (1997b). Regional assets can be supportive industrial policies set by proactive states; associational economies including indus-trial associations, chamber of commerce, and other business organizations; home-based advantages like cluster economies, localized supply networks, and social-ethic communities; or large domestic markets (see Sect. 2.2 in Chap. 2). Embedded in these regional assets, local firms may give TNCs more incentives to share or co-develop knowledge with them. Because regional assets are territorially bounded, transaction costs increase for non-local actors to get access. Local firms have certain advantages based on social-cultural familiarity, though these assets are not entirely exclusive to non-local actors.

The third condition refers to *the complexity of competitive dynamics* in GPNs that is more relevant on a global scale. It points to competition between TNCs at the top hierarchy of their value chains. This condition has a strong impact on TNCs' decisions to cooperate with other partners due to competitive pressures within GPNs. To local firms, the more complicated that competitive dynamics is, the more upgrading opportunities they may identify.

There are three basic types of competitive dynamics, *cost, flexibility*, and *speed (time to market)*, which are pushing global lead firms to deepen cooperation with their local partners so that they can further sharpen their competitive cutting edges (Lüthje 2002; Yeung 2009). Meanwhile, competitions between global lead firms and platform developers also provides new opportunities for contract manufacturers and suppliers to implement functional upgrading (Galvin and Morkel 2001; Lüthje 2002, 2004; Feenstra and Hamilton 2006; Sturgeon and Kawakami 2011). For instance, they can purchase and internalize turn-key technologies from platform developers within the same GPN, thus directly upgrading into owned-brand manufacturers to compete with lead firms. In this case, lead firms have not power to block this upgrading because lead firms can only exert control upon their value chains but not the whole GPN.

In sum, by recognizing these institutional–spatial conditions (contexts), we can identify more strategies of local upgrading. Taking advantages of various institutional–spatial conditions, local firms may leverage the governance power of TNCs without challenging them. Interactions among key actors thus present vivid scenarios configured by different incentives, strategies, and dynamic power relations. How does local upgrading vary in different scenarios? The next section attempts to answer this question by theorizing different patterns of strategic coupling that in turn leads to different upgrading outcomes.

3.4 Strategic Coupling and the Dynamics of Industrial Upgrading

The above section has elaborated on the analytical framework in relation to key actors, knowledge gaps, and power dynamics within strategic coupling. This section attempts to reveal casual relations between the variety of strategic coupling and the dynamic outcomes of upgrading. The general process of industrial upgrading is reinterpreted as shown in Fig. 3.3. Coupled actors in latecomer regions try various means to reduce or overcome knowledge gaps. Power relations are shaped and reshaped by actors' strategies of upgrading. These efforts lead to the changing patterns of strategic coupling and thus produce correspondent outcomes of upgrading. When firms get upgraded, they will face new knowledge gaps (Fig. 3.4).

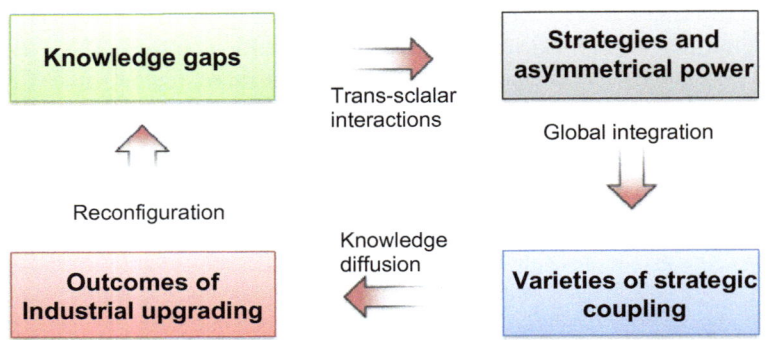

Fig. 3.4   General mechanisms of industrial upgrading (compiled by author)

3.4.1   Variety of Strategic Coupling

Based on collective endeavor from a journal special issue in *Regional Studies* in 2009, Yeung (2009) summarized three basic types of strategic coupling based on the development trajectories of six globalizing regions in East Asia. They are:

1. *International partnership* where lead firms from outside the region forge direct linkages with local firms as key nodes within global networks
2. *Indigenous innovation* where local firms develop greater technological capacities so as to occupy a better position when engaging with lead firms in GPNs
3. *Production platforms* where local firms strengthen capacities of systematic integration and specialize in manufacturing works for serving global lead firms.

Although this category of coupling has shed light on the pattern of integration between latecomer regions and GPNs, the current conceptualization is insufficient for explaining industrial upgrading. It is summarized through different strategies that latecomer regions have deployed. Hence, it is not a theoretically consistent topology for further analyses. The first type refers to a type of relationship; and the second type refers to a strategy of local firm; while the third refers to a type of position in GPNs. In contrast to this ontological ambiguity, Schmitz (2007) has offered an relevant account about latecomer strategies for global integration (see Table 3.2).

Schmitz's (2007) category is logically coherent because it is built on a fourfold configuration, according to the extent of technology and market gaps. But this policy-oriented category is too pragmatic to capture the ongoing dynamics of global integration. Basically, the strategies are overlapping with each other. For instance, strategies of attracting FDI and technological licensing actually are virtually the same as the strategies of inserting into global value chains. When firms pursue original design manufacturing, they may also develop joint venture with other firms for absorbing some cutting-edge technologies from the partners. Another pitfall is that this category overlooks the influences of institutional–spatial contexts (see Sect. 3.3.3 in this chapter). Technology and market assets are not necessarily bounded within firms,

Table 3.2 Four strategies for integrating into the global economy [Adapted from Fig. 3.2 in Schmitz (2007: 422)]

Market gap	Technological gap	
	Large	Small
Large	1. Access to technology and market is a severe problem for local firms. Foreign direct investment is a preferred strategy	2. Key challenge is not technology, but marketing. Integrating into value chains coordinated by global buyers seems best
Small	3. Challenge is not in marketing, but technology. Acquiring technology through licensing or joint ventures seems the best option	4. Technology and marketing gaps are narrow. Local firms can export own-designed complete products directly

but can be provided by other non-firm actors. Overall, Schmitz's (2007) account provides some solutions for latecomer regions, but fails to showcase the pattern of their integration into the global economy. Apart from these critiques, this category of latecomer strategies is insightful, because it implies the relationship between power asymmetry and knowledge gaps. This study synthesizes both Yeung (2009) and Schmitz (2007) and reinterprets the typology of strategic coupling as shown in Fig. 3.5. In a broader sense, the typology represents different relationships between latecomer regions and GPNs; in a narrow sense, the typology represents relationships between local firms and TNCs. This typology is regarded as an explanatory variable toward the dynamic outcomes of industrial upgrading.

Captive Coupling

Captive coupling refers to a situation in which late comers are highly dependent on foreign firms within GPNs in terms of technology and market resources. Due to the existing of huge knowledge gaps, latecomer regions must possess some assets to meet the demands of TNCs, such as lower production cost, preferential business environment, better fiscal incentives, or specific natural resources. If there are no

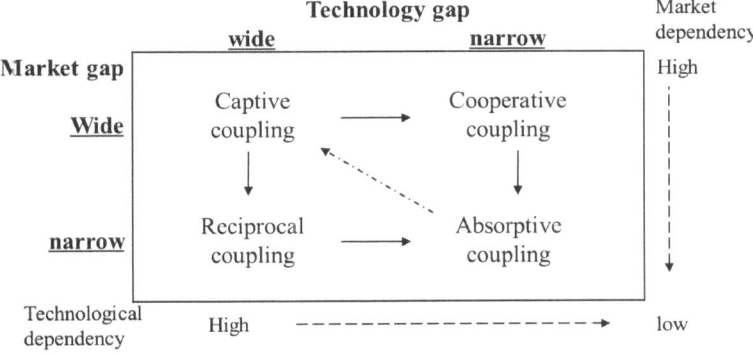

Fig. 3.5 Typology of strategic coupling (compiled by author)

such assets, coupling would not happen no matter how much effort by latecomer regions.

In this pattern, local firms are at a marginal position within GPNs. TNCs have dominant power in product definition, supply chain management, and price setting, whereas local firms play a subordinated role. Local firms and regional institutions have less bargaining power because the assets they provide are substitutable by other latecomer regions. This pattern is similar to captive governance in the GVC literature (Gereffi et al. 2005). Local firms are willing to depend on TNCs, as TNCs also like to lock-in suppliers in order to maintain production stability. Local firms need TNCs' help to bridge the knowledge gaps so as to catch up quickly instead of relying on their own efforts.

Cooperative Coupling

When technology gap is narrow, but market gap is wide, *cooperative coupling* tends to prevail. It refers to a situation that local firms in a latecomer region develop a complementary relationship with foreign firms within GPNs. The power of complementarity is built on mutual interests in terms of competitive advantages in labor division or co-development. Latecomer firms do not have to possess equivalent power as foreign firms. But at least they must have qualified technological capabilities or identify certain competitive advantages so that they can have autonomy in selecting strategic partners and their upgrading strategies. TNCs have incentives to treat local firms as strategic suppliers so as to reduce transaction costs.

This pattern is similar to the relational governance in Gereffi's et al. (2005) account which is based on non-cost transactions that are governed by social mechanisms, such as mutual trusts, reputation, or family/ethnic ties. The difference is that cooperative coupling has a broader definition which also includes cost-based transactions. Cooperative coupling also looks like coupling through being production platforms in Yeung's (2009) account. But it has a nuance meaning in that TNCs have also developed certain dependence on these production platforms. Otherwise, they are hard to keep cost competitive, comparing with the others which have developed cooperative coupling with latecomer firms. In this pattern, power relations are still asymmetrical, but in a moderate mode. Local firms and TNCs would mutually influence on the basis of various cooperative agreements, either formal or informal, in terms of production, transaction, marketing, and R&D activities. Overall TNCs cannot exert overwhelming control to local firms. This mutual dependency can be regulated through trust-based cooperation, contract-based commitment, or other social mechanisms. Within these relations, local firms and TNCs both impose costs on maintaining the stability of cooperation.

Reciprocal Coupling

When technology gap is large, but market gap is small, reciprocal coupling tends to occur. It reflects a situation in which actors develop coupling relationships for exchanging technology and market resources possessed exclusively by each actor. To latecomer upgrading, it specifically refers to a situation that TNCs comply with specific criteria from states and local firms, so as to get access to localized assets, such as local market. The state criteria often require them to provide additional assistance to local firms, or provide other benefits for the local economy. Power relations in this pattern are highly regulated by the intervention of state actors. The reciprocity of resource exchange is the key mechanism for developing such coupling. Forms of coupling can be technological licensing/cooperative agreements, joint ventures (either based on capital or technology), strategic alliances, or other forms of cooperation.

This pattern is similar to the situation of 'obligated embeddedness' theorized by Liu and Dicken (2006). The difference is that Liu and Dicken (2006) only referred to the situation in which market access was utilized by states as critical assets to increase their bargaining power. In this study, the reciprocal coupling can be built on other potential assets, such as national/regional business systems, monopoly industries, domestic logistic systems, natural resources, institutional arrangements, or social/ethnic ties (Storper 1997a, b; Cooke and Morgan 1998; Whitley 2000; Zhou and Tong 2003; Qiu 2005). In the GVC literature, this type of coupling is absent as state actor is not explicitly incorporated into their conceptual framework.

Absorptive Coupling
When technology and market gaps are both small, absorptive coupling tends to take place. It refers to a circumstance that local firms are capable of serving directly both domestic and global markets with their indigenous capabilities. Meanwhile, they still would like to couple with TNCs for absorbing state-of-art knowledge. Overall, TNCs are still occupying a leading position in their own value chains. But local firms are actively plugged into GPNs and manage to channel knowledge and identify various industrial opportunities.

This is a more matured and ideal level of global integration and it is also the most difficult stage for latecomer firms and regions to achieve. Power in absorptive coupling is more or less balanced in which local firms have sufficient independence in selecting partners, partnerships, and market niches. Local firms have greater bargaining power to require more knowledge diffusion from TNCs, but local firms do not override TNCs' power. Again, this pattern of coupling is absent in the GVC literature, because the GVC literature believes that local firms cannot possibly build up such balanced power relation with global lead firms, unless local firms quit the value chain and construct their own chains.

3.4.2 Producing Industrial Upgrading: How Does Strategic Coupling Matter?

The formation of strategic coupling is driven by the power of complementarity where the constituents of relationships benefit from each other's co-presence and engagement. Generally, when the power of complementarity in strategic coupling is greater, it will be more possible for upgrading to be produced based on higher synergy and lower tension. Four propositions are developed to elaborate on this mechanism in relation to the variety of coupling.

Proposition 1 *In captive coupling, whereby TNCs dominate knowledge diffusion, the deeper local firms become captive to TNCs, the faster will upgrading be facilitated. But the upgrading is limited and tends to be restricted in process and product upgrading.*

In *captive coupling*, TNCs exert strict governance on local firms by defining the content of local upgrading such as setting production parameters and allocating manufacturing tasks. The content of knowledge is more related to production and processing technologies, while not technologies in product development/design. Knowledge spillover from TNCs is limited in the sense that only standard and simple technologies will be diffused through formal traded relations. Market knowledge is rarely diffused from TNCs since there is no incentive to share it. In order to improve the supply capability of local firms, TNCs would like to assist local firms to upgrade more quickly. For instance, TNCs may import advanced machines for local firms or provide basic labor training. To achieve these helps, local firms are required to give up certain rights of control of their own corporate functions, such as management of production systems.

In order to receive more technological assistance from foreign partners, local firms should focus on developing technological capabilities that meet TNCs' demands, particularly in some technologies with asset specificity. TNCs may encourage these local efforts because their bargaining power may increase once local firms are technologically locked into them. Hence, the deeper local firms are dependent on TNCs, the more technological assistance local firms may be received. Functional upgrading is almost impossible because local firms are kept out of design technologies and marketing skills. There is no incentive or return for TNCs to share the knowledge. Indigenous efforts of functional upgrading will also create tension to the coupling relation.

Regional institutions in captive coupling often encounter a dilemma (see Sect. 3.3.2). They need to decide whether to put the strategic needs of local firms or foreign firms as their top priority. To help local firms, regional policy makers can provide much preferential assistance and invest intensively in constructing a regional learning system, but this process is time-consuming and costly. Local firms may also leave the region after successful upgrading. To give preference to foreign firms, regional policy makers can simply provide substantial fiscal incentives and give more priority to the needs of foreign firms. This strategy may serve as a critical shortcut for 'upgrading' regional economies. But this kind of regional upgrading would be shallow i f bcal firms are further marginalized or discriminated, such as the formation of technological enclaves in developing regions (Wang and Lee 2007; Wang and Lin 2008). The region may also become vulnerable due to over-dependence on TNCs (Chapman 2005). My detailed empirical investigation in Chap. 5 points to this process and outcome in the PRD's electronics industry.

Proposition 2 *In cooperative coupling, the more developed are complementarity and mutual interests between foreign and local firms, the higher is the potential for local upgrading.*

Ways of knowledge diffusion are rich within cooperative coupling. Since local firms can provide qualified technological services, TNCs are interested in developing various cooperation partnerships with local firms. Once TNCs treat local firms as strategic suppliers or partners, they tend to provide substantial helps to local firms so that the latter can conform to the former's demands, such as special training in developing OEM/ODM business. Meanwhile, TNCs may provide market feedbacks and may even share some knowledge in design to suppliers so as to meet rapid changing market demands. Therefore, the more TNCs are interested in cooperative with local firms, the more possible upgrading will be achieved. Product upgrading would be more prosper than other types of upgrading because it satisfies TNC's need of rapid product change for competing in the global market (Lüthje 2004; Staritz et al. 2011). But functional upgrading remains unwelcomed by TNCs, because local firms may grow up as a new competitor. However, once the mutual interest is built on exploiting new markets rather than challenging the original market shares of TNCs, functional upgrading would be possible. In other words, the more mutual interests are developed, the more upgrading possibilities can be realized in local firms.

Based on upgrading initiatives, local firms may invest a lot in familiarizing with the rules of the global market and in seeking global business opportunities. However, this effort not only requires intensive investment in capital, but also brings them into direct competition with a number of TNCs that have established world-wide brands, global distribution networks, and tremendous retail terminals. Given time and cost constrains, local firms would prefer to stay as contract manufacturers for global lead firms and improve their competitiveness by developing cutting-edge production technologies. Chapter 6 illustrates this proposition based on local upgrading in the apparel industry in the PRD.

Proposition 3 *In reciprocal coupling, the more balanced are power relations, the more synergy is there for upgrading.*

In reciprocal coupling, the extent and content of exchanged resources determine the ways of knowledge diffusion and power relations between local firms and TNCs. The power for regional institutions comes from their legitimized administrative rights on their territories. Local firms do not have this administrative power, but they have bargaining power because they are familiar with territorialized assets which are rooted in national bureaucratic systems and social-cultural networks. The outcomes of upgrading are quite diverse because all types of knowledge may diffuse according to specific criteria proposed by the local party.

TNCs are not passive to the local demands of knowledge transfer, but will try various efforts to defend their leading positions in GPNs. For instance, they may enforce a modular pattern of production organization so as to internalize their competent technologies within modularized components. TNCs may only transfer know-*how*, but may continue to block the transfer of know-*why*. They also may increase the complexity of knowledge sharing by enforcing exclusive industrial standards or setting specialized production parameters. Hence, local firms may also be technologically locked into them due to high asset specificity.

The niche of maintaining reciprocal coupling is a balanced power relation in which each party does not override the other. If local party request substantial knowledge sharing while does not provide corresponding benefits, TNCs may take a short-term strategy in the coupling without any intent of upgrading. If TNCs' power overrides the local party, they may be replaced unless they have technological monopoly in the global industry. In Chap. 7, this book exemplifies this proposition in the PRD's automotive industry.

Proposition 4 *In absorptive coupling, the more capable are local firms in multi-tasking within GPNs, the more upgrading will occur.*

Absorptive coupling is an ultimate stage of latecomer upgrading. It is also the most difficult stage of development for local firms to achieve. Although TNCs still have greater power in terms of technological advance and market control, local firms already have certain independence in selecting partners to couple with. In this case, TNCs have to prepare for the potential challenges derived from further local upgrading. TNCs may resist sharing their original newly advanced technologies or even enforce specific agreements in the coupling to hinder local upgrading. They may also raise industrial entry barriers (e.g., new industrial standards) to impede local firms' entry into the global market (Nadvi and Wältring 2004; Nadvi 2008; Tewari 2008).

How can local firms leverage the power of TNCs for better upgrading? The GVC literature suggests two strategies for local firms (Schmitz 2004). First is to launch joint action with other local firms. Second is to insert into multiple value chains rather than highly depend on one single chain. However, the first strategy may increase tension within coupling and the second strategy does not make much difference if local firms merely serve undifferentiated global lead firms. Reviews in Chap. 2 have shown some alternative local upgrading strategies. For instance, local firms can be deeply embedded in GPNs and serve multiple functions, such as conducting OEM/ODM/OBM business or developing different market niches simultaneously. I term this strategy as *multi-tasking* in GPNs through which local firms develop various partnerships with different types of TNCs which can be global buyers, branded lead firms, platform developers, or intermediate traders. This strategy may enable local firms to diversify knowledge channels and identify more competitive dynamics within GPNs (see Sect. 3.3.3). In doing so, local firms may maximize upgrading opportunities by synthesizing resources at different localities or positions within GPNs. Empirical investigations of this study found that none of the industries, cities, or clusters in the PRD has yet developed absorptive coupling. However, the potential of absorptive coupling is emerging at some cases. This book discusses this potential in Chap. 8.

In sum, this section has elaborated on the mechanisms of latecomer upgrading in relation to different types of strategic coupling. Patterns of knowledge diffusion vary among different industries. Power relations are not pre-determined by the pattern of industrial governance. Instead, they are subject to the patterns of coupling, resources possessed by each party and the strategies of firms that are embedded in various institutional–spatial contexts. This is the evolutionary nature of strategic coupling that leads us to appreciate the ongoing dynamics of local upgrading in globalizing latecomer regions.

3.5 The General Mechanism of Industrial Upgrading

The central theoretical attempt of this book is to conceptualize the dynamics of local upgrading according to different types of strategic coupling. This effort bridges the theoretical gaps between geographical and non-geographical studies by embracing key influential factors (industrial governance, embeddedness, and state intervention) and linking multi-scalar forces within a coherent analytical framework (see Fig. 3.2). It thus contributes to the literature on industrial upgrading by offering a more realistic account of the mechanism of local upgrading. In contrast to the regionalism literature, my framework recognizes both endogenous and exogenous forces in a more balanced way. Comparing with the GVC literature, my framework provides a useful lens for appreciating the influence of various non-firm (non-profit) actors on the process of upgrading. More importantly, it reveals the influence of institutional–spatial contexts on value-chain governance in which power relations may be reconfigured. Without privileging any specific scale or actors, this framework examines how the interactions of key actors within strategic coupling lead to various outcomes of upgrading. My analyses show that the driving forces of local upgrading are not as rigid as the GVC literature and development studies have predicted (see Chap. 2). This is basic contribution of this book.

The most critical contribution comes from my conceptualization of the typology of strategic coupling. Critically revisiting the concept of strategic coupling, this chapter further conceptualizes the concept in relation to different configurations of knowledge gaps and power relations. The fourfold typology serves as a key variable for explaining the dynamics of upgrading. This effort links together the regionalism literature and the GPN studies and helps readers understand the geography of upgrading in the context of globalization. Without any rigid and pre-determined trajectory, the process of local upgrading is dynamic and contingent to the interactions among key actors. Power relations and responsive strategies are critical factors that shape ways of knowledge diffusions. The interpretation of this typology illustrates the importance of political economy within GPNs in which the power relations of key actors and their bargaining processes are embedded in specific institutional–spatial contexts. While the content of knowledge diffusion is highly influenced by inter-firm governance pattern, synergy can be fostered to nurture more local upgrading. Within strategic coupling, besides the power of complementarity, there are also mutual interests and the reciprocity of resource exchange that produces synergy.

Another effort made by this chapter is related to the discussion of power dynamics within strategic coupling. It is pointed out that local actors can utilize resources embedded at different scales to leverage the governance power of foreign firms. This effort opens out many other possibilities for local firms to increase bargaining power or bypass the control of TNCs. Particularly, upgrading opportunities would emerge when local actors manage to synthesize different resources. This interpretation complements to development studies by offering more alternative of local upgrading strategies. The problem is whether local firms are capable of identifying these opportunities. The overall efforts of this chapter verify my central argument that local upgrading is subject to interactions among key actors, rather than the dominant power of global lead firms or state strategies alone. Four propositions are developed based on each type of strategic coupling. The rest of this book devotes four empirical chapters to exemplify the propositions, including one general chapter about strategic coupling in the PRD and three industry-specific chapters demonstrating different scenarios.

References

Allen, J. (2003). *Lost geographies of power*. Oxford: Blackwell.

Amin, A. (1998). Globalisation and regional development: A relational perspective. *Competition and Change, 3*, 145–165.

Amin, A. (2002). Spatialities of globalisation. *Environment and Planning A, 34*, 385–399. https://doi.org/10.1068/a3439.

Appleyard, M. M. (1996). How does knowledge flow? Interfirm patterns in the semiconductor industry. *Strategic Management Journal, 17*(2), 137–154.

Barney, J. (1991). Firm resources and sustained competitive advantage. *Journal of Management, 17*(1), 99–120.

Bathelt, H., & Glückler, J. (2003). Toward a relational economic geography. *Journal of Economic Geography, 3*(2), 117–144.

Beeson, M. (2004). The rise and fall (??van Diermen) of the developmental state: The vicissitudes and implications of East Asian interventionism. In L. Low (Block), *Developmental states: Relevancy, redundancy or reconfiguration?* (pp. 29–40). New York: Nova Science Publishers.

Boggs, J. S., & Rantisi, N. M. (2003). The 'relational turn' in economic geography. *Journal of Economic Geography, 3*(2), 109–116.

Boschma, R. A. (2004). Competitiveness of regions from an evolutionary perspective. *Regional Studies, 38*(1), 1001–1014.

Boschma, R. A., & Frenken, K. (2006). Why is economic geography not an evolutionary science? Towards an evolutionary economic geography. *Journal of Economic Geography, 6*, 273–302.

Boschma, R., & Frenken, K. (2009). Some notes on institutions in evolutionary economic geography. *Economic Geography, 85*(2), 151–158. https://doi.org/10.1111/j.1944-8287.2009.01018.x.

Boschma, R. A., & Lambooy, J. G. (1999). Evolutionary economics and economic geography. *Journal of Evolutionary Economics, 9*(2), 411–429.

Cammett, M. (2007). Business-government relations and industrial change: The politics of upgrading in Morocco and Tunisia. *World Development, 35*(11), 1889–1903. https://doi.org/10.1016/j.worlddev.2007.01.003.

Chapman, K. (2005). From 'growth centre' to 'cluster': Restructuring, regional development, and the Teesside chemical industry. *Environment and Planning A, 37*(4), 597–615.

Cho, D.-S., Kim, D.-J., & Rhee, D. K. (1998). Latecomer strategies: Evidence from the semiconductor industry in Japan and Korea. *Organization Science, 9*(4), 489–505. https://doi.org/10.1287/orsc.9.4.489.

Clark, G. L., & Kim, W. B. (1995). *Asian NIEs and the global economy: Industrial restructuring and corporate strategy in the 1990s*: The Johns Hopkins University Press.

Coe, N. M., Dicken, P., & Hess, M. (2008a). Global production networks—Debates and challenges. *Journal of Economic Geography, 8*(3), 267–269. https://doi.org/10.1093/jeg/lbn006.

Coe, N. M., Dicken, P., & Hess, M. (2008b). Global production networks: Realizing the potential. *Journal of Economic Geography, 8*(3), 271–295. https://doi.org/10.1093/jeg/lbn002.

Coe, N. M., & Hess, M. (2011). Local and regional development: A global production network approach. In A. Pike, A. Rodriguez-Pose, & J. Tomaney (Eds.), *Handbook of local and regional development* (pp. 128–138). Abingdon: Routledge.

Coe, N., Hess, M., Yeung, H. W.-C., Dicken, P., & Henderson, J. (2004). 'Globalizing' regional development: A global production networks perspective. *Transactions of the Institute of British Geographers, 29*(4), 468–484.

Cooke, P., & Morgan, K. (1998). *The associational economy. Firms, regions, and innovation.* Oxford: Oxford University Press.

Dicken, P (1976). The multiplant business enterprise and geographical space: Some issues in the study of external control and regional development. *Regional Studies, 10*(4): 401–412

Dicken, P (2007). *Global shift: Mapping the changing contours of the world economy* (5th ed.). London: Sage.

Dunning, J. H. (1979). Explaining changing patterns of international production—In defence of the electric theory. *Oxford Bulletin of Economics and Statistics, 41*(4), 269–295.

Dunning, J. H. (1988). The eclectic paradigm of international production—A restatement and some possible extensions. *Journal of International Business Studies, 19*(1), 1–31.

Dunning, J. H. (1995). Reappraising the Eclectic paradigm in an age of alliance capitalism. *Journal of International Business Studies, 26*(3), 461–491.

Dunning, J. H. (2000). The eclectic paradigm as an envelope for economic and business theories of MNE activity. *International Business Review, 9,* 163–190.

Ettlinger, N. (2001). A relational perspective in economic geography: Connecting competitiveness with diversity and difference. *Antipode, 33*(2), 216–227.

Evans, P. (1995). *Embedded autonomy: States and industrial transformation.* Princeton, NJ: Princeton University Press.

Feenstra, R., & Hamilton, G. (2006). *Emerging economies, divergent paths: Business groups and economic organization in South Korea and Taiwan.* New York: Cambridge University Press.

Galvin, P., & Morkel, A. (2001). The effect of product modularity on industry structure: The case of the world bicycle industry. *Industry and Innovation, 8*(1), 31–47.

Gereffi, C. (1994). Capitalism, development and global commodity chains. In L. Sklair (Block), *Capitalism and development* (pp. 211–231). London: Routledge.

Gereffi, C. (1999). International trade and industrial upgrading in the apparel commodity chain. *Journal of International Economics, 48*(1), 37–70.

Gereffi, G. (2001). Beyond the producer-driven/buyer-driven dichotomy—The evolution of global value chains in the Internet era. *Ids Bulletin-Institute of Development Studies, 32*(3), 30–40.

Gereffi, G., Humphrey, J., & Sturgeon, T. (2005). The governance of global value chains. *Review of International Political Economy, 12*(1), 78–104. https://doi.org/10.1080/09692290500049805.

Gibbon, P (2001). Upgrading primary products: A global value chain approach. *World Development, 29*(2), 345–363.

Henderson, J., Dicken, P., Hess, M., Coe, N., & Yeung, H. W.-C. (2002). Global production networks and the analysis of economic development. *Review of International Political Economy, 9*(3), 436–464. https://doi.org/10.1080/09692290210150842.

Hess, M. (2004). 'Spatial' relationships? Towards a reconceptualization of embeddedness. *Progress in Human Geography, 28*(2), 165–186. https://doi.org/10.1191/0309132504ph479oa.

Hess, M. (2008). Governance, value chains and networks: An afterword. *Economy and Society, 37*(3), 452–459. https://doi.org/10.1080/03085140802172722.

Hess, M., & Coe, N. (2006). Making connections: Global production networks, standards, and embeddedness in the mobile-telecommunications industry. *Environment and Planning A, 38,* 1205–1227.

Hess, M., & Yeung, H. W. C. (2006). Whither global production networks in economic geography? Past, present, and future. *Environment and Planning A, 38*(1), 1193–1204. https://doi.org/10.1068/a38463.

Hobday, M. (1995). East-Asian latecomer firms—Learning the technology of electronics. *World Development, 23*(1), 1171–1193.

Hoskisson, R. O., & Johnson, R. A. (1992). Corporate restructuring and strategic change—The effect of diversification strategy and research and development intensity. *Strategic Management Journal, 13*(8), 625–634.

Humphrey, J. (2003). Globalization and supply chain networks: The auto industry in Brazil and India. *Global Networks, 3*(2), 121–141.

Humphrey, J., & Schmitz, H. (2002b). How does insertion in global value chains affect upgrading in industrial clusters? *Regional Studies, 36*(1), 1017–1027. https://doi.org/10.1080/0034340022000022198.

Jones, M. (2009). Phase space: Geography, relational thinking, and beyond. *Progress in Human Geography, 33*(4), 487–506.

Jones, C., Hesterly, W. S., & Borgatti, S. P. (1997). A general theory of network governance: Exchange conditions and social mechanisms. *Academy of Management Review, 22*(4), 911–945. https://doi.org/10.2307/259249.

Lecraw, D. (1984). Bargaining power, ownership, and profitability of transnational corporations in developing countries. *Journal of International Business Studies, 15*(1), 27–43.

Liu, W. D., & Dicken, P. (2006). Transnational corporations and 'obligated embeddedness': Foreign direct investment in China's automobile industry. *Environment and Planning A, 38*(1), 1229–1247. https://doi.org/10.1068/a37206.

Lüthje, B. (2002). Electronics contract manufacturing: Global production and international division of labor in the age of the internet. *Industry and Innovation, 9*(3), 227–247.

Lüthje, B. (2004). Global production network and industrial upgrading in China: The case of electronics contract manufacturing.

MacKinnon, D., Cumbers, A., & Chapman, K. (2002). Learning, innovation and regional development: A critical appraisal of recent debates. *Progress in Human Geography, 26*(3), 293–311.

Martin, R., & Sunley, P. (2006). Path dependence and regional economic evolution. *Journal of Economic Geography, 6*(4), 395–437. https://doi.org/10.1093/jeg/lbl012.

Massey, D. (1979). In what sense a regional problem? *Regional Studies, 13*(2), 233–243.

Meyer-Stamer, J., Maggi, C., & Seibel, S. (2004). Upgrading in the tile industry of Italy, Spain and Brazil: insights from cluster and value chain analysis. In H. Schmitz (Block), *Local enterprises in the global economy* (pp. 110–139). UK: Edward Elgar.

Morgan, K. (1997). The learning region: Institutions, innovation and regional renewal. *Regional Studies, 31*(5), 491–503.

Nadvi, K. (2008). Global standards, global governance and the organization of global value chains. *Journal of Economic Geography, 8*(3), 323–343. https://doi.org/10.1093/jeg/lbn003.

Nadvi, K., & Wältring, F. (2004). Making sense of global standards. In H. Schmitz (Block), *Local enterprises in the global economy: Issues of governance and upgrading*. Cheltenman: Edward Elgar.

Ozawa, T. (2005). *Institutions, industrial upgrading, and economic performance in Japan- the 'Flying-Geese' paradigm of catch-up growth*. Northampton, MA: Edward Elgar.

Qiu, Y. (2005). Personal networks, institutional involvement, and foreign direct investment flows into China's interior. *Economic Geography, 81*(3), 261–281.

Schmitz, H. (2004). *Local enterprises in the global economy*. UK: Edward Elgar.

Schmitz, H. (2007). Reducing complexity in the industrial policy debate. *Development Policy Review, 25*(4), 417–428.

Sit, V. F.-S., & Yang, C. (1997). Foreign-investment-induced Exo-urbanisation in the Pearl River Delta, China. *Urban Studies, 34*(4), 647–677.

Staritz, C., Gereffi, G., & Cattaneo, O. (2011). Shifting end market and upgrading prospects in global value chains: Editorial. *International Journal of Technological Learning, Innovation and Development, 4*(1/2/3), 1–13.

Storper, M. (1997a). *The regional world: Territorial development in a global economy.* London and New York: Guilford Press.

Storper, M. (1997b). Regional economies as relational assets. In R. Lee & J. Wills (Eds.), *Society, place, economy: States of the art in economic geography* (pp. 248–257). London: Edward Arnold.

Sturgeon, T. (2002). Modular production networks: An American model of industrial organization. *Industrial and Corporate Change, 11*(3), 451–496.

Sturgeon, T., & Kawakami, M. (2011). Global value chains in the electronics industry: Characteristics, crisis, and upgrading opportunities for firms from developing countries. *International Journal of Technological Learning, Innovation and Development, 4*(1/2/3), 120–147.

Sturgeon, T., & Lester, R. (2004b). The new global supply-base: New challenges for local suppliers in East Asia. In S. Yusuf, A. M. Anjum., & K. Nabeshima (Eds.), *Global production networking and technological change in East Asia.* Oxford UK: Oxford University Press.

Sturgeon, T., Memodovic, O., Biesebroeck, J. V., & Gereffi, G. (2009). Globalisation of the automotive industry: Main features and trends. *International Journal of Technological Learning, Trade and Development, 2*(1), 7–24.

Sunley, P. (2008). Relational economic geography: A partial understanding or a new paradigm? *Economic Geography, 84*(1), 1–26.

Tewari, M. (2008). Varieties of global integration: Navigating institutional legacies and global networks in India's garment industry. *Competition & Change, 12*(1), 49–67.

Trippl, M., Todtling, F., & Lengauer, L. (2009). Knowledge sourcing beyond buzz and pipelines: Evidence from the Vienna Software sector. *Economic Geography, 85*(4), 443–463.

Van den Bulte, C., & Moenaert, R. K. (1998). The effects of R&D team co-location on communication patterns among R&D, marketing, and manufacturing. *Management Science, 44*(11), 1–18.

Wang, J.-H., & Lee, C.-K. (2007). Global production networks and local institution building: the development of the information-technology industry in Suzhou, China. *Environment and Planning A, 39*(8), 1873–1888. https://doi.org/10.1068/a38428.

Wang, C., & Lin, G. C. S. (2008). The growth and spatial distribution of China's ICT Industry: New geography of clustering and innovation. *Issues and Studies, 44*(2), 145–192.

Whitley, R. (2000). The institutional structuring of innovation strategies: Business systems, firm types and patterns of technical change in different market economies. *Organization Studies, 21*(5), 855–886.

Yeung, H. W.-C. (1994). Critical reviews of geographical perspectives on business organization and the organization of production—Toward a network approach. *Progress in Human Geography, 18*(4), 460–490.

Yeung, H. W.-C. (2009). Regional development and the competitive dynamics of global production networks: An East Asian perspective. *Regional Studies, 43*(3), 325–351.

Yeung, H. W.-c. (2005). Rethinking relational economic geography. *Transactions of the Institute of British Geographers, 30*(1), 37–51.

Zhou, Y, & Tong, X. (2003). An innovative region in China: interaction between multinational corporations and local firms in a high-tech cluster in Beijing. *Economic Geography, 79*(2), 129–152.

Chapter 4
Industrial Upgrading and Evolutionary Strategic Coupling in the Pearl River Delta

Since the 'open-door' reform in 1979, China has been transformed from an isolated country into one of the world's leading producers, traders, and destinations for FDI. In the first half year of 2010, China overtook Japan and became the second largest economy in the world with the GDP of $2.6 trillion.[1] However, this remarkable economic growth has been questioned. There is an ongoing debate about whether the performance of China's economic is driven mainly by productivity growth or by factor accumulation (Wang and Meng 2001; Wang and Yao 2003). It is unclear whether FDI or human capital is more influential. The role of FDI in domestic knowledge spillover and national exports is also controversial (Cheung and Lin 2004; Xu and Lu 2009).

Specific to industrial upgrading, when the performance of the Chinese economy has been improved, whether Chinese local (domestic) firms have achieved corresponding upgrading is still in question (Young and Lan 1997; Sun 2007; Huang 2008). There are two different strands of thoughts. In a pessimistic view, Steinfeld (2004: 1971) argues that 'Chinese enterprises have become extensively linked with the global economy, yet in a shallow manner. They remain stuck in commodity manufacturing, undifferentiated activities for which innovation is absent'. Huang (2008) believes that SOEs have made a major contribution to the growth of domestic economies. But the contribution is at the expense of a huge amount of state investments utilized in a very inefficient way. Steinfeld (2010) also critiques that Chinese firms will not be the threat to the West, due to their lagging-behind speed in technological innovation in comparison with Western TNCs.

In contrast to these critiques, other studies embody an optimistic view to the achievement of upgrading in China, such as the formations of industrial districts and the changing patterns of regional development (Marco and Marco 2005; Sun 2007; Wei et al. 2007, 2009); the improving capabilities of innovation in domestic firms (Zhou and Tong 2003; Lazonick 2004; Ernst 2007; Fan 2007; Zhou 2008); the enhancement of the institutional environment (Lin 2009a; Zheng et al. 2009);

---

[1] Source: National Bureau of Statistics, http://www.stats.gov.cn/tjsj/jdsj/t20100716_402657756.htm.

Y. Liu, *Local Dynamics of Industrial Upgrading*, Economic Geography, https://doi.org/10.1007/978-981-15-4297-8_4

and so on. These studies consider export-oriented industrialization and indigenous absorptive capabilities as the key to achieve innovation and industrial upgrading (Zhou and Wei 2011). Scholars in the literature of developmental state hold a similar view. They argue for export-driven forces as the primary and superior impetus for industrial growth and technological upgrading to latecomer economies (White 1988; Amsden 1989; Hobday 1995; Lall and Urata 2003; Beeson 2004).

Situating in such a debate, this book does not attempt to offer an exhausted account of the progress of industrial upgrading or to argue whether foreign firms or China's states are the key driver of domestic industrial growth. Drawing upon the case of the PRD, it focuses on an issue that these China studies have not yet clearly articulated: How does the interplay among foreign firms, domestic firms, and state institutions affect local upgrading?

Chapter 3 has theorized the causal mechanism between strategic coupling and the dynamics of latecomer upgrading. From this chapter through to Chap. 7, I will operationalize the relational framework and exemplify the upgrading mechanism based on the case of the PRD over three decades of development. As the first empirical chapter, this chapter focuses on three topics: the types of strategic coupling that have been developed in the past decades; the extent to which the PRD has achieved upgrading and the key drivers of this upgrading; and the features of changing pattern of coupling.

4.1 Changing Dynamics in the Pearl River Delta: Beyond a World Factory

The post-reform development of the PRD can be reinterpreted as three stages in relation to institutional reforms historically. From 1978 to 1992, the PRD was in a period of restricted policy experiment. Strategic coupling was developed in which the central government mediated this region to meet the demands of industrial relocation of Hong Kong and other East Asian NIEs such as Japan. This period was meant for exploring institutional reforms and learning the manipulation of capitalism (Xu 1988; Lu 2001). Before 1986, all reform policies were only available within two special economic zones in the PRD (Shenzhen and Zhuhai). Township and village enterprises (TVEs) were encouraged by local states within rural areas in the rest of the PRD. Foreign investors, mainly from Hong Kong, were allowed to establish export-processing enterprises (EPEs) in the PRD. The preliminary success of industrialization encouraged China's central government to remove the restriction after 1986. Industrialization was speeding up. From 1986 to 1992, the total industrial output of the PRD increased by 32% annually; and land used for urban and industrial development expanded by 60,000 ha.

During the 1990s, strategic coupling was reinforced in which the PRD experienced very rapid industrialization with further market liberalization. The initial success and the Southern inspection tour of Deng Xiaoping (in 1992) served as catalysts that brought more institutional supports to the (Gan and Gan 1994; Li 1997; Fang and Luo 1999; Tang and Tian 2002). In 1994, the PRD was officially established as an independent economic zone with more autonomy for attracting foreign investments and leveraging institutional reforms (Wu 2005). Meanwhile, the implementation of new fiscal law stimulated prefecture governments as the key actors of industrial development because they became heavily dependent on land transfer fees as revenues (Liu and Lu 2002; Lin 2009b). From 1990 to 1993, the amount of utilized FDI in the PRD reached $14 billion, which was twice of the total amount in the 1980s. From 1993 to 1997, the PRD underwent rounds of economic booms in the stock market and the real estate market (commercial and industrial). Billions of domestic capitals and millions of migrant workers flowed into this region. However, this rapid development was slowed down by the 1997 Asian Financial Crisis during which Hong Kong experienced a very serious recession and significant negative impacts on the PRD occurred (Jao 2001; Lin and Chen 2003).

After 2000, China's accession into WTO made the PRD more open to international competition in which local firms enjoyed less export rebates, import subsidies, and tax reduction as before (Sit 2001; Yeung 2002; Chen and Wang 2010). During this period, strategic coupling was enhanced in two ways. First, Hong Kong was further integrated with the PRD under the Mainland and Hong Kong Closer Economic Partnership Arrangement (CEPA). This arrangement was an economic cooperative framework launched in 2004, including tax-free policies, market opening in the service industries, and investment facilitation.[2] The mission of CEPA was partly meant for upgrading the PRD's economy by attracting more producer-service industries from Hong Kong (Yang 2005).

Second, the PRD's regional authorities have implemented various new industrial policies to stimulate industrial upgrading. As introduced in Chap. 1, the PRD has adopted the dual-transformation policy since 2008. When this policy was implemented, tension emerged between local and regional authorities in defining the usage of industrial land (Yang 2012; also see Chap. 6). Meanwhile, regional authorities implemented a new policy—Guangdong Technology Correspondent Project—to help local upgrading. The project was aimed at building up regional innovation networks by establishing connections between universities/institutes and local firms. Selected technicians were allocated to local firms for at least one year and were required to participate in at least one project pertinent to upgrading or innovation, such as process improvement, new product development, or equipment redevelopment. By 2010, about 1000 technicians were allocated to 932 firms. About 80% of the firms located in the PRD, and more than 50% were electronics enterprises.[3] During this period, the PRD has also been challenged by its economic sustainability, such as

---

[2] Since 2004, about 300 products have been treated as tax-free products for manufacturing, covering industries like electronics, apparel, medical, and chemical. Four main industrial markets in the PRD were open for Hong Kong firms to participate in, and hundreds of manufacturing components were treated as free-tax goods. Macao was included in the agreement later on.

[3] http://cxy.gdstc.gov.cn/HTML/tzgg/1276738766866665523469706315577545.html.

the exhausting land resources, raising labor wages, environmental degradation and increasing raw material costs, and so on (Huang and Chen 2009). All these problems pointed to industrial upgrading as an ultimate solution (Yu and Zhang 2009).

4.2 Characteristics of Industrial Upgrading

Throughout three decades of export-oriented industrialization, the PRD has achieved upgrading to a significant degree. The region is transformed from an agricultural backwater into one of the world's leading manufacturing hubs. From 1978 to 2010, GDP in the PRD grew by 15–17% annually (GDSY 2010). By 2009, the PRD took up 3% of the world exports with a value of $234 billion. Within China, the PRD has become a national economic vanguard. Since 1990, the PRD has accounted for more than 28% of export value in the country's total. Since 2000s, the annual GDP of the PRD has consistently exceeded 8.5% of the national total. This rapid industrial growth was accompanied by the improvement of performance at the firm level. A measurement based on industrial value added (IVA) illustrates this tendency.

As shown in Table 4.1, the total IVA of the region increased from 6.1 billion *yuan* in 1980 to 1529 billion *yuan* in 2009. This significant growth resulted from improved efficiency of firms. From 1980 to 2009, IVA per enterprise continuously grew from 0.4 to 37 million *yuan*. The IVA per capita also achieved a remarkable growth of 23.5 times. During the same period, the number of firms only increased by 2.5 times, and

Table 4.1 Industrial development and upgrading in the Pearl River Delta (Guangdong Statistic Yearbook 1990–2010; Pearl River Delta and Yangzi River Delta Statistic Yearbook 2001, 2006, 2011, 2016; Guangdong Industrial Census 2004)

Category	Unit	1980	1990	1995	2000	2005	2010	2015
GDP	billions	12	101	408	842	1828	3767	6227
# PRD/Nation	%	2.6	5.4	6.7	8.5	9.8	9.1	9.1
IVA	billion	6.1	29	120	263	815	1908	2368
No. enterprises	thousand	16.3	25.1	19.5	15.7	28.2	41.4	31.8
No. employees	million	3.1	5.3	9.1	4.6	9.2	13.2	11.8
IVA per enterprise	millions	0.4	1.2	6.2	16.8	28.9	46.0	74.5
IVA per capita	thousand	2.0	5.5	13.2	57.2	88.6	144.3	200.3
ELI	unit	190	211	467	293	326	319	372
ETI	thousand	49.7	340.2	2383.3	3804.4	5651.9	7157.5	16,800.2
Profit ratio	%	N.A.	3.5	3.1	3.5	4.8	7.2	6.42

Note Expect for figure in GDP, all data refer to enterprises above designated size that an annual turnover more than 5 million *yuan*. These enterprises accounted for the majority of total industrial output in the PRD which was more than 85% before 2000 and about 95% by 2009. *IVA* industrial value added; *ELI* enterprise labor intensity = employment per enterprise; *ETI* enterprise technology intensity = annual net value of equipment and instrument per enterprise; profit ratio = gross profit/total turnover

the number of workers grew 10 times. These growth rates were much slower than the ones in IVA per enterprise and per capita.

By comparing the ratios of labor intensity and technology intensity, a watershed of the regional trajectory can be seen. Around 2000, the figure of labor intensity reached a peak level and then dropped slowly. In contrast, the ratio of technology intensity kept increasing continuously. This trend implies that firms in the PRD were less dependent on utilizing massive labor as before. Instead, significant investments were devoted to improving the technological capabilities of firms. It should be noticed that the figure of technology intensity here only refers to expenditures on new facilities and equipment renewal. Overall, the profit ratio of the PRD's firms was enhanced from 3.5% in 1990 to 6.1% in 2009.

The revealed competitive advantage (RCA) index is applied to reflect the changing competitiveness of the PRD in the 2000s. The RCA index is widely used in international economics for calculating the relative advantage or disadvantage of a certain country/region in a certain class of goods or services as evidenced by trade flows (see Balassa 1979; Li et al. 2012). Results in Table 4.2 show that the region has been upgrading its competitiveness in the past decade with an increasing RCA index from 0.11 to 0.17, in spite of negative impacts from the Global Financial Crisis in 2008.[4] The most competitive industries were textile, apparel (including footwear, headgear, and so on), stone products, miscellaneous manufacture, and workers of art collectors. The competitiveness of machinery and electronics products also achieved the moderate extent of growth from 0.15 to 0.23. But the international competitiveness of the automotive sector was reducing (see products of vehicles and aircraft vessels).

Besides the upgrading of firm performance, functional upgrading was also achieved at the regional level in the sense that the PRD has upgraded from a processing base into one of local economic powerhouses with horizontally agglomerated industries, vertically integrated production networks, and a growing body of R&D and innovation activities (Enright et al. 2003, 2005; Yang and Liao 2009; Yu and Zhang 2009). Dozens of industrial clusters, national/provincial industrial parks, and development zones were developed in various sectors, such as electronics, home appliances, telecommunication equipment, toys, automobile vehicles, watches and clocks, garments, footwear, plastics products, and ceramics.

As I have shown in Chap. 1, the industrial structure of the PRD is moving toward and concentrating on higher-value-added sectors (see Fig. 1.3) The dominant role of the electronics industry, including electronics product, ICT, and electronic machinery, has been reinforced. In contrast, the influence of the textile and apparel industries is declining over time. As a newly emerging industry with higher value added, the transport equipment industry stands as the industry with most significant growth.

Along with the transformation of industrial structure, the positions of these industries in GPNs are also improved. Currently, the PRD's electronics industry is not made up of low-value-added processors in a marginal position. Instead, the PRD has taken

---

[4]The massive drop of the RCA index in 2004 mainly resulted from the huge increase in imports in plant products, medical instruments and equipment, clocks and watches, musical instruments, and so on. These export amount of these products originally exceeded import before 2000.

Table 4.2 RCA index of foreign merchandise trade in Guangdong Province

Years	1998	2004	2009	2014
Total	0.11	0.07	0.17	0.20
Live animal	0.33	0.25	0.02	−0.14
Vegetable products	0.09	−0.49	−0.63	−0.76
Animal or vegetable fats	−0.36	−0.90	−0.86	−0.71
Prepared foodstuff	0.44	0.37	0.31	0.10
Mineral products	−0.24	−0.77	−0.56	−0.66
Chemical products	−0.37	−0.52	−0.33	−0.28
Plastics	−0.36	−0.42	−0.35	−0.18
Leather, furs and related products, travel articles, handbags	0.41	0.27	0.43	0.52
Wood and products	**−0.27**	**−0.08**	**0.14**	**−0.36**
Wood pulp	−0.44	−0.30	0.07	0.17
Textile	**0.35**	**0.36**	**0.63**	**0.71**
Footwear, headgear, umbrellas, feather	**0.96**	**0.97**	**0.97**	**0.97**
Stone products	**0.42**	**0.47**	**0.67**	**0.56**
Jewelry, coins	0.07	0.27	0.15	0.29
Base metal	−0.31	−0.24	−0.20	0.10
Machinery, electric product	**0.15**	**0.12**	**0.23**	**0.24**
Vehicles aircraft vessel	**0.32**	**0.15**	**0.08**	**0.33**
Instruments, medical/optical instruments	**0.34**	**−0.20**	**−0.16**	**−0.05**
Miscellaneous manufacture	**0.94**	**0.93**	**0.93**	**0.93**
Works of art collectors	**0.98**	**0.95**	**0.93**	**0.77**
Special trading goods	0.18	−0.89	−0.80	−1.00

Note The RCA of net exports as a percentage of gross exports plus imports, given by

$$\text{RCA}_{\text{xat}}^{X-M*} = \frac{X_{\text{xat}} - M_{\text{xat}}^*}{X_{\text{xat}} + M_{\text{xat}}^*}$$

where

X_{xat} is the region x's export value of commodity at time t

M_{xat} is the region x's import value of commodity at time t

Ceteris paribus the closer the index is to +1.0; the more competitive an industry is in the global economy, and vice versa: that is, RCA ≥ 0 implies comparative advantage while RCA ≤ 0 implies a competitive disadvantage

Source Export and import data of main merchandise in Guangdong Statistic Yearbook in multiple years. Data specific for the PRD are unavailable. Provincial data are deployed and regarded as representative because the PRD's foreign trading accounted for more than 90% of the entire province in the 2000s

up a much more central role in the electronics' GPNs. This industry comprises manufacturing plants of many global lead firms in consumer electronics such as Sony, Kyocera, Toshiba, Samsung, LG, Nokia, and Motorola; key electronics manufacturing service (EMS) providers like Foxconn, Flextronics, Quanta, Compal, Wistron, Inventec, and Delta; and promising local or domestic Chinese firms like Huawei and ZTE (telecommunication), Media and TCL (home appliance), and Lenovo (computer), and so on. Integrated with thousands of suppliers, these leading electronics firms agglomerate within dozens of industrial clusters/parks in the PRD, particularly in Shenzhen, Dongguan, and Zhuhai (see details in Chap. 5).

In the apparel industry, thousands of competent local firms agglomerate in clusters and product-specific specialized towns. They are manufacturing countless products for most of the global branded retailers ranging from Louis Vuitton, Prada, and Armani in Europe; to Levis, LEE and A&F in the USA. Although the importance of the apparel industry in the PRD has been shrinking, this industry still accounted for 5% in total world export in 2009. This portion led ahead many developing countries such as Turkey, India, Vietnam, and Indonesia (see details in Chap. 6). In the automotive industry, the PRD has been upgraded into a key automotive industrial base supplying to the large domestic market of China. The key change in this industry occurred in the three joint ventures between SOEs and leading Japanese auto assemblers (Toyota, Honda, and Nissan). A vertically integrated production network was constructed by these joint ventures, their origin suppliers, and new local Chinese suppliers (see details in Chap. 7).

According to my empirical survey of 69 interviewed firms in 2010, product upgrading was the most significant type of upgrading with a value of 2.16 (see Fig. 4.1). Process upgrading stood second and was followed by functional upgrading. Sectoral upgrading was less significant with only a score of 0.57 within a scale of zero to 3. The overall tendency shows that the surveyed firms have achieved significant upgrading within the same sector.

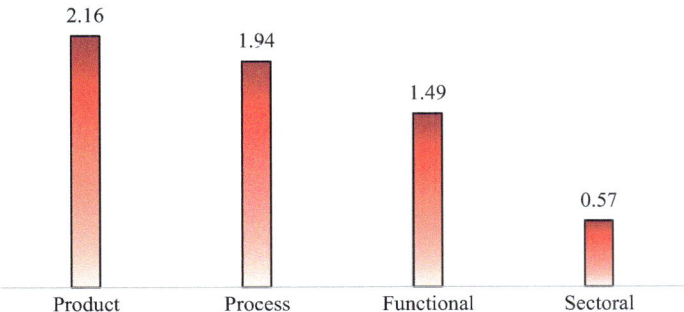

Fig. 4.1 Industrial upgrading in the surveyed firms. *Note* Informants were requested to evaluate the extent of upgrading in four types. A value ranged from absent (0) to very high (3) was attributed. The result is averaged (author's survey on 69 firms in the PRD in 2010)

4.3   Captive Coupling, Knowledge Diffusion, and Upgrading

The above section has shown the development stages and characteristics of upgrading in the PRD. The analytical foci of this section are the formation of captive coupling and how it led to a limited outcome of upgrading.

4.3.1   Formation of Captive Coupling

In the case of the PRD, the initial pattern of coupling belonged to *captive coupling*, referring to a state in which local firms were highly dependent on foreign-invested firms (FIEs, either TNCs or foreign investors) in terms of capital, technology, and market. The formation of captive coupling resulted from multi-scalar forces as shown by Fig. 4.2.

At a global scale, the PRD faced extremely huge technology and market gaps with the global economy because of its lack of industrial base (see Chap. 1). The PRD could only satisfy the basic profit-seeking imperative of TNCs which tended to relocate labor-intensive segments to localities with lower production costs. At the beginning of the 1980s, the average wage in manufacturing SOEs in the PRD was about $5 per month (Yu 2008). Before the Asian financial crisis in 1997, the monthly wages in manufacturing were merely increased to $100 in the PRD (Gu and Yang 1999). This cost-based complementarity was attractive to TNCs.

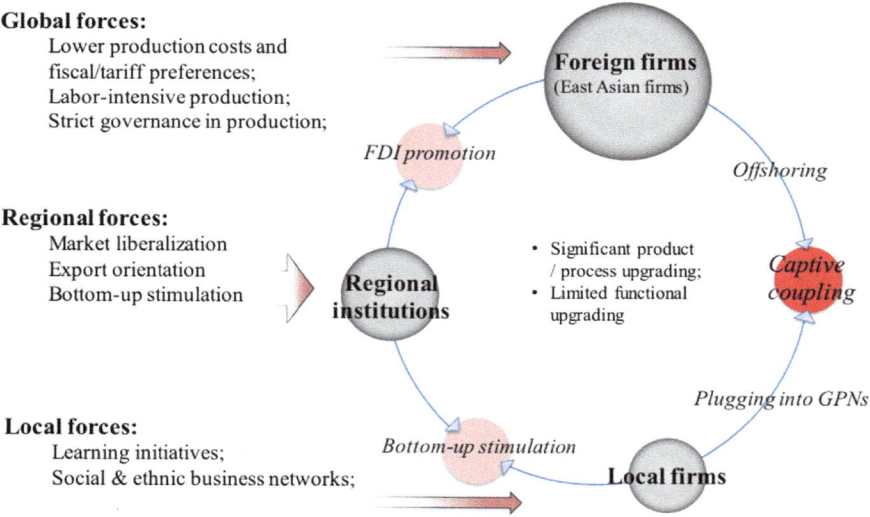

Global forces:
    Lower production costs and
    fiscal/tariff preferences;
    Labor-intensive production;
    Strict governance in production;

Foreign firms
(East Asian firms)

FDI promotion

Offshoring

Regional forces:
    Market liberalization
    Export orientation
    Bottom-up stimulation

Regional institutions

- Significant product / process upgrading;
- Limited functional upgrading

Captive coupling

Plugging into GPNs

Local forces:
    Learning initiatives;
    Social & ethnic business networks;

Bottom-up stimulation

Local firms

Fig. 4.2   Captive coupling in the PRD (compiled by author)

At the regional scale, with a liberal policy framework, regional governments in the PRD managed to facilitate the formation of captive coupling. This institutional leeway satisfied both the interests of local entrepreneurs and global capitalists. They both preferred a more flexible administrative environment so that they could practice capitalism without violating relevant laws and directives (e.g., public ownership) in China (Xu 1988; Chen and Pu 1999; Enright et al. 2003). Hong Kong firms played a critical intermediate role during this process. This point can be illustrated by the view of an owner of a Hong Kong-based OEM company in the apparel industry:

My big boss [investor] was actually from the U.S. When he decided to outsource jeans to China in 1982, he chose the PRD for its cheap labor costs and liberalizing environment. He set up a company in Hong Kong first for coordinating his business. This was because this big boss was skeptical of opening directly a factory in China since he had heard a lot of negative comments about the unstable politics and arbitrary local cadres of China. He also did not fully understand how to do business in China. That was why I was chosen to be a partner. (Interview 100325, on 25 March 2010 in Guangzhou)

At the local scale, captive coupling was reinforced by a bottom-up approach of FDI promotion. In the beginning of the 1980s, Guangdong Province had little financial capital in its regional banking systems. Without additional capital investments from the central government, the Guangdong provincial government had little capability to launch large-scale construction projects or to nurture competent SOEs. Hence, the provincial government further decentralized power and promoted foreign investments at the local scale such as counties, towns, and villages, which led to a scattered form of FDI distribution in the PRD (Xu 1988; Yang and Sit 1995; Cui 1999). Local governments were highly incentivized because they could retain the bulk of the revenue generated under a specific arrangement of 'fiscal contract' (Cai Zheng Bao Gan). As Table 4.3 shows, the category of 'others,' including small cities, counties, towns, and villages, accounted for most of the FDI with the highest growth rate between 1980 and 1993. These local governments served as flexible and proactive actors to satisfy the needs of foreign investors. The former chief planner

Table 4.3 Distribution of actual utilized foreign capital in the PRD (1980–1983) (Guangdong Statistics on Regional Economic Development, 1980–1993)

Urban scale (population)	1980 (%)	1993 (%)	1980–1993 (%)	Annual growth rate (%)
Mega city (>1 million)	28.1	13.2	14.2	43
Big city (0.5–1 million)	26.3	22.3	29.5	52
Middle city (100–500 thousand)	22.0	18.1	21.2	51
Others (<100 thousand)	23.6	46.5	34.7	55
Total amount (million, $)	101.2	6428	20,094	

Note Others include small cities, counties, towns, and villages

in Guangzhou Urban Planning and Design Institute has conceptualized this phenomenon as the 'small dog economy' which contributed to the formation of captive coupling considerably:

> Dongguan is a typical city that is highly dependent on FDI. At that time, all 33 towns were mobilized to attract foreign investments at the same time, like a local tournament. The municipal governments almost had no restriction on them or industrial plan for them, expect setting an unwritten but fixed annual criteria of FDI attraction to be achieved. I called it as 'small dog economy' in which all the dogs [towns] were running round and competed with each other for food [FDI]. It was quite flexible and efficient for development in the beginning, but it was a rough way of resource utilization in terms of lands and environment. (Interview, 100417, on 17 April 2010 in Guangzhou)

Social and ethnic business networks in the PRD also played a positive role in facilitating captive coupling. These connections enabled the region to enjoy good accessibility to information about the global market, state-of-art technologies, and modern managerial skills. They either introduced the PRD to wider audiences or directly shaped the relocation decisions of TNCs based on personal networking or preferences, particularly when the decision makers or brokers were ethnic Chinese (Hsing 1996; Yeung 1997; Olds and Yeung 1999; Qiu 2005). For example, many of the apparel industrial clusters in the PRD benefited from the overseas relatives of local entrepreneurs (see details in Chap. 6). Zhuhai City attracted many Japanese firms by constructing a specific social network. In the mid-1980s, Zhuhai governments hired several Chinese returnees from Japan as senior officers in the Zhuhai Bureau of Foreign Economy and Trade. These returnees actively organized several official business trips to Japan for promoting FDI. Meanwhile, the returnees mobilized their social connections in Japan to get in touch with Japanese lead firms in the electronics industry. As a result, Zhuhai successfully brokered a large amount of Japanese electronics companies to offshore their manufacturing segments to Zhuhai, such as Canon (1990, camera and printer), Mitsum (1991, transformers and magnetic head), and Panasonic (1993, motor and battery). By 2000, Zhuhai had hosted about 240 Japanese electronics companies and continuously attracted more Japanese firms based on this agglomeration effect. Within a single year in 2006, 100 Japanese electronics firms established branch plants in Zhuhai with a total investment over US$10 million.[5] Apart from providing fiscal incentives for these Japanese firms, Zhuhai governments also actively built up several industrial parks to accommodate them and even provided help in recruiting workers, technicians, and engineers.

4.3.2 Limited Upgrading in Captive Coupling

Due to large knowledge gaps, liberalizing regional environment, and local initiatives, the integration pattern of the PRD initially turned out to be a form of captive

---

[5]Source: author's interviews in Zhuhai in June, 2010, with four interviewees: two directors and a senior officer of three industrial parks, and a vice-director of the Foreign Economy and Trading Bureau of Zhuhai.

coupling. Local economies were captive to foreign firms which provided capitals and technologies by establishing a large number of FIEs. This captive coupling led to rapid industrialization in the PRD in which product and process upgrading was significantly realized based on the synergy between local entrepreneurs and foreign investors. However, the upgrading was limited. The limited upgrading was embodied by the prevalence of export-processing enterprises (EPEs) and Hong Kong firms in the PRD.

EPEs were called the *San Lai Yi Bu* enterprises in China, which is also termed as process and assemble firms (Yeung 2001). These enterprises refer to three forms of processing works[6] and compensation trade. These enterprises have no domestic sale quota, and all finished goods must be exported. It should be noticed that investments in EPEs are excluded from the conventional definition of FDI and are regarded as 'other forms of foreign investments' in Chinese statistical terms. EPEs are similar to the *maquiladora* in Mexico which emerged in the 1960s and became prevalent after the establishment of NAFTA in 1994 (Kamel and Hoffman 1999). The difference is that EPEs have greater flexibility in material procurement. They do not necessarily process materials designated or provided by foreign partners, while enjoy certain autonomy in sourcing in global markets (Xu 1988; Song et al. 1989; Gan and Gan 1994).

EPEs have been prevalent in the PRD for three decades which means that the region has highly depended on this type of enterprises in which local firms are captive to foreign investors. In 1980, investments in EPEs accounted for 61% of total utilized foreign capital in the PRD. Though the portion was decreasing, it still took up a share of 48% in 1990 (GDSY 2001). Data from the custom regime show the significant role of EPEs in the foreign trading of the PRD. In 1990, EPEs accounted for 82% of total export value and 80% of total import value in the PRD. A decade later, the portion was reduced a little bit with 78% in export and 70% in import. By 2009, EPE still played a major role in foreign trading, accounting for 57% of export value and 54% of import value in the PRD.[7]

Due to geographical proximity, social–cultural networks and deliberated national strategies, Hong Kong firms became the primary players in establishing EPEs in the PRD. Taiwanese firms followed after the mid-1980s (Leung 1993; Tuan and Ng 2004; Yu 2008). By 1985, Hong Kong-origin investments ($670 million) accounted for 90% of total utilized foreign capital in the PRD.[8] Most of them were concentrated on the apparel and electronics industries (Chui et al. 1997). The prevalence of Hong Kong firms formed a regional production pattern between the PRD and Hong Kong, termed as the 'front-shop-back-factory' (FSBF) pattern. As shown in Fig. 4.3, Hong Kong played a dominant role as a front shop which received orders from global markets and completed manufacturing works by thousands of EPEs in the PRD (Sit

---

[6](1) manufacturing with designated designs and templates from foreign partners; (2) manufacturing with provided raw materials from foreign partners; (3) manufacturing with imported materials from foreign partners.

[7]Guangdong Statistic Yearbook in multiple years, 1995–2010.

[8]Guangdong Statistics Yearbook in multiple years, 1991–2010.

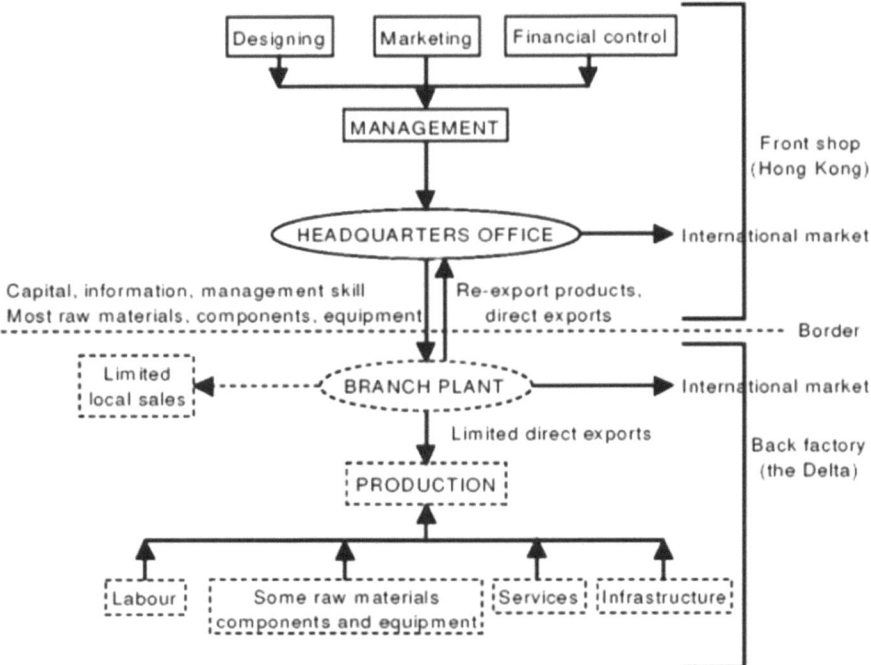

Fig. 4.3 Front-shop-back-factory pattern of production in the PRD (Fig. 3 in Sit and Yang 1997: 657)

and Yang 1997; Sit 1998). The FSBF pattern largely boosted the competitiveness of Hong Kong firms by offshoring and outsourcing labor-intensive segments to the PRD hinterland. Many Hong Kong-based FIEs participated in this pattern later on by subcontracting orders to local manufacturers rather than establishing EPEs.

There was synergy for nurturing upgrading within EPEs. In terms of labor division, foreign investors were in charge of investing in facilities (including machines, plants, and basic equipment), importing parts of raw materials, providing designs and managerial assistance, and exporting final products to global markets. With very low entry barriers, local firms provided all other resources such as land, workshops, and low-waged workers, except capital and technologies. In terms of profit sharing, local firms earned a fixed amount of processing fees and tax reimbursements, while foreign firms appropriated all other profits. Therefore, foreign investors had incentives to improve production efficiency by upgrading product ranges and processing technologies in EPEs. Local partners were willing to follow the governance of foreign investors as this was the best learning opportunity for them when their indigenous capabilities were rather weak.

Knowledge diffusion took place through the efforts of foreign investors in three general steps: providing product definitions and designs, constructing production lines (equipment, facilities, and even factories), and labor training. For instance, during the 1980s, there were about $3 billion machines imported into the PRD by foreign investors. A comment from the owner of Changjiang Textile and Apparel Company interprets knowledge diffusion within EPEs:

> We knew nothing at all at that time [the 1980s]. We would be better off by just following the instructions set by foreign businessmen. We did what they told us to do. They taught us how to set up a factory, organize a production and management system, although sometimes we did not know why we should do it that ways. Our business boomed quickly. Many workers from states owned enterprise hopped to my factories, because in my factory, they could earn more and learn more. (Interview 100427, on 27 April 2010 in Guangzhou)

Though there was synergy, functional upgrading was limited within EPEs. By defining production and organization, foreign investors had overwhelming power toward local partners from production to delivery. Local firms served as affiliated processors at a truncated and marginal position within EPEs. This position was disconnected from information about market demand, marketing, procurement, logistics, the management skills of production system, and supply chain. Foreign investors had no incentive to transfer any of these types of knowledge to local firms.

Being situated in such a disadvantaged position, local firms had litter power to bargain for a better position with more learning opportunties. Regional assets, such as liberalizing institutional environment, proactive developmental states, and overseas social–cultural networks, could only facilitate the process of industrialization, whereas could not support local firms to reshape power relations with foreign investors (Cui 1999; Li 2002). The weak power of local governments and firms was described by the director of Guangdong Development Research Institute as below:

> At that time [the 1980s], policy was our only treasure for development. We kept persuading foreign firms to invest in the PRD, while at that time, we could not ask for too much. It was good enough once those business-men were willing to invest in. Therefore, local governments rushed to attract FDI by lowering production costs. As I remembered, many towns and counties even waived land rents. At the same time, all industries came in, unselectively, such as low end and processing industries, or highly polluted or highly energy-consuming industries. (Interview 100518, on 18 May 2010 in Guangzhou)

Institutional inertia was also developed within EPEs that further hindered local functional upgrading. Comparing with FIEs, foreign investors in EPEs only have to pay processing fees. Operating in the forms of EPEs had lower managerial costs and earned more marginal profits. Moreover, workers in EPEs were employed under short-term labor contracts without any coverage of pension or social insurance (Gu and Yang 1999). Therefore, foreign investors hardly had interests in upgrading EPEs into FIEs, unless they wanted to develop the domestic market. To local authorities in townships and villages, they also preferred to stay with EPEs for earning administrative and processing fees. Once EPEs were upgraded into normal enterprises, local authorities could only reap profits from land leasing. This was why local authorities resisted the new regional-upgrading policy in 2008 which aimed for relocating EPEs in the PRD.[9]

---

[9]An online media report about the bargaining between local and regional authorities about restructuring EPEs, at: http://finance.ifeng.com/city/cskx/20091101/1414570.shtml.

To sum up, the economic takeoff of the PRD resulted from the formation of captive coupling based on multi-scalar forces: the global imperative of industrial relocation, regional liberalizing tendency, and local initiatives. Synergy within captive coupling nurtured rapid industrial growth as well as limited product and process upgrading in the region. Functional upgrading was impeded organizationally and institutionally. Nevertheless, the PRD was not dominated by this captive coupling throughout three decades of development. Strategic coupling has been evolving since the 1990s. Next section addresses this dynamics.

4.4 Impetus of Change: Evolutionary Strategic Coupling

The formation of captive coupling occurred between the 1980s and the early 1990s. Beginning in the mid-1980s, FIEs started to increase their influence in the region through establishing joint exploration of resources and three types of FIEs (ventures): equity joint venture, contractual joint venture, and wholly foreign-owned venture. Different from EPEs, these FIEs not only benefited the regional economy through the effects of knowledge spillover, and also nurtured local firms as their suppliers. Since the 1990s, FIEs became much more influential and replaced EPEs as the key driving force. Meanwhile, local firms were also catching up with FIEs and managed to develop more comprehensive partnerships with foreign investors by utilizing various new regional assets. This section illustrates the evolutionary tendency of strategic coupling in three dimensions: (1) the changing regional profiles of foreign trade which reflect the evolving pattern of integration; (2) the divergent performance of firms which present the reconfiguration of driving forces to local upgrading; and (3) local upgrading strategies which are embedded in various spatial–institutional conditions. I argue that these changes provide new opportunities for local firms to leverage the governance power of foreign firms in their pursuit of local upgrading.

4.4.1 Changing Patterns of Foreign Trades: Moving Away from Captive Coupling

By examining the changing profiles of foreign trade data in the PRD, this study identifies two distinctive features related to the evolution. First, as shown in Table 4.4, the PRD has been directly articulated into the global economy, rather than depended heavily on the intermediate role of Hong Kong. From 1990 to 2009, the dominant role of Hong Kong was overtaken by firms from the USA, Japan, Taiwan, and other EU members. Although Hong Kong was still the most important partner in the export market, its share declined from 81 to 32%. In the import market, there was evidence of Hong Kong's shrinking share from 80% in 1995 to 7% in 2000 and to 2.4% in 2005. Moreover, Hong Kong was excluded from the top five importers in 2009. In

Table 4.4 Main trading partners of Guangdong Province (1990–2015) (Guangdong Statistics Yearbook, 1991–2016)

Rank	1990	1995	2000	2005	2010	2015
Export						
1	HK (81)	HK (87)	HK (34.3)	HK (39)	HK (37.3)	HK (31.9)
2	USA (3.8)	USA (3.1)	USA (28)	USA (25)	USA (18.6)	USA (16.8)
3	Japan (2.7)	Japan (2)	Japan (8.4)	Japan (6.2)	Japan (4.7)	Japan (3.77)
4	Macao (1.6)	Taiwan (2)	German (3.5)	Netherland (3)	German (3.1)	South Korea (3.7)
5	Singapore (1.3)	Macao (0.8)	UK (2.87)	German (2.5)	Netherlands (2.2)	UK (2.59)
Import						
1	HK (66)	HK (80)	Taiwan (19)	Taiwan (18)	Japan (14.1)	Taiwan (14)
2	France (8)	Taiwan (11)	Japan (18)	Japan (17)	Taiwan (13.2)	South Korea (11)
3	Macao (6.4)	Japan (3)	South Korea (9)	South Korea (9)	South Korea (9.0)	Japan (10)
4	Japan (4.4)	USA (1.2)	USA (6.8)	USA (4.2)	Malaysia (4.7)	USA (5.4)
5	UK (4.0)	Sweden (1)	HK (6.7)	HK (2.4)	USA (4.3)	Malaysia (4.5)

Unit: %

the export market from 1990 to 2009, the USA overtook Hong Kong's role with an increase from 4 to 19%. During the same period in the import market, Hong Kong was replaced by Japan, Taiwan, and South Korea. Particularly, Japan became the third important trade partner of the PRD. This tendency implies that the PRD is moving from a marginal node into a more central position within GPNs. The region has articulated into global markets by building up trade relationships with many of the most important developed and developing countries. Second, as shown in Table 4.5, the PRD was reducing dependence on EPEs in its international trade markets. In export trade, the share of EPEs declined from 82% in 1990 to 57% in 2009. In import trade, it was reduced from 80% in 1990 to 54% in 2009. Correspondently, ordinary trade kept growing and exceeded the share of EPEs. The articulation into global markets and the fading influence of EPEs implies that the PRD has been moving away from captive coupling. Both foreign and local firms in the PRD increasingly export more sophisticated products than EPEs.

Table 4.5 Changing patterns of foreign trades in the PRD (1990–2015) (Guangdong Statistic Yearbook 1992–2015, Currency: US$, billion)

Year	Total	Ordinary trade (%)	EPE trade (%)	Others (%)
Export				
1990	22.2	18	82	0.6
1995	56.6	19	80	0.4
2000	91.9	19	78	0.3
2005	238.2	22	65	0.0
2010	453.2	33	57	3.8
2015	643.5	43	44	3.7
Import				
1990	19.7	18	80	2.0
1995	47.4	16	83	0.7
2000	78.2	27	70	0.8
2005	189.8	26	61	0.6
2010	331.7	36	53	0.4
2015	379.3	41	42	0.7

Note EPE trade refers to trades based on export-processing firms. Others include trades based on the bonded warehouse, donations, and so on

4.4.2 Divergent Performance of Key Actors: Who Are the Drivers?

While the pattern of captive coupling is evolving, who are the key drivers of this change? By investigating the performance of different firms, this study finds that the driving forces of the PRD have been reconfigured constantly in the last two decades. By and large, SOEs have the best performance but least influence in the PRD. The region is still led by FIEs. But local private firms are quickly catching up with FIEs (see Table 4.6).

During the 1980s, SOEs were playing a dominant role in the regional economy. By 1992, more than 7000 SOEs produced the majority of output with 25 billion *yuan* IVA. Collective-owned enterprises (COEs) were the second largest forces accordingly. From then on, SOEs and COEs have lost their influence. The number of SOEs and COEs shrank incredibly. In 2009, there were only 294 SOEs and 612 COEs. Meanwhile, their contribution to IVA in the PRD became very insignificant. In 2009, SOEs contributed only 83 billion *yuan* IVA which was 10% of the FIEs' total, while the COEs' outputs were much less. However, the SOEs turned out to be highly efficient in terms of their growing figures of IVA per enterprise and IVA per capita which were ranked top among all firms in the last decade.

This distinctive trajectory of the SOEs/COEs largely resulted from the radical national reform during the 1990s (Wu 2005). Due to the unsatisfactory outcome of

Table 4.6 Enterprise performance in the PRD (1991–2009) (Guangdong Statistic Yearbook 1996–2010; the PRD and the YRD Statistic Yearbook, 2005–2010; Guangdong Economic Census 2004 and 2008)

Year	SOE	COE	PE	#FIE	FIE (HTM)	Others
Industrial value added (billion)						
*1991	25	15	1.2	5	12	N.A.
1999	33	21	30	41	97	29
2005	38	11	197	255	290	55
2009	83	12	530	429	407	68
Number of enterprises (unit)						
*1991	7172	20,499	N.A.	N.A.	N.A.	N.A.
1999	1304	2801	1914	1261	5776	N.A.
2005	1047	974	8909	3931	9810	N.A.
2009	294	612	14,727	5364	11,720	N.A.
IVA per enterprise (million)						
*1991	3.5	0.7	N.A.	N.A.	N.A.	N.A.
1999	25.2	7.5	14.2	32.5	16.8	N.A.
2005	87.3	11.3	22.1	64.9	29.5	N.A.
2009	281.4	19.6	36.0	79.9	34.7	N.A.
IVA per capita (thousand)						
*1991	14	7	N.A.	N.A.	N.A.	N.A.
1999	84	29	73	82	45	N.A.
2005	290	39	101	123	75	N.A.
2009	469	43	154	148	87	N.A.

Note SOE refers to state-owned enterprise; *COE* refers to collective-owned enterprises; *PE* refers to private-invested enterprise; *FIE* (HTM) refer to FIEs originated from Hong Kong, Taiwan, and Macao; and Others refer to all firms with annual revenue lower than 5 million *yuan* plus EPEs
*Data in 1991 refer to the whole Guangdong Province. Currency: *yuan*
#FIEs refers to foreign-invested enterprise excluding the ones from Hong Kong, Taiwan, and Macao

the SOEs reform in the 1980s, China implemented two radical policies in implementing managerial and structural reform among SOEs which were termed as 'Zhua Da Fang Xiao' (grasping the big and let go the small) and 'You Jin You Tui' (selective industrial development). These policies significantly consolidated the number of SOEs through intra- and inter-regional mergence and acquisition, massive employment layoff, and privatization (Steinfeld 1998, 2004; Huang 2002). In doing so, SOEs became giant corporate groups and possessed a huge amount of fixed assets and dominated in monopolistic industries, such as petroleum, power supply, railway, and telecommunication (Wang 2011). By 1998, the number of SOEs in China was reduced to about 60,000 and then further to 20,000 in 2009, while most of them were highly profitable due to monopoly.[10]

Since 1990, EPEs have been losing their importance in the regional economy. In Guangdong Province, while EPEs accounted for 60% of foreign investments in the 1980s, this portion significantly declined to about 25% in around 1995 and further shrank to 12% in 2005 and to 4% in 2009 (GDSY 2001). When EPEs, SOEs, and COEs became less influential, FIEs emerged as the key driver of the regional economy. As shown in Table 4.6, FIEs had accounted for the largest share of IVA and the numbers of firms since 1999. Among private firms, FIEs and FIEs-HTM (firms from Hong Kong, Taiwan, and Macao), FIEs had the best performance, and FIEs-HTM became the least efficient recently in terms of IVA per enterprises and per capita.

The dominance of FIEs resulted from the further market liberalization in the PRD during the 1990s and the 2000s (Yu and Zhang 2009). As Steinfeld (2004: 1979) described, 'the reformers [in this period] pursued arguably the most liberal FDI policy of any Asian developing country'. Incentivized by the new taxation law since 1994, urban authorities became a very proactive force in mobilizing large-scale development projects in the PRD. Because land conveyance became one of the most important sources of revenue, regional governments tended to increase their income by 'selling' land for industrial and urban development (Lin 2009b). By 2006, 30 development zones and industrial parks were established in the PRD, covering an area of 28,266 ha. These industrial districts were used for attracting the relocation of TNCs, particularly those in high- and new-technology industries (Wong and Tang 2005; DRCGP 2009).

In order to improve local supply stability and international competitiveness, FIEs did not merely relocate non-core processing segments to the PRD, but progressively transplanted their suppliers to the region. Within respective production networks, incumbent and new technologies were diffused from their R&D centers and headquarters to the production sites in the PRD. This mechanism of FDI-driven development has been discussed in many previous studies (Lin 1997; Sit and Yang 1997; Enright et al. 2003; Yang 2005, 2009; Yang and Liao 2009). My interpretation of captive coupling in Sect. 4.3 is generally consistent with their explanations.

While FIEs are leading the regional economy, private firms have achieved the most significant growth. As shown in Table 4.6, private firms were quite insignificant in 1991, contributing to less than 3% of the regional IVA. But they have made remarkable progress within two decades. In 2009, they contributed one-third of the regional total. In 1999, the performance of private firms was lower than most of the other firms in terms of IVA per enterprise. But in the last decade, the number of private firms increased dramatically from about 2000 to 15,000. Meanwhile, they managed to upgrade their production capabilities by substantially improving efficiency: The

---

[10]In 2009, with a profit of $20 billion, China Mobile Communications Corporation was evaluated as the most profitable corporation in the world; the total profit of all SOEs was US$137 billion, while top six monopolistic SOEs accounted for 63%.

figures of IVA per enterprise and IVA per capital more than doubled. These figures showed higher efficiency than FIE-HTM. It also should be noted that data in Table 4.6 only refer to firms with a minimal annual turnover of 5 million *yuan*. As this study's estimation is based on multiple sources of statistical yearbooks, there were about 140,000 enterprises in the PRD lower this minimal annual turnover in 2009, contributing to merely 5% of the regional total IVA. These smaller firms employed millions of workers and were struggling for their survival.

4.4.3 Strategies of Local Upgrading

The above elaboration has demonstrated that the PRD is moving away from captive coupling to a certain extent. The regional economy is no longer dependent on EPEs to stimulate rapid industrialization. Firms in the PRD are moving from a highly truncated mode to a more central position within GPNs. Meanwhile, the PRD is no longer fully dependent on FIEs in driving regional growth. Local firms have caught up with FIEs and become another key driving force in shaping regional upgrading. What are the trajectories of local upgrading? What are the key strategies adopted by local firms? Is there anything new beyond previous studies that emphasize the importance of indigenous innovation? The rest of this chapter attempts to answer these questions on the basis of the empirical investigation of this study.

To account for the remarkable industrial growth and upgrading in China, previous studies have pointed to a key answer in relation to the contributions of knowledge spillover from TNCs, strong state investments, and intensive endogenous innovation, such as in the cases of Lenovo and Huawei (Lazonick 2004; Fan 2006, 2007, 2011; Ernst 2007; Li 2009; Lin and Wang 2009; Yang 2009). However, my empirical investigation shows that the majority of local firms in the PRD do not conform to this catching-up trajectory.

By examining the performance of high-tech industries in the PRD, this study finds that innovation does not play a significant role in the past decade. Innovation here refers to the use of new technologies, methods or ideas.[11] As shown in Table 4.7, from 1998 to 2008, high-tech enterprises achieved significant growth and accounted for 31% of the regional industrial output. Within the output value of high-tech products, the share of new products progressively grew from 13 to 17% during the same period. Meanwhile, the amount of R&D expenditures, issued patents, and employment for R&D all had an impressive growth. Nonetheless, if we take the increasing number of firms into account, the achievement of innovation was not significant and was even disappointed to a certain degree. From 1998 to 2008, the average R&D expenditure of high-tech firms increased from 6.8 to 9.2 million *yuan*, but the ratio between R&D expenditures and output value decreased by 0.4%.

---

[11]Innovation differs from invention in that innovation refers to the use of a new idea or method, whereas invention refers more directly to the creation of the idea or method itself.

Table 4.7 Performance of the high-tech industries in Guangdong Province (Guangdong Scientific Development Yearbook, 1998–2008)

	1998	2000	2002	2004	2006	2008
General						
• High-tech products in total industrial output (%)	11.2	17.2	21.6	23.5	30.5	30.9
• Value of new products in high-tech products (%)	12.7	13.9	12.9	13.5	13.9	16.7
• Number of high-tech firms	815	1173	1730	3065	4673	7831
R&D and patent						
• R&D expenditures of high-tech firms (million)	5600	11,300	16,200	24,100	38,500	71,800
# per enterprise	6.8	9.9	9.4	7.9	8.2	9.2
# in high-tech output (%)	3.6	3.9	3.5	2.8	2.5	3.2
• Issued patents (item)	10,707	15,799	22,760	31,446	43,516	62,031
# per enterprise	13.1	13.9	13.2	10.3	9.3	7.9
• R&D employment (people)	21,100	53,400	69,400	76,300	127,100	197,500
# per enterprise	26	47	40	25	27	25

Note According to the official category from National Bureau of Statistics of China (2006), high-tech industries include eight key sectors: nuclear fuel processing, chemical-information products, medicine manufacturing, aerospace manufacturing, electronics and communication products, computer and Internet equipment, medical equipment and instrument, and public software. See more detail at: http://www.stats.gov.cn/tjbz/t20061123_402369836.htm. Data specific for the PRD are not available. But the PRD accounted for more than 80% of output in high-tech industries in the 2000s. Hence, provincial-level data are considered as representative

Although the total amount of issued patents increased sixfold, the average amount per firm declined from 13.1 to 7.9. In a similar trend, while the PRD's high-tech firms were employing more technicians for conducting R&D activities, the average number of R&D technicians did not experience the corresponding increase. It indeed grew from 26 in 1998 to 47 in 2000. After that, the average number was dropping and it eventually declined to 25 in 2008.

If not innovation, what will be the local strategies of upgrading in the PRD? My empirical investigation has observed different strategies that local firms have frequently deployed in their pursuit of upgrading. These strategies are related to changing institutional conditions at different spatial scales.

At the local scale, while serving as the suppliers or subcontractors of foreign firms, local firms preferred to develop more external cooperation with both firms and institutional actors so as to identify more learning opportunities. The increasing cooperative type of firms was a sign to support this point. From 1995 to 2009, among FIEs in the PRD, the proportion of Chinese-foreign joint ventures had increased from 20 to 29%. Before 1995, the majority of the SOEs were wholly owned by the state. This configuration was reshaped. Among about 1000 SOEs in 2009, only 300 of them were wholly owned by the state. The others were state-holding companies either with

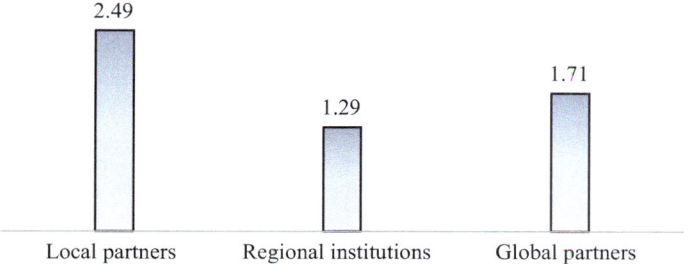

Fig. 4.4 Importance of external partners to local upgrading. *Note* Informants were requested to evaluate the importance of external collaborators in the upgrading of their companies. A value ranged from absent (0) to very high (3) was attributed. The result is averaged. *Source* Author's survey on 45 local firms

private firms or FIEs (GDSY 2010). The increasing number of cooperative enterprises diversified external linkages that enabled more knowledge diffusion among local firms. According to my field survey (see Fig. 4.4), cooperation with local partners had the most significant influence on the upgrading strategies of local firms. Global partners were the second most important type of collaborators. Regional institutions were less significant with a score of 1.29.

At the regional level, local firms tended to utilize emerging new assets to increase their bargaining power and upgrading opportunities. Apart from the liberalizing environment, there were at least three new assets available for local firms in the PRD. First was the emergence of China's huge domestic markets. This market did not exist in the 1980s to most of the firms. It was originally small in size and regionally fragmented due to limited household incomes and the state-controlled pricing system. But currently China's domestic markets have become quite large based on the incredible industrial growth and the increasing purchase power of firms and individuals (Wu 2005; Gadiesh et al. 2007; Ma 2009). Second was the growing body of regional supply networks. Different from the condition in the 1980s, the PRD has now developed such a production network based on thousands of TNCs, the transplanted suppliers, and the growth of local firms. The third asset was the emergence of regional associational economies (e.g., industrial associations) which served as the channels of knowledge diffusion in the PRD.

Figure 4.5 articulates the influence of these assets on local upgrading among the surveyed firms. Domestic markets served as the most important asset to local firms in upgrading. The availability of technologies in the PRD stood as the second important factor, followed by the factors of regional supply-based capabilities and production-cost advantages. Particularly, 90% of the informants affirmed that their companies had increased local sourcing content and reduced component importation in the past decade. About 70% of the informants confirmed that they had sourced more than 50% components and materials from local supply networks within the PRD. In comparison with these factors, associational economies and social–cultural advantages mattered less. Governmental support was the least significant. This result reminds us that the

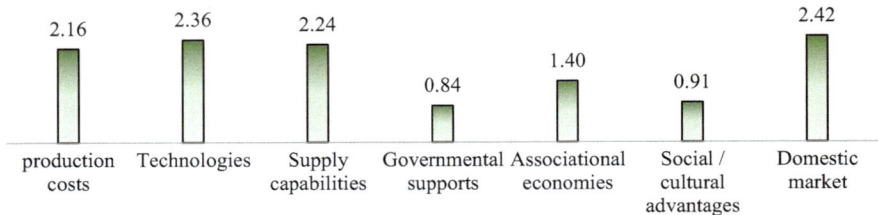

Fig. 4.5 Importance of regional assets to local upgrading. *Note* Informants were requested to evaluate the degree of importance of regional assets during the upgrading of their companies. A value ranged from absent (0) to very high (3) was attributed to each type of regional assets. The result was averaged. *Source* Author's survey on 45 local firms

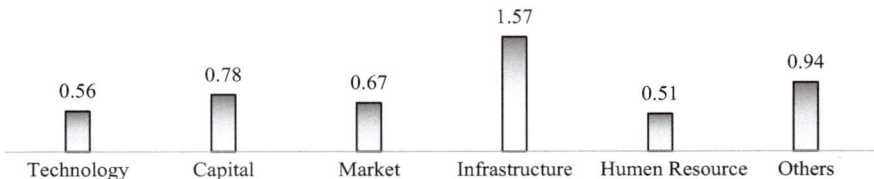

Fig. 4.6 Importance of supports from governments and institutions. *Note* Informants were requested to evaluate the degree of importance of governmental supports during the upgrading of their companies. A value ranged from absent (0) to very high (3) was attributed to each type of supports. The result was averaged. *Source* Author's survey on 45 local firms

role of regional institutions in the PRD should not be over-emphasized, even though the proactive China's state institutions have been well recognized in the literature (Huchet 1997; Fan 2007; Ma 2009). In Fig. 4.6, governmental support was only effective in constructing infrastructures (with a value of 1.57). All other governmental support was not influential on local upgrading such as technologies, capital, market, and human resource.

At the global level, local firms tended to look for more upgrading opportunities by taking advantages of competitive dynamics within GPNs. This strategy was implicitly generalized from different viewpoints by my informants. It enabled local firms to bypass the control of foreign firms and cooperate with a wider range of foreign partners. The disintegration of the FSBF pattern (see Sect. 4.3.2) between Hong Kong and the PRD is a good example.

Within the FSBF pattern, Hong Kong firms' governance power was vulnerable. Overtime, the PRD's local firms became familiar with international markets and trading regulations. They went to Hong Kong to establish their own shops and receive orders from global buyers directly. At the same time, when domestic institutional environment became more liberal, global buyers also preferred to bypass Hong Kong traders and to develop their own suppliers in the PRD. This tendency was facilitated by more frequent international trade fairs, business exhibitions, or other events hosted in the PRD (Yeh and Xu 2006). The reunion of Hong Kong and China and the

Asian financial crisis also facilitated this process (Jao 2001; Shen 2003). Eventually, the governance power of Hong Kong firms was bypassed. Hong Kong no longer served as the 'front shop' of the PRD. It gradually shifted to providing professional sourcing/trading services for global buyers and logistic services for the PRD firms, respectively (Tewari 2006; Yeh and Xu 2006). This change is reflected in the comment by a senior committee member of the Fashion Designer Association of Hong Kong who is also the CEO of Alter Design Corporation:

> After the reunion, global buyers [lead firms] preferred to cooperate directly with firms from mainland China. Everybody knows that middle man [Hong Kong's firms] must take some money, so why not we just move further to deal with the producer. I must say, that the crisis [in 1997] gave the PRD an opportunity. Because China' well performances within the crisis, those buyers had faith to deal with Chinese firms, and they soon found that PRD's local firms were not bad actually. So things got changed. A lot of [Hong Kong] bosses needed to find another way to make money, like turning to the logistics and financial industries. Hong Kong sill has certain expertise in these kinds of industries. (Interview 100602, on 2 June 2010 in Guangzhou)

The above empirical observations have introduced three general strategies of local firms adopted in their pursuit of upgrading. These strategies are not exclusive to each other and can be synthesized. In Chaps. 6–8, I provide further detailed case studies to demonstrate how local firms deploy these strategies to leverage the governance power of foreign firms. For instance, domestic markets serve as a crucial source of profits in the electronics industry (Chap. 5), while it is utilized by local firms to practice marketing skills in the apparel industry (Chap. 6). In the automobile industry, domestic markets are deployed as an exchange for knowledge diffusion from TNCs (Chap. 7). In reducing knowledge gaps, local firms in the electronics industry mainly learn from their TNCs clients (Chap. 5). But in the apparel industry, they accumulate knowledge through diverse channels (Chap. 6). In the automotive industry, local firms absorb knowledge from their foreign partners (Chap. 7). The overall finding resonates with Viotti's (2003: 653) view that innovation tends to be 'a phenomenon alien to late industrializing economies'. Many local firms in the PRD actually adopt 'a strategy of learning that focuses on the mastering and improving the absorbed technologies of production'.

4.5 Dynamic Outcomes of Local Upgrading

In most of the contemporary China studies, the PRD has been recognized as one of the world's leading manufacturing bases and the vanguard of China's national economy (Cartier 2001; Chen and Li 2006). Scholars interested in the PRD mainly attribute the success of PRD's development into four factors: (1) export-oriented strategies; (2) knowledge spillover from FIEs (mostly from Hong Kong and Taiwan); (3) economic power decentralized by the central government that allows regional policy makers to construct a business-friendly institutional environment; and (4) local initiatives of coupling facilitated by ethnic-based social networks (Hsing 1996; Sit 1998; Ng and

Tang 2004; Enright et al. 2005; Yeh et al. 2006; Smart and Lin 2007). These studies generally come to an agreement that while the PRD experiences upgrading through learning from and benchmarking against TNCs, it is now becoming less promising due to exhausted land resources, increasing labor costs, and deteriorative environment (Liao and Chan 2009; Lin 2009b; Yang 2009). Some scholars have argued for greater endogenous technological innovation to overcome this diminishing return (Fan 2011; Zhou and Wei 2011). Otherwise, industrial development will reach a bottle-neck soon and upgrading is bound to be impeded as Steinfeld (2004) has predicted.

Although the above assertions are plausible and have been supported with some empirical facts, they mainly hold a static view of the captive coupling pattern of integration. In contrast to them, this chapter offers an alternative interpretation by investigating the relation between strategic coupling and local upgrading in the PRD.

By reviewing three decades of development in the PRD, this chapter found that the development trajectory of the PRD cannot be accounted for the developmental state literature. A developmental state did not appear in the PRD. Instead, the region underwent a liberalizing process continuously which was mediated by the central government's desire for promoting export-oriented industrialization. More recently, a regional imperative of upgrading emerged that tended to relocate labor-intensive manufacturing industries within the region. Empirical examination has shown that the PRD managed to achieve upgrading in various dimensions, such as corporate performance, international competitiveness, and structural and functional changes. The region is moving into a world manufacturing hub, rather than processing and assembling base.

Through the relational framework, this chapter reinterpreted the economic take-off of the PRD in relation to the formation of captive coupling among foreign firms, regional institutions, and local firms. The prevalence of EPEs reflected how synergy within captive coupling led to rapid industrial growth as well as the improvement of the processing capabilities of local partners. A historical analysis of the operation of EPEs demonstrated that synergy within captive coupling was not predetermined by value-chain governance. In contrast, it was subject to specific institutional arrangements and spatial conditions where EPEs were embedded. The asymmetrical power relation within EPEs hindered the prospect of local upgrading, such as functional upgrading. Local firms had little power to escape from the disadvantaged position. However, my further analyses illustrated that captive coupling was not static but evolutionary and subject to changing knowledge gaps and institutional–spatial conditions.

Section 4.4 has largely articulated the impetus of changes. Since the 1990s, there were many ongoing trends implying that the PRD was moving away from captive coupling, such as the new regional profile of foreign trading and the divergent performance of firms. The new regional trading profile indicated that the PRD was no longer captive to Hong Kong for participating in the global trading. It became more capable of engaging with trading partners from most of the developed countries in a more comprehensive manner. During this process, the driving forces of the regional economy were reconfigured substantially. EPE, SOEs, and COEs, the key players before 1990s, lost their influences significantly. In contrast, FIEs became the most significant economic force, while local private firms caught up quickly. Interestingly, local firms had already performed better than FIEs from Hong Kong, Taiwan, and Macao by 2009.

While previous studies have emphasized the importance of indigenous innovation in nurturing local upgrading, the PRD case does not conform to this phenomenon. Drawing on the performance of the high-tech industries, this chapter identified that the influence of innovation was less significant. In contrast, the empirical survey of my study showed that local firms would like to adopt three alternative strategies related to different resources and opportunities rested at different scales.

This chapter so far has revealed the evolutionary tendency of strategic coupling. The unresolved issues are that: What type of coupling is the PRD evolving toward, and what are the subsequent impacts on industrial upgrading? My interpretation of three local strategies remains preliminary at this stage and insufficient to provide conclusive answers. Next three chapters will detail the evolutionary strategic coupling and subsequent upgrading in three different industries: electronics, apparel, and automotive. The electronics industry reflects the most important technological/capital-intensive industry of the contemporary global economy in terms of output value and production volume; the apparel industry represents the labor industry that accounts for a major share of employment for many developing countries; the automotive represents the sophisticated industry that requires capital, technological, and labor inputs.

References

Amsden, A. H. (1989). *Asia's next giant: South Korea and late industrialization*. New York: Oxford University Press.

Balassa, B. (1979). The changing pattern of comparative advantage in manufactured goods. *Review of Economic and Statistics, 61*(2), 259–266.

Beeson, M. (2004). The rise and fall (?) of the developmental state: The vicissitudes and implications of East Asian interventionism. In L. Low (Block), *Developmental states: Relevancy, redundancy or reconfiguration?* (pp. 29–40). New York: Nova Science Publishers.

Cartier, C. (2001). *Globalizing South China*. Oxford: Blackwell.

Chen, G. H., & Li, S. (2006). Evolving trends in the development of manufacturing industry in the PRD. In A. G.-A. Yeh, V. F.-S. Sit, G. Chen, & Y. Zhou (Eds.), *Developing a competitive Pearl River Delta in South China under one country-two systems* (pp. 27–45). Hong Kong: Hong Kong University Press.

Chen, J. & Pu, X. (Eds.). (1999). *'The fifty years of Guangdong'—Official statistics report of Guangdong Provincial Government (in Chinese)*. Beijing: China Statistics Press.

Chen, J., & Wang, Q. (2010). The reform, opening, and development of China's industrial economy. In F. Cai (Block), *Transforming the Chinese economy* (pp. 39–84). Leiden: Brill.

Cheung, K.-Y., & Lin, P. (2004). Spillover effects of FDI on innovation in China: Evidence from the provincial data. *China Economic Review, 15*(1), 25–44.

Chui, S. W.-K., Ho, K.-C., & Lui, T.-L. (1997). *City-states in the global economy: Industrial restructuring in Hong Kong and Singapore*. Boulder: Westview Press.

Cui, G. H. (1999). Bottom-up mechanism of urbanization in China (in Chinese). *Journal of Geography, 54*(2), 17–34.

DRCGP. (2009). *Research on the development of high-tech industries in Guangdong Province in a new era*. Guangzhou: Development and Reform Commission of Guangdong Province and Sun Yet-Sen University.

Enright, M. J., Chang, K. M., Scott, E. E., & Zhu, W. (2003). *Hong Kong and the Pearl River Delta: The economic interaction*. Hong Kong: The 2022 Foundation.

Enright, M. J., Scott, E. E., & Chang, K. M. (2005). *Regional powerhouse: The greater Pearl River Delta and the rise of China*. Singpore: Wiley.

Ernst, D. (2007). Beyond the 'Global Factory' model: Innovative capabilities for upgrading China's IT industry. *International Journal of Technology and Globalisation, 3*(4), 437–459.

Fan, P. (2006). Catching up through developing innovation capability: Evidence from China's telecom-equipment industry. *Technovation, 26*(3), 359–368. https://doi.org/10.1016/j.technovation.2004.10.004.

Fan, P. (2007). China's technology catching up: An introduction. *International Journal of Technology and Globalisation, 3*(4), 337–340.

Fan, P. (2011). Innovation, globalization, and catch-up of latecomers: Cases of Chinese telecom firms. *Environment and Planning A, 43*(4), 830–849.

Fang, Y.-H., & Luo, J.-S. (1999). Comparison between the expor-processing (San Lai Yi Bu) enterprises and foreign invested enterprises in Guangdong (in Chinese). *International Economics and Trade Research, 2,* 49–54.

Gadiesh, O., Leung, P., & Vestring, T. (2007). The battle for China's good-enough market. *Harvard Business Review, 85*(1), 81–89.

Gan, Z.-X., & Gan, L.-P. (1994). Background and prospects of the "San Lai Yi Bu" enterprises in coastal areas (in Chinese). *Economic Crisscross, 5*(1), 28–31.

GDSY. (2001). *Guangdong statistic yearbook (in Chinese)*. Beijing: Guangdong Provincial Bureau of Statistics.

GDSY. (2010). *Guangdong statistic yearbook (in Chinese)*. Beijing: Guangdong Provincial Bureau of Statistics.

Gu, Q.-L., & Yang, Y.-X. (1999). *The development of the China apparel industry*. Beijing: China Textile University and Harvard Center of Textile and Apparel Research.

Hobday, M. (1995). East-Asian latecomer firms—Learning the technology of electronics. *World Development, 23*(1), 1171–1193.

Hsing, Y.-T. (1996). Blood, thicker than water: Interpersonal relations and Taiwanese investment in Southern China. *Environment and Planning A, 28*(12), 2241–2261.

Huang, Y. (2002). Selling China: Foreign direct investment during the reform era. In *Cambridge modern China series*. Cambridge University Press.

Huang, Y. (2008). *Capitalism with Chinese characteristics: Entrepreneurship and the state*. New York: Cambridge University Press.

Huang, Y., & Chen, S. (2009). *Crisis of industrialization in the Pearl River Delta* (EAI Background Brief No. 444). Singapore: East Asia Institute.

Huchet, J.-F. (1997). The China circle and technological development in the Chinese electronics industry. In B. Naughton (Block), *The China circle: Economics and electronics in the PRC, Taiwan, and Hong Kong* (pp. 254–289). Washington, DC: Brookings Institution Press.

Jao, Y. (2001). *The Asian financial crisis and the ordeal of Hong Kong*. Westport: Greenwood.

Kamel, R., & Hoffman, A. (Eds.). (1999). *The maquiladora reader: Cross-border organizing since NAFTA*. American Friends Service Committee.

Lall, S., & Urata, S. (Eds.). (2003). *Competitiveness, FDI and technological activity in East Asia*. Cheltenham: Edward Elgar.

Lazonick, W. (2004). Indigenous innovation and economic development: Lessons from China's leap into the information age. *Industry and Innovation, 11*(4), 273–297.

Leung, C. K. (1993). Personal contacts, subcontracting linkages and development in the Hong Kong-Zhujiang Delta region. *Annals of the Association of American Geographers, 83*(2), 272–302.

Li, L.-X. (1997). Characteristics of township and village enterprises in Pearl River Delta (in Chinese). *Tropical Geography, 17*(3), 16–21.

Li, X. (2002). Urban competition and cooperation among cities in Pearl River Delta (in Chinese). *Guangdong Social Science, 4*(2), 24–29.

Li, X. (2009). China's regional innovation capacity in transition: An empirical approach. *Research Policy, 38*(2), 338–357.

Li, L., Dunford, M., & Yeung, G. (2012). International trade and industrial dynamics: Geographical and structural dimensions of Chinese and Sino-EU merchandise trade. *Applied Geography, 32*(1), 130–142.

Liao, H., & Chan, R. (2009). Industrial relocation of Hong Kong manufacturing firms: Towards an expanding industrial space beyond the Pearl River Delta. *GeoJournal,* 1–17. https://doi.org/10.1007/s10708-009-9316-3.

Lin, G. C. S. (1997). *The red capitalism in South China: Growth and development of the Pearl River Delta.* Vancouver: UBC Press.

Lin, G. C. S. (2009a). *Developing China: Land, politics, and social conditions.* London: Routledge.

Lin, G. C. S. (2009b). Scaling-up regional development in globalizing China: Local capital accumulation, land-centred politics, and reproduction of space. *Regional Studies, 43*(3), 429–447.

Lin, X.-Y., & Chen, Z.-N. (2003). Pattern of integration and strategies in metropolitan area in Pearl River Delta (in Chinese). *Economic Frontier, 2*(3), 32–34.

Lin, G. C. S., & Wang, C. (2009). Technological innovation in China's high-tech sector: Insights from a 2008 survey of the integrated circuit design industry in Shanghai. *Eurasian Geography and Economics, 50*(4), 402–424.

Lu, D. (2001). Three development stages and main achievements of the reform in Guangdong Province (in Chinese). *Special Zone Economy, 7*(1), 7–10.

Ma, L. J. C. (2009). China's authoritarian capitalism: Growth, elitism and legitimacy. *International Development and Planning Review, 31*(1), 1–12.

Marco, B., & Marco, R. D. T. (2005). The case of specialized towns in Guangdong, China. *European Planning Studies, 13*(5), 707–729.

Ng, M. K., & Tang, W. S. (2004). The role of planning in the development of Shenzhen, China: Rhetoric and realities. *Eurasian Geography and Economics, 45*(3), 190–211.

Olds, K., & Yeung, H. W. C. (1999). (Re)shaping 'Chinese' business networks in a globalising era. *Environment and Planning D-Society & Space, 17*(5), 535–555.

Qiu, Y. (2005). Personal networks, institutional involvement, and foreign direct investment flows into China's interior. *Economic Geography, 81*(3), 261–281.

Shen, J. F. (2003). Cross-border connection between Hong Kong and mainland China under 'two systems' before and beyond 1997. *Geografiska Annaler: Series B, Human Geography, 85*(1), 1–17.

Sit, V. F. S. (1998). Hong Kong's "transferred" industrialization and industrial geography. *Asian Survey, 38*(1), 880–904.

Sit, V. F. S. (2001). Economic integration of Guangdong Province and Hong Kong: Implications for China's opening and its accession to the WTO. *Regional Development Studies, 7,* 129–142.

Sit, V. F.-S., & Yang, C. (1997). Foreign-investment-induced exo-urbanisation in the Pearl River Delta, China. *Urban Studies, 34*(4), 647–677.

Smart, A., & Lin, G. C. S. (2007). Local capitalisms, local citizenship and translocality: Rescaling from below in the Pearl River Delta region, China. *International Journal of Urban and Regional Research, 31*(2), 280–302. https://doi.org/10.1111/j.1468-2427.2007.00732.x.

Song, L.-J., Mu, F.-G., & Li, G.-L. (1989). Problems and suggestions to the export-processing (San Lai Yi Bu) enterprises (in Chinese). *China Reform, 3,* 23–24.

Steinfeld, E. S. (1998). *Forging reform in China: The fate of state-owned industry.* Cambridge: Cambridge University Press.

Steinfeld, E. S. (2004). China's shallow integration: Networked production and the new challenges for late industrialization. *World Development, 32*(11), 1971–1987. https://doi.org/10.1016/j.worlddev.2004.04.003.

Steinfeld, E. S. (2010). *Playing our game: Why China's rise doesn't threaten the West*. New York: Oxford University Press.

Sun, P. (2007). Is the state-led industrial restructuring effective in transition China? Evidence from the steel sector. *Cambridge Journal of Economics, 31*(3), 601–624.

Tang, W.-J., & Tian, B. (2002). Comparison of institutional evolution between Pearl River Delta and Yangzi River Delta (in Chinese). *Urban Economy and Special Zone Economy, 8*(2), 55–58.

Tewari, M. (2006). Is price and cost competitiveness enough for apparel firms to gain market share in the world after quotas? *Global Economy Journal, 6*(4), 1–46.

Tuan, C., & Ng, L. F. Y. (2004). FDI and industrial restructuring in post-WTO greater PRD: Implications on regional growth in China. *World Economy, 27*(10), 1609–1630.

Viotti, E. B. (2003). National Learning Systems: A new approach on technological change in late industrializing economies and evidences from the cases of Brazil and South Korea. *Technological Forecasting and Social Change, 69*(1), 653–680.

Wang, X.-T. (2011). Status of state owned enterprise reform and the tendency. *Modern Business Trade Industry, 17,* 1–2.

Wang, X., & Meng, L. (2001). A reevaluation of China's economic growth. *China Economic Review, 12*(4), 338–346.

Wang, Y., & Yao, Y. (2003). Sources of China's economic growth 1952–1999: Incorporating human capital accumulation. *China Economic Review, 14*(1), 32–52.

Wei, Y. H. D., Li, W., & Wang, C. (2007). Restructuring industrial districts, scaling up regional development: A study of the Wenzhou model, China. *Economic Geography, 83*(4), 421–444.

Wei, Y. H. D., Lu, Y. Q., & Chen, W. (2009). Globalizing regional development in Sunan, China: Does Suzhou Industrial Park fit a neo-Marshallian district model? *Regional Studies, 43*(3), 409–427.

White, G. (Block). (1988). *Developmental states in East Asia*. New York: St. Martin's Press.

Wong, S.-W., & Tang, B.-S. (2005). Challenges to the sustainability of 'development zones': A case study of Guangzhou Development District, China. *Cities, 22*(4), 303–316.

Wu, J.-L. (2005). *Understanding and interpreting Chinese economic reform*. Singapore: Thomson/South-Western.

Xu, X. Q. (1988). Accelaration of urbanization in the Pearl River Delta through the opening reform (in Chinese). *Journal of Geography, 43*(3), 201–210.

Xu, B., & Lu, J. (2009). Foreign direct investment, processing trade, and the sophistication of China's exports. *China Economic Review, 20*(3), 425–439.

Yang, C. (2005). Multilevel governance in the cross-boundary region of Hong Kong–Pearl River Delta, China. *Environment and Planning A, 37*(12), 2147–2168. https://doi.org/10.1068/a37230.

Yang, C. (2009). Strategic coupling of regional development in global production networks: Redistribution of Taiwanese personal computer investment from the Pearl River Delta to the Yangtze River Delta, China. *Regional Studies, 43*(3), 385–407.

Yang, C. (2012). Restructuring the export-oriented industrialization in the Pearl River Delta, China: Institutional evolution and emerging tension. *Applied Geogrpahy, 32,* 143–157.

Yang, C., & Liao, H. (2009). Backward linkages of cross-border production networks of Taiwanese PC investment in the Pearl River Delta, China. *Tijdschrift Voor Economische En Sociale Geografie, 101*(2), 199–217.

Yang, C., & Sit, V. F. S. (1995). Integration of socialist market economy with the world market: Foreign investment in the Pearl River Delta, China. *Asia Profile, 23*(1), 1–16.

Yeh, A. G. O., & Xu, J. (2006). Turning of the dragon head: Changing role of Hong Kong in the regional development of the Pearl River Delta. In A. G.-O. Yeh, V. F. S. Sit, G. Chen, & Y. Zhou (Eds.), *Developing a competitive Pearl River Delta: In South China under one country-two system*. Hong Kong: Hong Kong University Press.

Yeh, A. G. A., Sit, V. F. S., Chen, G., & Zhou, Y. (Eds.). (2006). *Developing a competitive Pearl River Delta in South China under one country-two systems*. Hong Kong: Hong Kong University Press.

Yeung, H. W.-C. (1997). Critical realism and realist research in human geography: A method or a philosophy in search of a method? *Progress in Human Geography, 21*(1), 51–74.

Yeung, G. (2001). *Foreign investment and socio-economic development in China: The case of Dongguan*. Basingstoke: Palgrave.

Yeung, G. (2002). WTO accession, the changing competitiveness of foreign-financed firms and regional development in Guangdong of Southern China. *Regional Studies, 36*(1), 627–642.

Young, S., & Lan, P. (1997). Technology transfer to China through foreign direct investment. *Regional Studies, 31*(1), 669–679.

Yu, Y.-F. (2008). *Road to the fashion: Transformation of apparel industrial cluster in Humen (in Chinese) (Development of Guangdong industrial specialized towns)*. Guangzhou: Guangdong People Press.

Yu, H., & Zhang, Y. (2009). *New initiatives for industrial upgrading in the Pearl River Delta* (EAI Background Brief) (p. 16).

Zheng, J. H., Bigsten, A., & Hu, A. G. (2009). Can China's growth be sustained? A productivity perspective. *World Development, 37*(4), 874–888. https://doi.org/10.1016/j.worlddev.2008.07.008.

Zhou, Y. (2008). *The inside story of China's high-tech industry: Making Silicon Valley in Beijing*. Lanham, MD: Rowman & Littlefield Publishers.

Zhou, Y., & Tong, X. (2003). An innovative region in China: Interaction between multinational corporations and local firms in a high-tech cluster in Beijing. *Economic Geography, 79*(2), 129–152.

Zhou, Y., & Wei, Y. H. D. (2011). Globalization, innovation, and regional development in China. *Environment and Planning A, 43*(4), 781–785.

Chapter 5
Captive Coupling in the Electronics Industry: Relocation, Localization, and Local Upgrading

5.1 Situating Latecomer Upgrading in the Electronics Industry

The electronics industry is one of the most important sectors in the world because it employs more workers, generates greater revenue, and stimulates innovation across entire economies than any other sector (Mann and Kirkegaard 2006). In the PRD, the electronics industry is the most influential industry in terms of output and export value throughout three decades of development (see Chaps. 1 and 5). This chapter provides an examination of local upgrading in the PRD's electronics industry.

Contemporary studies have articulated the difficulty of latecomer upgrading in the electronics industry due to the strong intensity of technology and capital. In order to overcome this difficulty, the GVC literature suggests latecomer firms to insert into value chains and become the quick followers of global lead firms, so that latecomer firms can catch up through learning by doing technology sharing and organizational acquisition from global buyers to their suppliers (Schmitz 2004; Sturgeon and Lester 2004; Gereffi et al. 2005). However, these scholars also admit that upgrading opportunities are limited and restricted by industrial gate keepers based on the regular pattern of *modular* governance in this industry.

From a different perspective, scholars suggest that developmental state institutions can directly promote upgrading in the domestic electronics industry by heavily investing in indigenous innovation (White 1988; Douglass 1994; Johnson 1995; Beeson 2004). More recent studies of the electronics firms in China similarly argue that strategies like FDI promotion or export-oriented industrialization are not sufficient in fostering industrial upgrading, but have to be accompanied by intensive investments in local innovation in order to improve indigenous capabilities (Fan 2011; Zhou and Wei 2011). If we follow the logic of the above studies, local upgrading in the electronics industry in the PRD is bounded to be doomed, since the PRD almost lacks any of the assets listed above. Would local upgrading in the PRD be a less satisfactory story? This chapter conducts a critical investigation to answer this question.

© Springer Nature Singapore Pte Ltd. 2020
Y. Liu, *Local Dynamics of Industrial Upgrading*, Economic Geography,
https://doi.org/10.1007/978-981-15-4297-8_5

As elaborated in Chap. 4, the PRD's economic takeoff was initially led by the pattern of captive coupling. Local firms were positioned in a marginalized node within global GPNs and concentrated in the processing and assembly segments of value chains. However, recent dynamics has called for a re-examination of the pattern of coupling and the correspondent outcomes of upgrading in the electronics industry. At the local scale, the further localization of global lead firms has substantially strengthened the manufacturing capabilities of the PRD that leads to the amazing growth of such companies as Foxconn (see the opening story in Chap. 1). This localization would reduce knowledge gaps between local firms and TNCs because it provides more learning opportunities for local firms. At the national/regional scale, there are emerging new assets such as regional supply networks and domestic markets that may increase the bargaining power of local firms (see Sect. 4.4 in Chap. 4). At the global scale, increasing competition among global lead firms, platform developers, and contract manufactures has provided more opportunities for local firms to catch up (Sturgeon and Kawakami 2011). But these changing institutional–spatial conditions do not guarantee the success of local upgrading. There are still many tough obstacles for local firms to overcome, such as the prevalence of modular governance and rapid change in technologies. In this sense, learning by doing or reverse engineering would be difficult, because the limited absorptive capabilities of local firms will make their efforts seriously lagging behind the rapid speed of innovation in global lead firms (Steinfeld 2010). But what if local firms are not merely reliant on reverse engineering or learning by doing? What if global lead firms would like to cooperate with local firms for various interests beyond seeking low-cost suppliers?

Situated in such an industrial context, this chapter focuses on three issues: (1) the formation of captive coupling in the electronics industry and whether it has evolved since the 1990s; (2) the current achievements and limitations of industrial upgrading in the region; and (3) upgrading strategies adopted by local firms. The overall attempt of this chapter is to explain the ongoing dynamics of local upgrading in the PRD's electronics industry, rather than to take it for granted as another repeated story of latecomer development which gets stuck in labor-intensive activities.

This chapter starts by interpreting the key features of the global electronics industry and the potential power dynamics in its modular governance. By grounding the electronics industry in the PRD's context, the third section elaborates on why and how the pattern of captive coupling is developed and persistent over the decades and the current outcomes of upgrading. While the limitations of local upgrading are revealed, the fourth section provides a critical account of alternative upgrading strategies. Drawing on case studies, this penultimate section articulates three potential pathways of local upgrading. This chapter finally discusses how the PRD's electronics industry offers a different story beyond previous studies and sheds light on a geographical interpretation of value-chain governance.

5.2   Governance and Power Dynamics in the Global Electronics Industry

In this book, the electronics industry refers to a broad range of industries including semiconductor, information and communication technology (ICT), electronic machinery and equipment, and electronic products (e.g., home appliance, cell phone, liquid crystal display, and computer). This section probes into global industrial trends and power relations in the modular pattern of its value-chain governance. The discussion serves as a critical industrial context for understanding the development of the electronics industry of the PRD.

5.2.1   Global Industrial Shifts and Modular Governance

The global shift of the electronics industry generally departs from the global North to the global South in the past decades (Dicken 2007). From the 1960s to the 1980s, North American firms in the computer industry heavily outsourced low-value-added manufacturing segments to Mexico and East Asia that in turn enabled US firms to upgrade into more design-intensive activities in both electronic devices and platforms, such as the 'horizontal computer industry' in the Silicon Valley (Grove 1996) and the 'Wintelism' (Borrus and Zysman 1997). By taking this opportunity, contract manufacturers in East Asian newly industrialized economies built up regional production networks in more complex 'triangle manufacturing' arrangements that brought factories in Japan, South Korea, Singapore, Taiwan, and Hong Kong into an integrated production system (Gereffi 1999; Lüthje 2002). During this process, global lead firms served as industrial gate keepers based on their strong technological capacities and governance power. Their higher-tier suppliers, such as strategic partners in East Asia, also developed certain strong bargaining power due to their capabilities in systematic integration and supply chain management. The lower-tier suppliers and subcontractors had less power due to their substitutable nature.

Due to different firm strategies, national contexts and the competitive dynamics of cost, flexibility, and speed within GPNs, East Asian firms have gradually specialized in certain segments or products and formed an inter-regional division of labor to a certain degree (Lüthje 2004; Yusuf et al. 2004; Yeung 2009). Without radical product shift, Japanese producers mainly stay in consumer electronics and tend to specialize in developing new generations of dynamic random-access memory (DRAM), electronic machinery, and equipment (e.g., Toshiba). Meanwhile, many of them have upgraded into global lead firms in consumer electronics (e.g., camera, multimedia players, and home appliances). South Korean firms follow the pathway of Japan, but invest heavily in semiconductor, liquid crystal display, and mobile device technologies. Some of them also grow up and become global lead firms (e.g., Samsung and LG). In contrast, Taiwanese CMs specialize in the entire production chain of the semiconductor and personal computer by providing electronics manufacturing services (EMS), such as

TSMC, Foxconn, and Quanta. Singapore firms tend to develop strong expertise in process engineering and wafer fabrication, such as chartered semiconductor. Together with Hong Kong, the PRD joins in East Asian production networks but is situated in a marginal position for processing and assembling less sophisticated products (e.g., non-core electronics components, casings, or plastic parts). Components with sophisticated technologies or higher value added are produced and distributed by global lead firms and CMs outside the PRD (Lüthje 2002; Yeh et al. 2002; Yang 2007). Apparently, the PRD has limited space of industrial upgrading in such a position. The region is isolated from core knowledge in terms of production technologies, systematic integration skills, as well as marketing and distribution skills.

5.2.2   The Fragility of Governance Power

The electronics industry has become highly globalized production networks based on the prevalence of modularization and standardization which integrates a customer's need for direct monitoring and control (Sturgeon 2002; Principe and Honday 2003). This industrial specificity enhances interoperability in the sense that components and systematic elements can be substituted without redesigning the entire products (Ulrich 1995; Balconi 2002; Langlois 2003). Hence, electronics lead firms are able to engage in the twin strategies of outsourcing and offshoring over a long distance without losing their governance power in dealing with their suppliers. Meanwhile, by isolating sophisticated technologies within modularized components, they can reinforce their core competences and enforce parameter setting along with their value chains (Humphrey and Schmitz 2004; Frigant and Layan 2009). That is the alleged power of modular governance in favor of lead firms. Upgrading opportunities are offered by global lead firms to their local suppliers through parameter setting and product definition in value chains (Sturgeon 2002; Gereffi et al. 2005). The imperative of doing so is to reduce asset specificity and to take advantage of specialization.

Under modular governance, local firms in the PRD's electronic industry indeed receive some learning opportunities by serving as suppliers. But the barrier of upgrading is evident, because knowledge diffusion is defined and modularized by global lead firms. These types of knowledge are more related to the skills of know-how (e.g., processing technologies), while still have a way to reach the knowledge of know-why. When technology sharing goes beyond lead firms' interests, local suppliers would not receive any assistance from lead firms (Humphrey and Schmitz 2002; Schmitz 2004; Gereffi et al. 2005; Sturgeon and Kawakami 2011). Therefore, local firms tend to be kept at the most labor-intensive and lower-value-added segments of value chains, unless they receive substantial state supports, invest heavily in innovation, or manage to launch joint actions with other local firms (Humphrey and Schmitz 2002; Giuliani et al. 2005; Lowe 2009; Fan 2011; Zhou and Wei 2011). However, the dynamics of local upgrading does not always follow this rigid logic. As articulated in Chap. 3, there are three institutional–spatial conditions that may help latecomer firms to leverage the governance power of electronics lead firms: diversity of knowledge channels, regional assets, and competitive dynamics within GPNs. Particularly in the electronic industry, the complex and dynamic power relations within GPNs provide more opportunities for local firms to leapfrog.

Different from the apparel industry, an electronics GPN is not just made up by a simple dichotomy of global buyers and local suppliers in a linear structure, but is made up by at least four groups of key actors: (1) global lead firms (branded name firms presenting in end markets); (2) platform developers/specialized product providers; (3) contract manufacturers (e.g., EMS providers); and (4) local suppliers (Lüthje 2002; Sturgeon and Lester 2004; Gereffi et al. 2005; Dicken 2007; Yeung 2009).

Global lead firms premise their bargaining power on financial risks taken during their ordering and selling products. They invest heavily in product development, marketing, and distribution which are the core of their competitiveness. Compared with lead firms, contract manufacturers are less powerful because they are substitutable. Thus, they struggle in product and process upgrading to capture a lion share of market in which they have strong manufacturing expertise. Meanwhile, they also increase power by collecting bundles of capabilities so as to provide one-stop shopping for lead firms seeking regional and global supply solutions (Sturgeon and Lester 2004). Suppliers, particularly lower-tier suppliers are the least powerful actors due to their highly substitutable nature and vulnerable capacities. However, the rise of platform developers complicates power relations within GPNs by providing turnkey/platform solutions of product manufacturing in the form of software, hardware, or combination, such as the Intel Atom chipset, Microsoft, and Google's Android operating system (Sturgeon 2002; Lüthje 2004; Fixson and Park 2008). Upgrading opportunities are thus diversified.

For contract manufacturers and suppliers, they can purchase and internalize turnkey technologies from platform developers within the same GPN, thus directly upgrading into own-brand manufacturers to compete with lead firms. Latecomer firms do not necessarily upgrade to challenge global lead firms. Instead, they can upgrade into a turnkey product supplier, or even a new platform developer, such as the formation of Global Mobility Bazaar (GMB) alliance of VIA from Taiwan (Galvin and Morkel 2001; Lüthje 2002, 2004; Feenstra and Hamilton 2006). In this case, lead firms have no power to block this upgrading. They can only control their upstream suppliers and downstream customers along the same chain, but cannot control platform developers or specialized service providers in the same GPNs.

In sum, there are many alternative upgrading pathways for latecomer firms. These strategies do not necessarily challenge the governance power of global lead firms. The critical issue is whether local firms are able to identify the necessary assets and develop more synergy with their foreign partners during the process of local upgrading. This is the analytical focus of the next two sections.

5.3   FIE-Led Upgrading in Captive Coupling: Synergy and Limitations

The PRD has embraced the global economy through market liberalization and export-oriented industrialization after 1978. Based on outsourcing and offshoring strategies, electronics TNCs and their subcontractors took advantage of this opportunity and operated in the PRD in various forms of FIEs. This was the fundamental synergy that led to coupling between the PRD and the electronics GPNs. This section investigates the institutional contexts and synergy within captive coupling and how captive coupling leads to the progress and limitation of industrial upgrading.

5.3.1   Institutional Contexts of the Electronics Industry

Experience from the East Asian electronics industries has shown the important role of developmental states in nurturing domestic upgrading through investing in indigenous innovation and facilitating technological transfer (Wade 1990; Hobday 1995; Cho et al. 1998; Hobday 2001; Liu and Dicken 2006). But the PRD did not have this type of developmental state. All state support was allocated to other regions in East and North China (CCW 2004; Cao 2007).

Before the opening reform in 1978, China's electronics industries developed through import substitution (Liang 1999). However, this strategy eventually widened technological gaps between domestic firms and TNCs (Cao 2007). From 1982 to 2000, the national strategy for the electronics industry was shifted into export-oriented modernization (CW 2001). Many cooperative partnerships between SOEs and global lead firms were established in the forms of joint ventures, technological licensing, strategic alliances, or cooperative investment (Wang 1996; Liang 1999). This strategy significantly accelerated the development of China's semiconductor industry. However, none of the key SOEs was located in the PRD; they were instead concentrated in the Yangzi River Delta and Bohai Rim region (see Table 5.1).

From 2000 onward, China reinforced export-orientation strategy by liberalizing further the domestic market. In 2000, China's State Council established a remarkable directive known as *Policies for Encouraging the Development of Software and Integrated Circuit Industries* (NDRCSC 2001; see detail in Table 5.2). By providing fiscal incentives, this directive was meant for stimulating more TNCs to relocate higher value-added segments and R&D activities to China. This directive might appear to work effectively. It facilitated knowledge spillover from TNCs (CCW 2004). By 2010, the total sale value in China's electronics industry soared to near $1 trillion, while the value of exports accounted for 60% of the country's total (PDO 2011). There has been increasing localization of foreign firms in China in the forms of new production lines and factories, local management centers and R&D bases, as well as IC design segment (Li 2008: also see Table 5.1, Ding et al. 2010; Fan 2011). However, during this process, Chinese SOEs and private firms lost domestic market

Table 5.1   Key semiconductor enterprises in China (Liang 1999; Wang 1996 and authors' survey)

Type of cooperation	SOEs	Partner	Years	Key technologies
Technology licensing	Huangjing (Shanghai)	Lucent	1987	6 in. silicon wafer with a minimal feature size of 0.9 m
		Toshiba	1995	Intel 386SX microprocessor
	Shanghai Beijing	Indigenous	1988	4 in. wafer with a minimal feature size between 2 and 3 μm
		ISSI	1995	6 in. silicon wafer with a minimal feature size of 0.8 m
	Shanghai semiconductor	Indigenous	1992	5 in. wafer with a minimal feature size of 2.3 m
		North Tel	1994	6 in. silicon wafer with a minimal feature size of 0.8 μm
	Huayue (Shanghai)	Fujitsu	1998	Bi-CMOS, 5 in. silicon wafer with a minimal feature size of 2 μm
Joint ventures	Shanghai steel	NEC	1994	DRAM and micro-programmed control unit (MCU), 0.5 μm
		NEC	1997	DRAM and MCU, 0.35 μm
	Stone (Shanghai)	Mitsubishi	1996	Microprocessor
	SMICS (Chengdu)	UTAC (Singapore)	2005	Wafer fabrication
State owned	SMICS (Shanghai)		2000	Silicon wafer with a minimal feature size of 0.35 μm–45 nm; microprocessor
State owned	SMICS (Wuhan)		2006	Silicon wafer with a minimal feature size of 0.35 μm–45 nm; microprocessor

(continued)

Table 5.1 (continued)

Type of cooperation	SOEs	Partner	Years	Key technologies
Foreign-owned enterprises	• In Bohai Rim Region: Motorola in Tianjin (1993) • In the Yangzi River Delta: Samsung in Suzhou (1996), AMD in Shanghai (1997), Philip in Suzhou (2002), Gracesemi in Shanghai (2003), TSMC in Shanghai (2003), Hynix in Wuxi (2006), and so on • In West China: Intel in Chengdu (2003) • In North China: Intel in Dalian (2007)			

Table 5.2 Policies of encouraging the development of the software and IC industries (NDRCSC 2001; NDRC 2011)

Aims	Key items of the state directive in 2001	Key renewed items of the state directive in 2011
Taxation discount	All enterprises with endogenous-developed software products are only imposed by 17% value-added tax, while the amount of actual burden tax over 3% will be refunded to the firm for R&D expenditure (abolished since 2005 due the arbitration from WTO)	Enterprise income tax will be waived in enterprises which are conducing software development, integration and testing, integrated circuit design and testing
Taxation waiver	Certificated new high-tech enterprises in software or IC industries enjoy a specific tax favor called 'two plus three': full waiver of tax for the first two year, and 50% discount in the next three years	From 'two plus three' to 'five plus five': free income tax for the first five years and 50% discount in the next five years. Enterprises conducing IC testing and assembly activities are also involved within the preferential policy networks
Industrial pillar group	Key enterprises involved in national industrial planning are only imposed by 10% of enterprise income tax	Besides the national planning, inter-provincial emerging of SOEs is also encouraged for cultivating stronger SOEs
Market liberalization	All in situ enterprises in software and IC industries enjoy these polices regardless the ownership types	Electronic service industry is encouraged

share seriously, from 69% in 1999 to 29% in 2009 (MIIT 2003, 2010). While the production volume of integrated circuits (ICs) was huge, about 60% of the output came from packing and testing segments (APCO 2009). These problems put the policy effect on domestic upgrading in question.

5.3.2   *Captive Coupling and Synergy*

Before the reform in 1978, the PRD was still largely an agricultural-based economy and the electronics industry did not exist except several local SOEs producing lamps and wires (Sung et al. 1995; Lin 1997). Due to the absence of state support, captive coupling was developed as knowledge gaps (technology and market) were too wide to be bridged (see Fig. 5.1). As elaborated in Chap. 4, there were generally four factors that fostered synergy within captive coupling in the electronics industry: the locational advantage of the PRD; the liberalizing institutional environment; pre-existing ethnic-based business networks, and available low-waged labor pool. The synergy gave rise to the boom of EPEs and FIEs.

The opening reform of China made the PRD the prime hinterland, better than Southeast Asian countries, for accommodating the relocation of Hong Kong's electronics industry (Sung 1991; Clark and Kim 1995; Huchet 1997). Thousands of establishments in this industry constituted a major share of foreign investment in the PRD during the 1980s and 1990s (Chui et al. 1997). Following Hong Kong firms, Taiwanese firms in the computer industry joined this process by the end of the 1980s (Xue 2009). Currently, all key Taiwanese EMS providers, including Foxconn, Quanta, Compal, Wistron, Inventec, ASUS, and VIA, have built their production plants in the PRD. Shenzhen and Dongguan have the largest agglomeration of Hong Kong and Taiwanese firms, while Zhuhai attracts many Japanese firms.

Regional and local authorities were proactive actors in the formation of captive coupling. They were keen in attracting electronics TNCs, because these firms brought significant growth in GDP, foreign trade, and employment. These achievements could

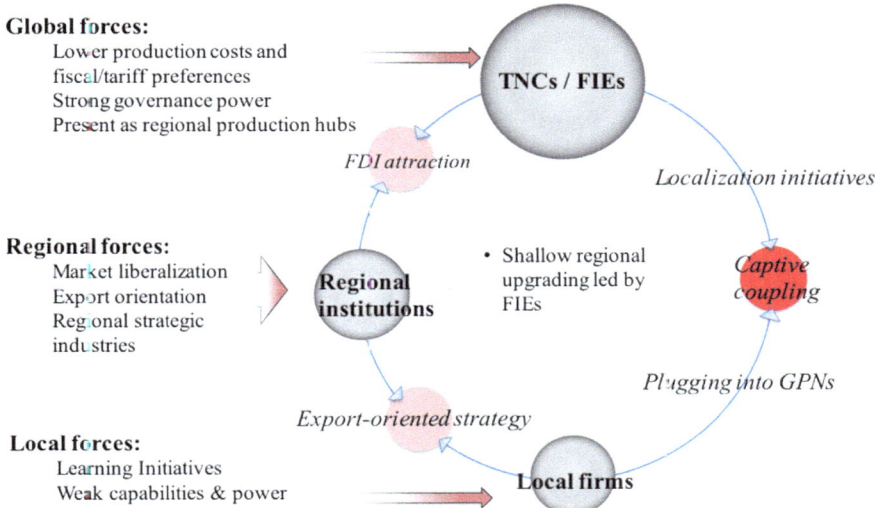

Fig. 5.1   Captive coupling in the electronics industry in the PRD (drawn by author)

prosper regional economy and benefit the political aspiration and promotion of local carders. Since the 1990s, all prefectural governments in nine PRD cities have targeted the electronics industry as their strategic industries with the top priority in investment promotion, preferential fiscal subsidies, and infrastructure construction (Xu 1988; Sit and Yang 1997; NDRC 2003).

5.3.3 Regional Upgrading Within Captive Coupling

Captive coupling led to substantial growth of the PRD's electronics industry. After three decades of development, it continues to play a dominant role in the regional economy (see Fig. 1.3). In 2009, it contributed to about US$ 25 billion in export value. This amount was about 25% of China's total, about 4% of the world total (GDSYST 2010). During this process, various types of upgrading were achieved.

In terms of product and process upgrading, the electronic firms and labor are more capable of producing higher value-added products in a more efficient manner. Table 5.3 shows this noticeable progress. In the past two decades, the number of firms and IVA received constant and substantial growth. Meanwhile, the production capabilities of firms and labor were both improved significantly. In 2009, the IVA per enterprise grew by nine times against 1991; and IVA per labor increased by four times during the same period. Compared with them, the number of employee per enterprise presented a different trend that grew relatively slow from 1991 to 2005 and then fell down a little bit after 2005. It means that electronics firms are less reliant on the intensive usage of labor, while achieving substantial improvement in efficiency.

Table 5.3 Upgrading in the electronics industry in the PRD (1991–2009) (Guangdong Statistic Yearbook 1992, 1996, 2000, 2006, 2010)

Year	No. firms	IVA	IVA-E	IVA-L	NEE
	Unit	Billion	Million	Thousand	Person
1991	969	6.8	7.0	24.5	287
2001	1315	63.3	48.1	86.0	560
2005	2790	191.4	68.6	101.9	673
2010	4455	408.9	91.8	132.4	693
2015	4515	623.6	138.1	195.5	707

Notes Currency is Chinese *yuan* at constant 2000 price. The electronics industry in the PRD's statistic data includes electrical equipment and products, ICT and computer-related products and electronic equipment and products. All data refer to enterprises above designated size that an annual turnover more than 5 million *yuan*
IVA industrial value-added; *IVA-E* industrial value-added per enterprise; *IVA-C* industrial value-added per capita; *NEE* number of employee per enterprises

During the upgrading of processing efficiency, the product ranges of the electronics industry have been upgraded. The PRD is no longer processing low-value-added and less sophisticated products (e.g., home telephones, cable, wires and non-core components), but is supplying the world with many high value-added and sophisticated electronics products, such as liquid crystal display products, multimedia players, computers, mobile phones, telecommunication equipment, medical/mechanical electronic devices, and all kinds of electronics components (Chen and Pu 1999; GDSY 2000; GDSYST 2010). In short, there has been a great deal of product and process upgrading in the forms described in the literature on latecomer upgrading (Humphrey and Schmitz 2002, 2004). Consistent with that literature, this study finds that foreign firms have played a very positive role in providing learning opportunities and assistance to their suppliers on the basis of arm-length market relations or subcontracting partnerships. Local firms have benefited from being captive to them. The trajectory of local upgrading is seen in a general manager of Lingyang Electronics in Shunde, as below:

> In the 1980s, Lingyang was just an EPE processing plastic casings and assembled thermoses for Hong Kong clients. After a decade, the clients became our partners. They suggested and trained us to make coffee machines and toasters for global customers. By then we upgraded into a full-package manufacturer. With the help of our Hong Kong partners, we focused on supplying a few global branded buyers. In order to be certificated as their OEM supplier, we worked closely with the Hong Kong partners and technical consultants from our buyers to improve substantially the designs and functions of our products, as well as our workspace and supply-chain management. Now we are not only a qualified OEM supplier, but also conducting OBM business in Middle East and Southeast Asian markets under an appropriate brand. This is functional upgrading in your words. (Interview 100415, on 15th April 2010 in Shunde)

During the 1980s, the electronics industry in the PRD was just a processing and assembly base largely composed by thousands of EPEs (Song et al. 1989; Gan and Gan 1994; Sung et al. 1995). Currently, the PRD has been gradually upgraded into a global manufacturing center comprising about 30 specialized industrial towns and clusters (see Fig. 5.2). Each town or cluster has more or less specialized in certain products or segments. A total of 23 of them are certificated as national industrial-specialized towns (NDRC 2008; DRCGP 2009; GDSYST 2010).[1] Leliu Town is one of the largest towns specialized in home appliances. Its industrial output exceeded 100 billion *yuan* in 2009. With about 40 billion *yuan* of industrial output in 2009, Shijie Town has been famous for manufacturing computer components in global markets. The total industrial output of these towns is unknown. Upon various news and statistical reports, this study has estimated that most of these towns had an output over 20 billion *yuan* by 2010.

Underpinned by the proliferation of industrial clusters, towns and parks, regional upgrading is achieved and it leads to an intra-regional division of labor. Shenzhen city has grown into a global center of the ICT and EMS industries comprising many highly competitive companies, such as Foxconn, Nokia, Philips, Huawei, and ZTE.

---

[1]Two criteria for the certification: (1) with an annual industrial output over 300 million *yuan*; (2) more than 70% of the output comes from the electronics industry.

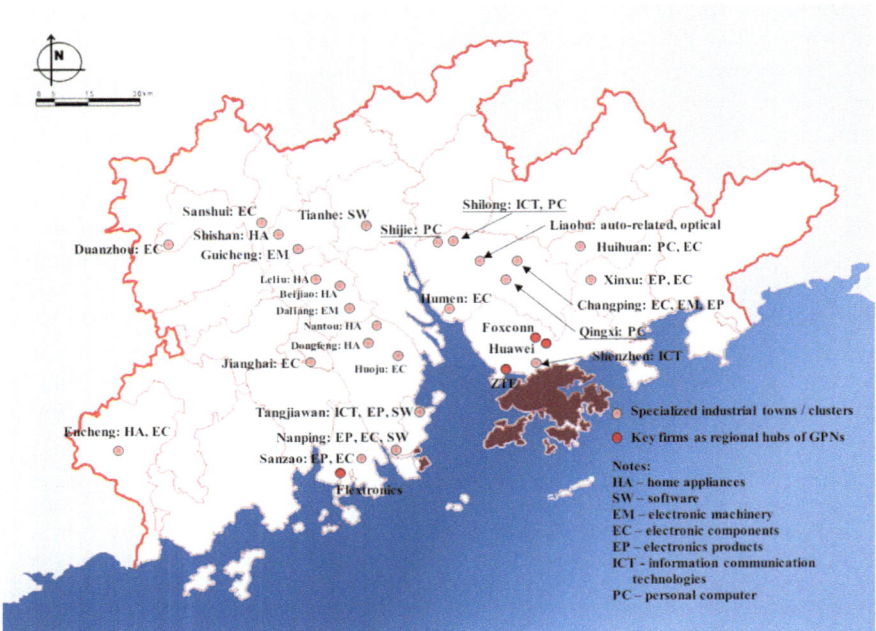

Fig. 5.2 Specialized industrial clusters and towns in the PRD's electronics industry [compiled by author based on the field work and the NDRC (2003, 2008)]

Dongguan and Huizhou accommodate a large number of Taiwanese CMs and currently contribute to 30–40% of the total output in the global personal computer industry (GDDRC 2009). Zhuhai has specialized in consumer electronics and IC products based on Japanese firms (e.g., Hitachi, Cannon, and SHIRAI). As the provincial capital with many universities and research institutes, Guangzhou has developed specialty in the software industry with about 1500 firms creating $1 billion of output value by 2009 (IARE 2010). The Northwest part of the PRD, including Foshan, Zhongshan, Jiangmen, and Zhaoqing, has matured as the largest manufacturing center of the home appliance industry in China, occupying about 60–70% of the domestic market value by 2008 (Lin 2009; Zhang and Xu 2010). Some of them have become international branded firms (e.g., Midea, Kelon, and Galanz). A comment from the vice chairman of the Electronics Industrial Association of Dongguan (EIAD) illustrates well this regional upgrading of the PRD:

> Dongguan has been well known for making easy-and-quick money for decades. But nowadays, we [the electronics industry] are no longer dependent on those low-end crabs [EPEs]. We are competing in the global market with qualified products based on multi-national FIEs and promising local firms located in specialized towns. In our survey during the economic crisis last year, we found out that labor wages in other developing countries such as Vietnam and Philippine were lower than here. But FIEs did not move away in a hurry because they cannot find a better supply base than here. Thirty years ago, you might make money by

importing components and then assembling here. But now, it is unaffordable to do so. It costs too much than local sourcing. (Interview 100807, on 17th Aug 2010 in Dongguan)

5.3.4 Persistence of Captive Coupling

Although regional upgrading is progressing in the PRD, the pattern of captive coupling is persistent. On the one hand, the region is still captive to the global industry for importing key electronics components. On the other hand, local firms are still captive to FIEs as their lower-tier suppliers. Fundamentally, the functional upgrading of the region is contributed by FIEs, rather than local firms.

According to the RCA index, the PRD's electronics industry has been improving its competitiveness in the global industry (see Table 5.4). Between 2000 and 2009, the index of general electrical and electronics products increased from 0.05 to 0.16. The index of high- and new-tech products also increased from −0.04 to 0.1. Computer and communication products (e.g., computer parts, cell phones, or network facilities) became the most competitive products in the PRD as their RCA index has grown from 0.37 to 0.59. However, trends from another two indexes show that the PRD is still heavily dependent on importing sophisticated components. Though having a noticeable drop, the index of products about computer-integrated technology was still at −0.48 in 2009. The index of electronic technology remained steady at about −0.7. The combination of these indexes implies that the PRD has become more able to manufacture and assemble electronic products within the region, but it still relies heavily on importing some sophisticated components and machinery.

Figure 5.3 generally shows that FIEs still considerably dominate the industry in the latest decade. The gap between FIEs and local firms was even enlarged. In terms of industrial value added, the share of FIEs increased from 60% in 1999 to 65% in 2008. During the same period, private firms had made great progress by increasing the share from 10 to 26%, but the share of SOEs dropped from 25 to 9%. In terms of export value, FIEs accounted for 75–80% of total exports. Private firms' share of

Table 5.4 RCA index of the electronics industry in the PRD (Guangdong Statistic Yearbook in multiple years, data before 2000 are unavailable)

Product types	2000	2003	2006	2009
General electrical and electronic products	0.05	−0.03	0.06	0.16
High- and new-tech electronic products	−0.04	0.03	0.08	0.10
Computer and communication	0.37	0.47	0.54	0.59
Electronic technology	−0.68	−0.77	−0.70	−0.67
Computer-integrated manufacturing	−0.83	−0.79	−0.73	−0.48

Notes Data are at the provincial level. But in the electronics industry, the proportion of the PRD accounted for more than 95% of total foreign trade value in the whole province. It is thus considered as representative

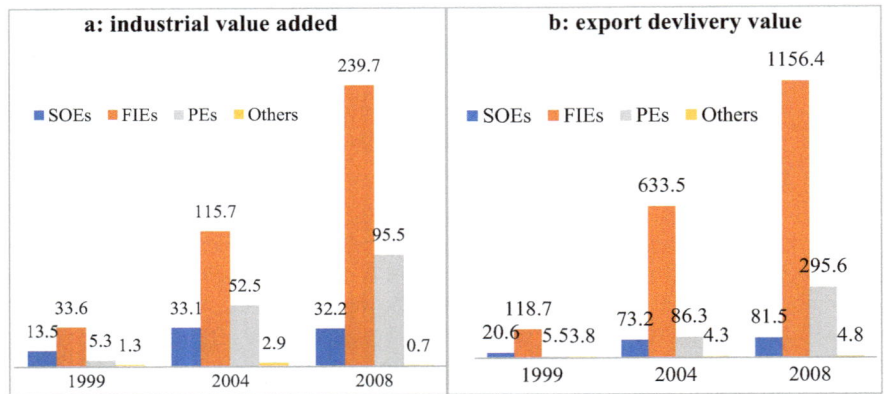

Fig. 5.3 Changing driving forces of the PRD's electronics industry. *Notes* SOEs state-owned enterprises; FIEs foreign-invested enterprises; PEs private enterprises; others collective-owned enterprises and enterprises with annual turnover lower than 5 million *yuan*. *Unit* billion *yuan* (the national economic census conducted in 2004 and 2008; Guangdong Industrial Census Yearbook 2000)

exports achieved the most significant increase from 4 to 19% and replaced the role of SOEs accordingly. It should be noted that the number of SOEs has declined sharply during this period. Therefore, at individual level, the value added per enterprise of SOEs would be much higher than FIEs and local firms. But at the regional level, the contribution of SOEs to regional upgrading was rather insignificant.

5.3.5 Limitations of Local Upgrading: Operating Under the Shadow of FIEs

The above analyses have demonstrated that the PRD's electronics industry has achieved noticeable regional upgrading in various ways. However, as the pattern of captive coupling is persistent, most of the upgrading outcomes are produced by FIEs. This finding echoes previous studies which have revealed the dependence of local firms on TNCs (Lin 1997; Naughton 1997; Sit 1998). Through knowledge spillover effects, FIEs provided learning/benchmarking opportunities for local firms to use new machines, adopt new product systems, and absorb matured managerial skills. However, local firms met great difficulties in further upgrading, because the regional production networks were substantially controlled by FIEs. These FIEs, particularly Taiwanese computer firms in Dongguan, tended to confine the knowledge within their backward linkages or the 'global pipelines' which are part of their GPNs (Xue 2009; Yang and Liao 2009; Xiao and He 2010). Although sophisticated components were exposed to local firms, the modular form of integration made reverse engineering less possible (Chesbrough and Kusunoki 2001). The circumstances in Shijie Town and Shilong Town illustrate this upgrading predicament.

Shijie is labeled as 'Delta Town' because it is entirely dominated by Delta Electronics, the world's largest producer of power supply units for personal computers from Taiwan. Within the town, Delta is surrounded by dozens of transplanted suppliers and about 200 local firms. This mini regional production network accounts for more than 80% of total output value in the town (IARE 2010). By 2010, just a few of local firms were serving as first-tier suppliers. All other local firms were satiated in manufacturing peripheral components and packing works. In a different sector, Shilong specializes in the optoelectronics industry led by a group of Japanese FIEs such as Kyocera, TKR, Konica Minolta, and Nidec Sankyo. In 2005, it was certificated as China's national base of the electronics industry with millions of annual production volume in various products including camera, copy machine, printer, and desktop computer (Zhu 2010). These Japanese firms originally were EPEs. Since the mid-1990s, they were encouraged to convert into FIEs. Japanese firms agreed with that but decided to acquire most of the best local firms rather than investing in new plants and factories. Local states devoted abundant efforts to satisfy the needs of these Japanese firms and even persuaded local firms to be acquired. This transformation turned most of the promising local firms into FIE's subsidiaries and diminished the possibility of local functional upgrading, as told by the vice chairman of EIAD:

> In order to convert the Japanese EPEs into FIEs, local states almost mobilized all available resources, such as providing additional institutional services, offering more fiscal incentives, training professionals and persuading local firms to be acquired. The joint ventures were proved to be effective and successful. But we did lose something. Now we hardly find promising local firms that are wholly private-owned in Shilong. None of them can be the first-tier suppliers of those Japanese FIEs. As I know, some of the local talent entrepreneurs have left to establish new business somewhere else. (Interview 100807, on 17 Aug 2010 in Dongguan)

Within these networks, some FIEs further integrated production vertically. This effort led to less and less space for skilled local firms to pursue further upgrading due to the increasing complexity of transactions and asset specificity. Foxconn and Flextronics are two relevant examples. As the world's largest EMS provider, Foxconn has integrated all production segments within several industrial parks in Longhua town in Shenzhen since 1988. This effort had shaped Longhua into a 'Foxconn Town' with more than 400,000 employees by 2009. This giant stood as the top export company in Shenzhen with a new record of $48 billion in 2010 (Wu 2011). This kind of huge industrial complex is what American plants cannot compete against (see the opening story in Chap. 1). The limited upgrading opportunity of Foxconn's suppliers can be seen in the comment of a former manager of Foxconn:

> The strong capability of vertical integration of Foxconn is not only a nightmare to its competitors, but also a serious headache to it suppliers in Shenzhen. Most of the suppliers can only earn a marginal profit, since Foxconn knows the procedures and costs very well. Whichever sophisticated components or products, Foxconn makes by itself. So I don't think there is a lot of knowledge spillover happening. Unless like me. When leaving it, I did carry away some knowledge. (Interview 100706, on 6th June 2010 in Guangzhou by telephone)

Similar to Foxconn, the world's second largest EMS provider, Flextronics, built its own industrial town in Zhuhai in 1996 and subsequently relocated all 13 key business units into the town. In 2009, Flextronics (Zhuhai) produced a total output value of $ 60 billion and also accounted for 41% of total export value in Zhuhai.[2] During this process, Flextronics upgraded the function of its Zhuhai base from printed circuit board (PCB) assembly into a full range of EMSs, such as mobile devices, automotive components, computing devices, touch displays, camera modules, and power suppliers. An exclusive local supply network was constructed in three steps: (1) transplanted 26 Flextronics' suppliers from elsewhere; (2) established 11 solely owned subsidiaries surrounding the industrial park; and (3) acquired four competent local suppliers directly. Its vice president noted that:

> Compared with Foxconn, we were a bit late [in the PRD]. So we moved faster. We asked our suppliers to come, established our own one, and even acquired local [private] firms. Those local firms were out suppliers originally in PCB manufacturing. As they were growing fast, we saw their competences as well as potential challenge. So we bought them with an irresistibly good price instead of relocating our owned factories from elsewhere. (Interview 100704, on 14th May, 2010 in Zhuhai)

In summary, captive coupling has been developed and reinforced in the electronics industry in the PRD throughout three decades of development. Regional upgrading is possible in various ways. But it is mainly contributed by FIEs. Although local private firms have been catching up quickly, they still lag behind substantially with limited functional upgrading under the shadow of FIEs. This phenomenon can be found in the examples of Shijie and Shilong, Foxconn (Shenzhen), and Flextronics (Zhuhai). Nevertheless, the prospect of local upgrading should not be viewed too pessimistically. There are some new institutional–spatial conditions that may give local firms a chance to upgrade via a different pathway.

5.4 Potential Pathways of Local Upgrading: Leveraging the Power of FIEs

The FIE-led upgrading within captive coupling resonates with many previous studies which assert that TNCs (or global lead firms) play a determinant role in defining latecomer upgrading in the electronics industry (Hobday 1995; Cho et al. 1998; Schmitz 2004; Gereffi and Fernandez 2011). However, as critiqued in Sect. 5.2, these studies overlook certain potential in local upgrading. Although captive coupling has been reinforced, local firms may utilize some resources embedded in changing institutional–spatial contexts to leverage the power of lead firms.

    In the PRD local firms in the electronics industry were leveraging the power of FIEs by utilizing two resources most frequently: new regional assets and competitive dynamics within GPNs. This section articulates three cases in relation to these strategies of upgrading. Specifically, the case of Shunde shows how emerging regional assets can increase the bargaining power of local firms in the home appliance industry. The case of CZC illustrates how local firms may bypass the control of

---

[2]Interview with a vice president of Flextronics on 14 Mar 2010 in Zhuhai.

TNCs and CMs by taking advantage of recent competitive dynamics in the computer and cell phone markets. Finally, the case of Jingtuo exemplifies how local firms can synthesize various assets to achieve product upgrading under the shadow of FIEs. It should be noted that these cases merely shed light on some possible new pathways of local upgrading. They do not mean that the entire electronics industry in the PRD has fully moved away from captive coupling.

5.4.1 New Regional Assets and the Home Appliance Cluster in Shunde

Compared with the historical moment in 1978, the institutional–spatial contexts of the PRD's electronics industry have substantially changed. Various regional assets have been developed during rapid industrialization in this region. Since the late 1990s, regional governments in the PRD have started to nurture many industrial associations (Xue 2009; Xiao and He 2010). A total of 20 Technology Innovation Centers were established in most of the specialized towns. However, these tech-innovation centers had little innovation content and merely functioned as public platforms for prototype experiment and testing. Half of them were even privatized before 2005 due to operational difficulties (Qiu and Yang 2008). Industrial associations were also facing difficulties in facilitating collective learning in the electronics industry, as noted by the vice chairman of EIAD:

> In the past decade, we did try a lot to build up the so called 'regional learning platform' by providing various business meetings, learning workshops and training programs, as requested by the Dongguan municipal governments. However, this outcome was less significant because technologies in the electronics industry were too diverse and sophisticated. The attendants had few common languages and became less and less interested. Thus we still more focused on our normal duties like organizing business trips and local trade fairs which seemed to be more effective. (Interview 100817, on 17 Aug 2010 in Dongguan)

While associational economies were not so effective, domestic markets became a rather important asset that gave rise of new upgrading opportunities. Originally, the electronics industry in the PRD relied highly on export markets since the 1980s. But the situation has changed now. China has become an emerging key market in many electronics sectors for global firms (Naughton 1997; Jin 2006; Gadiesh et al. 2007; APCO 2009). In the past decade, the PRD's electronics firms were selling more products in the domestic market than in the international markets. As shown in Table 5.5, in the electronic machinery and equipment products, the portion of sale value in the domestic market increased continuously from 41% in 1999 to 61% in 2008. The domestic share of electronics and ICT products also experienced a similar growth from 25% in 1999 to 36% in 2008. Interestingly, when FIEs are concentrating more in the domestic market, local private firms are focusing more on international markets.

Additionally, a regional supply network was emerging by the growth of local firms and the further localization of FIEs. This supply network comprised dozens

Table 5.5 Comparing the roles of market in PRD's electronics industry (the first and second Guangdong Economic Census in 2004 and 2008. All data referred to enterprises have an annual turnover over 5 million *yuan*)

Year	Total industrial sale value (billion *yuan*)	Global sale (%)	Domestic sale (%)	Total (%)
Electronic machinery and equipment				
1999	92.0	59.7	40.8	100
2004	304.0	49.7	50.3	100
2008	696.4	38.7	61.3	100
Electronics and ICT				
1999	175.0	75.1	24.9	100
2004	802.1	74.3	25.7	100
2008	1595.6	64.3	35.7	100
FIEs				
1999	151.6	78.3	21.7	100
2004	859.2	73.7	26.3	100
2008	1666.2	69.4	30.6	100
Private firms				
1999	50.8	11.8	89.2	100
2004	320.7	27.9	73.1	100
2008	870.1	34.0	66.0	100

of specialized industrial clusters and industrial parks with specialties in different segments in the electronic industry (see Sect. 5.3.3). Among 31 surveyed firms,[3] only 9 of them were largely based on regional supply networks in their early stage of development. But currently 24 of them said that the majority of supply chains were grounded in the PRD.

My survey found that the influences of regional assets varied toward local upgrading. As shown in Fig. 5.4, domestic markets, production costs, and regional supply networks were the three most important regional assets with values of 2.39, 1.97, and 1.94, respectively. Governmental supports and associational economies were less significant, and the social–cultural relations were the least important. According to my fieldwork, the combination of domestic markets, production costs, and regional supply networks increased the bargaining power of local firms, particularly in some products with lower technological entry barriers, such as home appliances. The advantage of lower production costs kept attracting global buyers and traders to subcontract their orders to the PRD. Assisted by the growing body of regional supply networks, local firms reduced technological dependency on global lead firms and gradually moved forward to develop OEM business, and then bargained for ODM business with global buyers. During the process, local firms reduced their market

---

[3] Among 37 interviewed firms, only 31 of them completed the questionnaire survey.

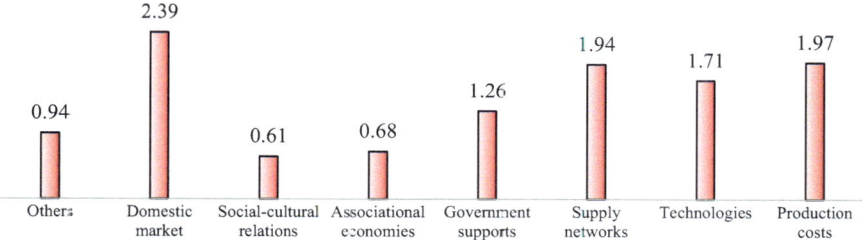

Fig. 5.4 Importance of regional assets in the electronics industry in the PRD. *Notes* Informants were requested to evaluate the degree of importance of regional assets during the upgrading of their companies. A value ranged from absent (0) to high (3) was attributed to each type of assets. The result was averaged (author's survey on 31 informants in the electronics industry)

dependency on global buyers by selling their products in the huge domestic market. Compared with products in the global market, their initial products were not competitive or less qualified. But the less-demanding domestic market gave them a critical opportunity for accumulating profits, production skills, and marketing knowledge. The success of home appliance clusters in Shunde exemplifies this mechanism of local upgrading.

As a district of Foshan City, Shunde is located in the Northwest part of the PRD. During the 1980s, Shunde was merely an export-processing base of electronic components and clothing products. It hosted hundreds of EPEs captive to Hong Kong firms. In the mid-1980s, a few firms were privatized from EPEs and began to make simple electrical products that were quite needed in domestic markets such as fans, water heaters, and electronic cookers later on. Without assistance from FIEs or TNCs, these local firms conducted reverse engineering to bridge the knowledge gap. The early electronic products from Shunde were poor in quality and functions, but those products were sold at an extremely low price in comparison with the ones made by Japanese and European lead firms. Hence, these products were 'acceptable good' to a certain extent (Gadiesh et al. 2007). By taking the opportunity of booming domestic markets, many local firms achieved functional upgrading into domestic branded name companies, such as Midea, Rongsheng, Kolen, Galanz, Macro, Dongling, and Wanhe.

The preliminary success of these local branded firms stimulated the further development of local suppliers. Some of them were privatized from EPEs or township and village enterprises (TVEs); some of them spanned off from the branded firms; and some of them were joint ventures between local firms and global lead firms (Liu et al. 2010). This supply network underpinned local branded firms to provide OEM services for global buyers, such as Electrolux, Hitachi and Mitsubishi during the mid-1990s. In 1995, Shunde contributed to about 80% of production volume in air conditioners and fridges in the China market (Lin 2009). By 2000, the sale records of many Shunde firms exceeded global lead firms in the China market, such as Panasonic, Electrolux, and Siemens (Li and Wang 2011). In 2006, Shunde was certificated as the 'National Town of Home Appliances' with more than 2000 competent local firms, about 20 domestic branded lead firms and vertically integrated production networks interwoven among three clusters: Leilu, Beijiao, and Daliang (see Fig. 5.2).

Midea is one of the most successful local branded firms in Shunde. It has supplied OEM products in global markets and OBM products in the domestic market since the 1990s. Midea has built up various partnerships with public research institutes in the PRD and also invested in other suppliers in Shunde. It has even set up an in-house training center called Midea College. In 1996, Midea made an important step by establishing a joint venture with Toshiba known as GMCC.[4] This joint venture realized the functional upgrading of Midea. The nuance power relation during this functional upgrading is well noted by a manager of the GMCC:

> There were three reasons contributed to the establishment of the joint venture. First, Toshiba had problems in acquiring land for building factories at that time and it needed some local partners to solve this problem. Second, it was also too costly for them to establish their own plants. More importantly, Toshiba had foreseen the huge potential of China markets and did not want to miss the opportunity. Hence Toshiba agreed to develop joint venture with Midea. If Toshiba declined, Midea would surely turn to other partners for the joint venture. (Interview 100902, on 2 Sep 2010 in Shunde)

GMCC was meant for making compressors (for air conditioners and fridges) for the China market based on Toshiba's X1C and X2C models. It initially sold compressors to many Chinese firms and then consolidated clients in a few domestic lead firms. During this process, Midea kept absorbing knowledge from GMCC through technological licensing, engineer rotation, and conducting co-development between Midea and GMCC. It then became the largest client of GMCC. Toshiba and Midea worked closely to develop new compressor models. Eventually, Midea purchased relevant intellectual property rights (IPRs) from Toshiba and acquired the share of Toshiba. In 2010, GMCC made the first turbo compressor based on Midea's proprietary IPRs.

What is the role of domestic and global markets in such local upgrading examples as Midea? An answer was provided by vice CEO of the Donglin Group. It should be cautioned that the domestic market here is not a necessary condition for local upgrading, but it does provide an opportunity for local firms to increase their bargaining power with global lead firms and to nurture their technological and marketing skills.

> China's domestic market is extremely important to us. All local firms [in Shunde] started by selling imperfect products in China in the 1980s. We then learned how to make them better and how to manage a brand. But I should admit that we learn the most significant technologies from our OEM customers. They bring us to understand the state-of-art technologies, new designs and rapid changing consumer behaviors in the global market. Nowadays we keep both domestic (OBM) and international (OEM) businesses for balancing risks in volatile market changes, such as the economic crisis last year [2009]. (Interview 100701, on 1st July 2010 in Shunde)

---

[4]http://www.chinagmcc.com.

5.4.2 Competitive Dynamics Within GPNs: The Functional Upgrading of CZC

Apart from the growing availability of regional assets, *competitive dynamics* within GPN is also a critical but implicit asset to local electronics firms. Since the mid-1990s, some new platform developers from East Asia have been challenging global lead firms in various product markets, such as the Creative Technology (Singapore, audio processing chipset), MTK (Taiwan, mobile phone baseband) and VIA (Taiwan, motherboard platform). Assisted by these turnkey solutions, many local firms in the PRD upgraded from component suppliers into branded manufacturers directly. Meanwhile, thousands of *Shanzhai* manufacturers[5] joined the game by making copy-cat products. The growth of these products led to a market shake out later on and only a few local firms survived such as K-Touch (mobile phone), OPPO (multimedia products), Seavo (desktop computer), and CZC[6] (netbook/tablet computer). These firms were mainly located in Shenzhen and Dongguan (Liu et al. 2010). This section specifically examines the case of CZC to illustrate how competitive dynamics have influenced local functional upgrading.

The upgrading strategy of CZC was to bypass the control of Taiwanese CMs and to develop new captive coupling with a distant platform developer. CZC was established in the mid-2000s to exploit the domestic market in netbook computers. Being captive to Taiwanese CMs for procuring key components, CZC supplied netbook motherboards for local branded firms including *Shanzhai* manufacturers. However, the problem of captive coupling kept CZC at bay, as told by the former vice director of CZC:

> About 80% of our components were sourced from top Taiwanese CMs. They fully controlled us by price and volume. Whenever they claimed that they were out of stock, we had to take it and stop our work. When they raised price, we could not say no. We could not escape from them. If we use other CMs' components, we will meet a problem of heat dissipation and systematic compatibility. (Interview 100907, on 7th Sep 2010 in Shenzhen)

An upgrading opportunity emerged through the availability of the Atom chipset solution from Intel. Atom was deliberately designed to solve the problems of heat dissipation, thus helping latecomer firms like CZC to reduce dependence on Taiwanese CMs. The incentive of Intel's strategy resulted from the competition between Intel and VIA for years.[7] Based on the Atom chipset, CZC quickly developed turnkey solutions in the S30 platform which was cheaper but less sophisticated than VIA's platforms (Pei and Hu 2009). This effort made CZC become a platform developer in

---

[5]Shanzhai product refers to Chinese imitation and pirated brands and goods, particularly in electronics industries. Shanzhai products are look alike, and low quality or with improved functions done in parody. Recent dynamics in many Shanzhai products shows that they are no longer pirated brands, but are still based on imitation from global lead firm strongly.

[6]Chuang Zhi Cheng Technology, established in Shenzhen.

[7]VIA launched the Global Mobility Bazaar (GMB) alliance in 2008 that challenged Intel's market shares by providing new turnkey solutions called the nano-platform. At: http://gmb.via.com.tw/resource/jsp/PartnersSolutions/PartnersSolutions.jsp.

the low end of the notebook computer market. The S30 platform was quite welcomed in the domestic market. In 2009, CZC hit the top seller record among its peers in China.[8]

To a certain degree, the CZC was functionally upgraded into a new platform developer but in a shallow form. The technological competence of CZC did not improve fundamentally. The S30 was still technologically lagged behind VIA's products, though it did capture some market shares from VIA. The growing local supply network in Shenzhen also sustained the upgrading of CZC. A comment from Mr Mao, the CEO of Hedy Holding, has described this change:

> The power of Taiwanese computer giants is weakening, with the rise of domestic OEM and ODM suppliers [such as CZC] and regional supply networks in the PRD. Now we can buy most of the components and the designs right here from the non-Taiwanese firms. (Interviewed by Nandu Daily, published on 3rd Jun 2009)

In 2011, after evaluating the cooperation of the Atom chipsets and the technological capabilities of CZC, Intel further authorized its Meego system (for tablet computer) to be used by CZC. The incentive of this strategy was derived from the competitive pressures between Intel and Microsoft, Apple, Google in operation systems occupying the top of the value-chain hierarchy. CZC was regarded as a strategic partner helping Intel to venture into the tablet computer market in China. Hence, CZC enjoyed certain privilege of installing the Meego system in its indigenously developed tablet computers. Domestic market opportunities increased the bargaining power of CZC in this deal. This Inter-CZC partnership is not unique in the PRD, but is a common phenomenon in the tablet computer market. As shown in Table 5.6, there were at least 32 branded domestic firms in 2010 that had developed cooperative partnership with 9 global platform developers in the PRD. Some of these local firms had already achieved good sale records in global markets. For instance, Zenithink's

Table 5.6 Global–local partnership in the tablet computer industry in the PRD (multiple media reports, interviews and author' fieldwork)

Platforms	Branded local firms
Intel, 450//455/470/Z530	CZC, Bben, LiveFan, G's Five Telsda, ViewPad, Idea, Jumper, Dianji
Qualcomm 7227/7627-T	Lenovo, Huawei, Voodoo
Freescale, iMX515/535	Grefu, Azpen, Eben
VIA, 8505/8650	1pad, Flytouch, Chuangshizhe, Shuziyin, Jinghan
Rockchip 2818/2918	TCL, Aoson, Hyundai, Simai, Yuandao
Infotmic, iMAPx210/220	Zenithink, Doken
Amlogic 8726	Zenithink, Ramos
Ranesas, Cortex A9	Linyun
Telechips, TCC8803/9201/8902	Emdoor, Yufeng

---

[8]Source: Nandu Daily on 3 Jun 2009, at: http://epaper.oeeee.com/D/html/2009-06/03/content_808524.htm.

product was ranked just after Apple's iPad and followed by Samsung, Archos, and Motorola in a global market survey in 2011.[9]

Taiwanese CMs had little power to block the functional upgrading of CZC. Although they were in the same GPN, the upgrading opportunity was given by Intel which Taiwanese CMs could control. This generation of opportunity looks like a trickle-down effect of competition on the top of the value-chain hierarchy. However, this functional upgrading should not be overemphasized. Local firms may encounter a modularity trap in which they become more and more captive to platform developers in technologies. In terms of functions and products, they indeed upgrade. But in technological capabilities, they do not. Moreover, the marketing capabilities of local firms are still greatly lagging behind global lead firms. How many local firms can survive in future market shake-out remains unknown.

5.4.3 Synthesizing Resources Under the Shadow of FIEs: Jingtuo Automatic

In contrast to Midea or CZC, many of the local electronics firms may not be able to increase bargaining power or bypass the control of FIEs. But they may leverage the power with FIEs by nurturing more mutual interests with them. The rest of this section draws upon the case of Jingtuo to illustrate a scenario: how asymmetrical power relations can be smoothed by better synergy and produce more product and process upgrading within captive coupling.

Jingtuo Automatic Equipment Ltd. (Jingtuo) was established in 2000 in Shenzhen to manufacture lower-cost soldering machines for substituting expensive imported machines costing 1 million *yuan* each at that time. Local markets boomed because of the rise of the local computer industry and *Shanzhai* manufacturers. In terms of quality and functions, Jingtuo's soldering machines were not competitive against imported machines from global leading manufacturers (e.g., ERSA). But Jingtuo developed a market niche by offering the machines at 40% of the international prices. Initially, the performance of Jingtuo's machines was unstable, while Jingtuo overcame this weakness by providing timely and intensive after-sale maintenance. Proximity to local market served as a crucial asset underpinning the growth of Jingtuo. As noted by the vice president of Jingtuo:

> Collocation with our customer makes our products accepted by the market. Indeed our products got many problems at the beginning, like operation halts or disordering temperature control. But our technician crews stand by 24/7 and can arrive at the factories in time. Even when our machines are operating quite well, I may bring some sellers and engineers together to visit the customers to see what we can improve or what they expect us to do. In doing so, we earned our reputation and collected a lot of useful feedbacks at the beginning. (Interview 100908, on 8th Sep 2010 in Shenzhen)

---

[9]Zenithink's tablet computers ranked at the second of worldwide costumer likelihood in 2011 according to a recent survey done by iSuppli; see http://lowendmac.com/inews/11ios/0829.html#8.

In the early 2000s, Jingtuo attracted the interest of Flextronics (Zhuhai) whereby captive coupling was developed between them. After further relocating major business units into Zhuhai, Flextronics had a strong imperative in cost reduction and they needed to replace thousands of soldering machines within every 3–5 years. As a designated key supplier with certain priority, Jingtuo was required to provide specialized design machines according to rapid-changing product ranges in Flextronics (Zhuhai). In return, Flextronics provided certain technological assistances and co-innovation opportunities for Jingtuo in product development. Synergy was well fostered based on long-term mutual interests. Jingtuo considered Flextronics as an important stepping stone to entry the global EMS industry, while Flextronics preferred Jingtuo's flexibility in engineering designs and efficiency in cost reductions. As told by a vice president of Flextronics:

> Our international suppliers [ERSA] mainly provide standardized machines with a few revisable functions. But Jingtuo works much more flexible. They are willing to revise the whole designs to fit our demands. We just tell them what we want and what the others can do. Sometimes we work together to figure out how we can improve the machines better, which saves us a lot of time and human costs. We now use quite a lot of machines from Jingtuo, apart from some high-end products in which we still use Siemens and ERSA's machines. (Interview 100514, on 14th May 2010 in Zhuhai)[10]

Based on the synergy with Flextronics, Jingtuo innovated and developed four series of machines in reflow soldering and wave soldering. Jingtuo even invented a dual-track soldering machine in 2008 that could process two types of product simultaneously within a single production line. The dual-track idea resulted from some complains of local customers about the complexity of IC designs. Again, local markets played an important testing role. Jingtuo initially sold the dual-track machines at half price to several local manufacturers and collected feedbacks before recommending it to Flextronics. Eventually, the dual-track machines were patented and adopted by Flextronics and other EMS providers. This product upgrading even pressured ERAS to develop a similar machine. But it was sold outside China so as to avoid being deemed as a follower or triggering IPR disputes. Jingtuo could upgrade into a small EMS provider for the local market that might eventually bring more profits. But Jingtuo gave up this upgrading action for maintaining synergy with Flextronics. As its vice president said:

> We can earn more profit by upgrading into an EMS supplier. Even many local entrepreneurs encouraged us to do so because they were tied of being controlled by Taiwanese CMs. But we decided not to do that because it would harm our relationship with Flextronics. We need this industrial name card and the learning opportunities in the global market in a long term. (Interview 100908, on 8 Sep 2010 in Shenzhen)

The revenue of Jingtuo in 2009 reached 400 million *yuan*. By 2010, Jingtuo held 30 patent rights and ten sets of software copyrights on the basis of only 80 technicians. All these patents and industrial reputation helped Jingtuo become a key supplier of

---

[10]Information about the exact amount and production lines that use JT's machines is kept as confidential by the interviewee.

global top EMS suppliers. Since 2009, Jingtuo has targeted developing photovoltaic equipment for the domestic market that was identified some ten years ago.

To sum up, the case of Jingtuo exemplifies how a local firm in the PRD can achieve upgrading in two steps: (1) deepening captive coupling with FIEs for better learning opportunities and (2) synthesizing various assets to increase bargaining power, such as cost advantages, local markets, proximity to customers, and a competent regional supply network. This book provides a reasonably good opportunity for local firms to leverage the power of FIEs and implement upgrading.

5.5 Seeking Alternative Pathways

On the mechanisms of upgrading in the electronics industry, previous studies tend to believe that modular governance has determined inter-firm power relationships and the effect of knowledge diffusion. Hence, it seems reasonable that indigenous innovation would possibly be the only option for latecomer upgrading. Since TNCs would not offer advance knowledge, local firms better make it by their own efforts. I regard this strand of discussions as a stereotype of latecomer upgrading. It appreciates neither the dynamics of power relations and synergy within inter-firm relationship, nor the institutional–spatial conditions that influence governance power. Once new mutual interests or the fragility of governance power is identified, power relations could be reshaped, despite that the pattern of strategic coupling may remain the same.

Understanding latecomer upgrading in this way, we can recognize many alternative pathways of regional development beyond the stereotypes of being a humble follower or an active innovator. Empirical investigations in this chapter have verified this point. Generally, this chapter offers a different story along three dimensions.

First of all, the PRD did not own promising regional assets in accordance with previous studies, such as strong state intervention, intensive indigenous innovation, regional innovation systems, or associational economies (Douglass 1994; Cooke and Morgan 1998; Lazonick 2004; Zhou and Wei 2011). Instead, this study found that upgrading in PRD's electronics industry was driven by captive coupling whereby local firms were highly dependent on FIEs in providing rapid-changing technologies and up-to-date information of market demands. This captive coupling led to substantial product and process upgrading in the PRD. But the dependence of local firms on TNCs was reinforced simultaneously. Regional functional upgrading was realized to a significant degree. The PRD was upgraded from a processing or subcontracting base to a global integrated manufacturing center. But the major contribution of this upgrading came from FIEs. During this process, the technological capacities and performance of local firms were improved, but were apparently still lagged behind FIEs.

Second, drawing upon several detailed case studies, this chapter has illustrated that the trajectory of upgrading is neither pre-determined by the pattern of global governance, nor restricted by the stereotypes of upgrading. Instead, it is subject to dynamic synergy within captive coupling and is constantly reshaped by changing mutual interests and firm strategies. The pattern of captive coupling has yet to be changed and FIEs still exert strong and strict control based on their modular governance of local firms. But FIEs cannot stop local firms in seeking upgrading potential within the broader and changing institutional–spatial conditions. In the PRD's electronics industry, local firms have managed to utilize various emerging assets to increase their bargaining power.

Third, my study found three local strategies as alternative pathways of local upgrading in the PRD's electronics industry. Local firms have increased bargaining power and earned more learning opportunities from foreign firms, such as those home appliance firms in Shunde; local firms also bypassed the control of foreign firms by utilizing opportunities embedded in competitive dynamics within GPNs, such as the case of CZC in Shenzhen; finally, local firms fostered more mutual interests with foreign firms and reduced the asymmetry of power relations, such as the cases of Jingtuo and Flextronics (Zhuhai). All these strategies point to the potential in the formation of cooperative coupling in future. In contrast to the electronics industry, cooperative coupling was more apparent in the apparel industry, as will be shown in the next chapter.

References

APCO. (2009). *Market analysis report: China's electronics industry* (pp. 1–33). APCO Worldwide, http://www.apcoworldwide.com/.

Balconi, M. (2002). Tacitness, codification of technological knowledge and the organisation of industry. *Research Policy, 31*(3), 357–379.

Beeson, M. (2004). The rise and fall of the developmental state: The vicissitudes and implications of East Asian interventionism. In L. Low (Block), *Developmental states: Relevancy, redundancy or reconfiguration?* (pp. 29–40). New York: Nova Science Publishers.

Borrus, M., & Zysman, J. (1997). Wintelism and the Changing terms of global competition. *BRIE working paper 96B.* Berkeley, CA: Berkeley Roundtable on the International Economy.

Cao, G. H. (2007). *Study on China's integrated circuit industry of independent innovation strategy.* Wuhan: Wuhan Polytechnic University (in Chinese).

CCW. (2004). Development history of semiconductor industry in China. *China Computer Weekly,* August 9, 2004 (in Chinese). http://it.icxo.com/htmlnews/2004/08/09/289823.htm.

Chen, J., & Pu, X. (Eds.). (1999). *'The fifty years of Guangdong'—Official statistics report of Guangdong Provincial government.* Beijing: China Statistics Press (in Chinese).

Chesbrough, H., & Kusunoki, K. (2001). The modularity trap: Innovation, technology phase shifts, and the resulting limits of virtual organizations. In L. Nonaka, & D. J. Teece (Eds.), *Managing industrial knowledge* (pp. 202–230). London: Sage Press.

Cho, D.-S., Kim, D.-J., & Rhee, D. K. (1998). Latecomer strategies: Evidence from the semiconductor Industry in Japan and Korea. *Organization Science, 9*(4), 489–505. https://doi.org/10.1287/orsc.9.4.489.

Chui, S. W.-K., Ho, K.-C., & Lui, T.-L. (1997). *City-states in the global economy: Industrial restructuring in Hong Kong and Singapore.* Boulder: Westview Press.

Clark, G. L., & Kim, W. B. (1995). *Asian NIEs and the global economy: Industrial restructuring and corporate strategy in the 1990s.* The Johns Hopkins University Press.

Cooke, P., & Morgan, K. (1998). *The associational economy. Firms, regions, and innovation.* Oxford: Oxford University Press.

CW. (200_). The Status Quo and Future of domestic market in China's integrated circuit industry [Market research]. *Computer World*, February 19, 2001 (in Chinese).

Dicken, P. (2007). *Global shift: Mapping the changing contours of the world economy* (5th ed.). London Sage.

Ding, W. W., Sun, J. X., & Kou, J. S. (2010). Development strategies of integrated circuit industry in China in new period. *Journal of Tianjin University (Social Sciences), 21*(6 , 482–488 (in Chinese).

Douglass, M. (1994). The 'developmental state' and the newly industrialised economies of Asia. *Environment and Planning A, 26*(4), 543–566.

DRCGP. (2009). *Research on the development of high-tech industries in Guangdong province in a New Era*. Guangzhou: Development and Reform Commission of Guangdong Province and Sun Yet-sen University.

Fan, P. (2011). Innovation, globalization, and catch-up of latecomers: cases of Chinese telecom firms. *Environment and Planning A, 43*(4), 830–849.

Feenstra, R., & Hamilton, G. (2006). *Emerging economies, divergent paths: Business groups and economic organization in South Korea and Taiwan*. New York: Cambridge University Press.

Fixson, S. & Park, J.-K. (2008). The power of integrality: Linkages between product architecture, innovation, and industry structure. *Research Policy, 37*(8), 1296–1316.

Frigant, V., & Layan, J.-B. (2009). Modular production and the new division of labour within Europe: The perspective of French automotive parts suppliers. *European Urban and Regional Studies, 16*(1), 11–25, https://doi.org/10.1177/0969776408098930.

Gadiesh, O., Leung, P., & Vestring, T. (2007). The battle for China's good-enough market. *Harvard Business Review, 85*, 81–89.

Galvin, P., & Morkel, A. (2001). The effect of product modularity on industry structure: The case of the world bicycle industry. *Industry and Innovation, 8*, 31–47.

Gan, Z.-X., & Gan, L.-P. (1994). Background and prospects of the "San Lai Yi Bu" Enterprises in Coastal Areas. *Economic Crisscross, 5*, 28–31 (in Chinese).

GDDRC. (2009). *Development of high-tech industries in Guangdong Province under New Era*. Guangdong Development and Reform Commission.

GDSY. (2000). *Guangdong statistic yearbook*. Beijing: Guangdong Provincial Bureau of Statistics (in Chinese).

GDSYST. (2010). *Guangdong statistic yearbook of science and technology*. Beijing: Guangdong Provincal Bureau of Statistics (in Chinese).

Gereffi, G. (1999). International trade and industrial upgrading in the apparel commodity chain. *Journal of International Economics, 48*(1), 37–70.

Gereffi, G., & Fernandez, S. K. (2011). *Global value chain analysis: A primer. Center on globalization*. Durham, NC: Governance & Competitiveness. Available at: http://www.cggc.duke.edu/pdfs/2011-05-31_GVC_analysis_a_primer.pdf.

Gereffi, G , Humphrey, J., & Sturgeon, T. (2005). The governance of global value chains. *Review of International Political Economy, 12*(1), 78–104, https://doi.org/10.1080/09692290500049805.

Giuliani, E., Pietrobelli, C., & Rabellotti, R. (2005). Upgrading in global value chains: Lessons from Latin American clusters. *World Development, 26*(2), 549–573. https://doi.org/10.1016/j.worlddev.2005.01.002.

Grove, A. (1996). *Only the paranoid survive. How to exploit the crisis point that challenge every company and career*. New York, London: Currency Doubleday.

Hobday, M. (1995). East-Asian latecomer firms—Learning the technology of electronics. *World Development, 23*(5), 1171–1193.

Hobday, M. (2001). The electronics industries of the Asia-Pacific: Exploiting international production networks for economic development. *Asian-Pacific Economic Literature, 15*(1), 13–29.

Huchet, J.-F. (1997). The China circle and technological development in the Chinese Electronics Industry. In B. Naughton, *The China circle: economics and electronics in the PRC, Taiwan, and Hong Kong* (pp. 254–289). Washington, DC: Brookings Institution Press.

Humphrey, J., & Schmitz, H. (2002). How does insertion in global value chains affect upgrading in industrial clusters? *Regional Studies, 36*, 1017–1027, https://doi.org/10.1080/0034340022000022198.

Humphrey, J., & Schmitz, H. (2004). Chain governance and upgrading: Taking stock. In H. Schmitz (Block), *Local enterprises in the global economy* (pp. 349–381). UK: Edward Elgar.

IARE (2010). *Industrial analysis report—Electronics industry in Guangdong 2009.* Guangzhou: Industrial Research Club, www.industrybbs.com.

Jin, J.-M. (2006). The current status of China's electronic information industry. *Economic Topics.* Tokyo: Fujitsu Research Institute. Available at http://jp.fujitsu.com/group/fri/en/column/economic-topics/200608/202006-200608-200618-200601.html.

Johnson, C. (1995). *Japan: Who governs? The rise of the developmental state.* New York: W. W. North.

Langlois, R. (2003). The vanishing hand: The changing dynamics of industrial capitalism. *Industrial and Corporate Change, 12*(2), 351–385.

Lazonick, W. (2004). Indigenous innovation and economic development: Lessons from China' leap into the information age. *Industry and Innovation, 11*(4), 273–297.

Li, K. (2008). State of art and tendencies of China's integrated circuit industry. *China Integrated Circuit, 8* (in Chinese).

Li, G., & Wang, X.-Y. (2011). Structural changes of home appliance industry in China. *China Review* (Vols. 11–7). China: Samsung Economic Research Institute (in Chinese).

Liang, G. L. (1999). Development of integrated circuit industry in China. *Electronic Chemicals, 10*(2), 6–9 (in Chinese).

Lin, G. C. S. (1997). *The red capitalism in South China: Growth and development of the Pearl River Delta.* Vancouver: UBC Press.

Lin, D. R. (2009). *Terrible Shunde: The national value of a county-level place.* Beijing: China Machine Press (in Chinese).

Liu, W. D., & Dicken, P. (2006). Transnational corporations and 'obligated embeddedness': Foreign direct investment in China's automobile industry. *Environment and Planning A, 38*(7), 1229–1247, https://doi.org/10.1068/a37206.

Liu, W. W., Liu, Y., & Li, X. (2010). The evolution and influential factors of the innovation networks of local firms in a globalizing region—A comparative study between Dolim group and Elec-Tech Group in the Pearl River Delta, China. *Economic Geography (Jing Ji Di Li), 30*(8), 1316–1323 (in Chinese).

Liu, Y, Y.-Y., Wang, X.-Y., & Kwon, S.-Y. (2010). Decoding Shanzhai Products. In *SERI China review* (Vol. 10, pp. 12). Beijing: Samsung China Research Institute (in Chinese).

Lowe, N. J. (2009). Challenging tradition: Unlocking new paths to regional industrial upgrading. *Environment and Planning A, 41*(1), 128–145, https://doi.org/10.1068/a40111.

Lüthje, B. (2002). Electronics contract manufacturing: Global production and international division of labor in the age of the Internet. *Industry and Innovation, 9*(3), 227–247.

Lüthje, B. (2004). Global production network and industrial upgrading in China: The Case of Electronics Contract Manufacturing.

Mann, C., & Kirkegaard, J. (2006). *Accelerating the globalization of America: The next wave of information technology.* Washington, DC: Institute for International Economics.

MIIT. (2003). National Statistic Bulletin of Electronics and Information Industries in 2009. Beijing: Ministry of Industry and Information Technology of the People's Republic of China. Available at http://news.xinhuanet.com/zhengfu/2004-04/27/content_1442441.htm.

MIIT. (2010). National Statistical Bulletin of Electronics and Information Industries. Beijing: Ministry of Industry and Information Technology of the People's Republic of China. Available at http://www.miit.gov.cn/n11293472/n11293832/n11293907/n11368223/13578902.html.

Naughton, B. (1997). *The China circle: Economics and electronics in the PRC, Taiwan, and Hong Kong.* Washington, DC: Brokking Institution Press.

NDRC. (2003). *Planning of the coordination and development of megalopolis in Pearl River Delta.* Guangzhou: National Development and Reform Commission (in Chinese).

NDRC. (2008). *The outline of the plan for the reform and development of the Pearl River Delta 2008–2020*. The National Development and Reform Commission.

NDRC. (2011). Policies for further encouraging the development of software and integrated circuit industries. Beijing: The National Development and Reform Commission.

NDRCSC. (2001). Policies for encouraging the development of software and integrated circuit industries. Beijing: The National Development and Reform Commission of State Council.

PDO. (2011). *China leads world in machinery, electronics exports in 2010*.

Pei, Y.-Q., & Hu, Y. (2009). The butterfly effect of netbook computers. *IT CEO World* (in Chinese).

Principe, A., A., & Honday, M. (Eds.). (2003). *The business of system integration*. UK: Oxford.

Qiu, H.-X., & Yang, L.-L. (2008). Operations and experiences of technological innovation centers in the PRD's industrial clusters. *Forum on Science and Technology in China, 7*(7), 46–54.

Schmitz H. (2004). *Local enterprises in the global economy*. UK: Edward Elgar.

Sit, V. F S. (1998). Hong Kong's "Transferred" industrialization and industrial geography. *Asian Survey, 38*(9), 880–904.

Sit, V. F-S., & Yang, C. (1997). Foreign-investment-induced exo-urbanisation in the Pearl River Delta, China. *Urban Studies, 34*(4), 647–677.

Song, L.-J., Mu, F.-G., & Li, G.-L. (1989). Problems and suggestions to the export-processing (San Lai Yi Bu) enterprises. *China Reform, 3,* 23–24 (in Chinese).

Steinfeld, E. S. (2010). *Playing our game: Why China's rise doesn't threaten the West*. New York: Oxford University Press.

Sturgeon, T. (2002). Modular production networks: An American model of industrial organization. *Industrial and Corporate Change, 11*(3), 451–496.

Sturgeon, T., & Kawakami, M. (2011). Global value chains in the electronics industry: Characteristics, crisis, and upgrading opportunities for firms from developing countries. *International Journal of Technological Learning, Innovation and Development, 4*(1,2/3), 120–147.

Sturgeon, T., & Lester, R. (2004). The new global supply-base: New challenges for local suppliers in East Asia. In S. Yusuf, A. M. Anjum., & K. Nabeshima (Eds.), *Global production networking and technological change in East Asia*. Oxford UK: Oxford University Press.

Sung, Y. W. (1991). *The China-Hong Kong connection: The key to China's open-door policy*. Cambridge: Cambridge University Press.

Sung, Y. W., Wong, R. Y.-C., & Lau, P. W. (1995). *The fifth Dragon: The emergence of the Pearl River Delta*. Singapore: Longman.

Ulrich, K. (1995). The role of product architecture in the manufacturing firm. *Research Policy, 24*(3), 419–440.

Wade, R. (1990). *Governing the market: Economic theory and the role of Government in East Asian industrialization*. Princeton: Princeton University Press.

Wang, Y. (1996). Market analysis of integrated circuit industry in China. *World Electronic Products, 3,* 31–35 (in Chinese).

White, G. (Block). (1988). *Developmental states in East Asia*. New York: St. Martin's Press.

Xiao, Z. X., & He, J. S. (2010). Industrial upgrading in electronic information product manufacturing in Pearl River Delta—Case in Dongguang Qingxi Town (in Chinese). *Special Zone Economy, 27*(3), 33–37.

Xu, X. Q. (1988). Accelaration of urbanization in the Pearl River Delta through the opening reform. *Journal of Geography, 43*(3), 201–210 (in Chinese).

Xue, J. (2009). Study of technological base and innovative network in clusters—Case of electronics industrial clusters in Shilong town, Dongguan city in China. *Science & Technology Progress and Policy, 26*(16), 66–71 (in Chinese).

Wu, D. Q. (2011). Foxconn ranks as the top exporter again in Shenzhen. Shenzhen Special Zone Daily, 6 Jan, 2011. Shenzhen: http://news.sznews.com/content/2011-01/06/content_5235501.htm.

Yang, C. (2007). Divergent hybrid capitalisms in China: Hong kong and Taiwanese electronics clusters in Dongguan. *Economic Geography, 83*(4), 395–420.

Yang, C., & Liao, H. (2009). Backward linkages of cross-border production networks of Taiwanese PC investment in the Pearl River Delta, China. *Tijdschrift Voor Economische En Sociale Geografie, 101*(2), 199–217.

Yeh, A. G.-O., Lee, Y.-S. F., Lee, T., & Sze, N. D. (Eds.). (2002). *Building a competitive Pearl River Delta region: Cooperation, coordination, and planning*. Hong Kong: The University of Hong Kong, Centre of Urban Planning and Environmental Management.

Yeung, H. W.-C. (2009). Regional development and the competitive dynamics of global production networks: An East Asian perspective. *Regional Studies, 43*(3), 325–351.

Yusuf, S., Altaf, M. A., & Nabeshima, K. (Eds.). (2004). *Global production networking and technological change in East Asia*. Washington, DC: The World Bank/Oxford University Press.

Zhang, S.-W., & Xu, L.-Y. (2010). Upgrading and transformation in the home appliance industry of China. In S.-R. Quan (Block), *SERIChina Review* (Vol. 10, pp. 14). Beijing: Samsung China Research Center at www.serichina.org (in Chinese).

Zhou, Y., & Wei, Y. H. D. (2011). Globalization, innovation, and regional development in China. *Environment and Planning A, 43*(4), 781–785.

Zhu, R.-H. (2010). *Relocation, upgrading and localization: The pattern of clustering and development in the electronics information Industry in Shilong Town in Dongguan*. Guangzhou: Guangdong People Press (in Chinese).

Chapter 6
Local Upgrading in the Apparel Industry: From Captive Coupling to Cooperative Coupling

6.1 Situating the Apparel Industry in the PRD

In Chap. 5, although clothing products are mostly low in value added and unsophisticated in technologies, the apparel industry serves virtually as the initial step of industrialization and even an important part of survival for latecomer economies (Dicken 2007). It is also considered as a primary industry that transfers upgrading opportunities from developed countries to developing economies during the process of globalization (Gereffi and Korzeniewicz 1994; Gereffi 1999). However, there is a bottleneck for latecomer firms to conduct functional upgrading from OEM into ODM/OBM in this industry, because global buyers discourage this upgrading (Bair and Gereffi 2001; Humphrey and Schmitz 2002b; Schmitz 2004). Moreover, latecomer firms also suffer competitive pressures as they are making undifferentiated products. They can be quite easily substituted by lower-cost producers (Hill and Fujita 1996; Ozawa 2005).

Situating in this paradoxical context, local upgrading in the apparel industry seems to be difficult. However, this study finds that the apparel industry in PRD has undergone a different trajectory of local upgrading. After three decades of development, the region has achieved functional upgrading to a certain degree. It has become a global manufacturing hub and a domestic design and fashion center, rather than just a 'world factory' full of sweatshops and low-skilled labor. This achievement goes beyond the explanations in previous studies. To address these dynamics, this chapter focuses on three issues in the PRD's apparel industry: (1) the progress of local upgrading and changing driving forces; (2) the formation and evolution of strategic coupling; (3) power dynamics and local strategies during the evolution of strategic coupling.

This chapter is organized into five sections. The next section interprets recent dynamics in the global apparel industry and critiques the potential of local upgrading in contemporary literature. After a brief review of the national institutional context, the third section analyzes the formation and evolution of strategic coupling driven by multi-scalar forces in the PRD. Drawing on two industrial-specialized towns (Humen and Xintang), the penultimate section addresses how the improvement of

© Springer Nature Singapore Pte Ltd. 2020
Y. Liu, *Local Dynamics of Industrial Upgrading*, Economic Geography,
https://doi.org/10.1007/978-981-15-4297-8_6

local capabilities and changing institutional–spatial conditions enables local firms to reshape their power relations with FIEs and global buyers. Key findings and theoretical implications are discussed in the last section.

6.2   Local Upgrading in the Apparel Industry

The apparel industry is primarily concerned with the design, manufacture, distribution, and retail of clothing products. In order to be consistent with the statistical term in China, the apparel industry in this chapter refers to clothes, underwear, footwear, headgear, processed feather, and other related products. It does not include textile, fabric, and machinery sectors. Generally, its technological and capital entry barriers are much lower than those in the automotive and electronics industries. While production technologies are increasingly standardized, the competitiveness of the apparel industry is more premised on the capabilities of design marketing and branding which are deeply embedded in popular culture, fashion trends, and geographically variegated consumer preferences (Aspers, 2010).

6.2.1   Global Tendencies in the Apparel Industry

In the past half century, the key episode of the apparel industry is a process of the global shift from old-established manufacturing hubs located in West Europe and North America to newly developing regions in Asia, Mexico, and Eastern Europe (Dicken 2007). The USA and EU, as well as Japan became the largest import markets. Most of the developing countries became exporters within globally dispersed production networks under the governance of Multi-Fiber Agreement (MFA, 1974–2005) and Agreement of Textile and Clothing (ATC).[1] The largest regional production network was constructed among East Asian NIEs.

During ATC and post-MFA period, the global trade of the apparel industry has consolidated on a limited number of large apparel exporters (Frederick and Gereffi 2011). In 1995, the 15 largest exporters accounted for 79% of the world export total. In 2009, the share of the top 15 increased to near 87%.[2] Together with Hong Kong, China became the largest exporter. Its share of exports grew from 22% in 1995 to 41% in 2009, representing an increase of export value from $33 billion to $123 billion.[3] Following China, the other developing countries (Bangladesh, India, Vietnam, Indonesia, Sri Lanka, Pakistan, and Cambodia) were increasing their export shares at the same period. Nevertheless, some other developing countries lost their market

---

[1] During 1995–2005, MFA was in a ten-year transition period under the Agreement on Textile and Clothing (ATC).

[2] The WTO data at: http://www.wto.org/english/res_e/statis_e/its2009_e/its09_toc_e.htm.

[3] World Trade Report 2010 from World Trade Organization, International trade and tariff data.

shares, such as countries in North and Central America, South Asia (e.g., Thailand and the Philippines) and Central Europe (e.g., Romania and Poland). While many East Asian latecomers have achieved substantial industrial growth, whether industrial upgrading has occurred and contributes significantly to regional development is still unclear.

Recent studies in China's apparel industry have shown the occurrence of industrial upgrading. As Frederick and Gereffi (2011) has argued, China has been a clear winner with significant technological upgrading according to its performance in global exports, the amount of imported machines, and the improvement of product quality, capacity, and diversity. Meanwhile, Mexico and Latin American countries are losing competitiveness because these regions lack integrated production networks, clusters, and sufficient investments in logistic facilities, machines, and so on. Apart from the advantage of lower production costs, China's apparel industry has also developed some non-cost-based competitiveness in timeliness and consistency. This competitiveness is supported by world-class distribution networks coordinated by intermediary trading firms from Hong Kong, Taiwan, and South Korea (Tewari 2006; Robinson 2010; Frederick and Gereffi 2011). A more recent study based on Sino-EU merchandise trade also reveals that China's apparel industry has been a highly competitive industry of this country. The revealed competitive index of textile products (including clothing products) was ranked fourth among all 14 key merchandises from 1996 to 2008 (Li et al. 2012). However, this remarkable national industrial growth should not be overemphasized because the content of local upgrading has yet to be unknown. If FIEs contribute to the majority of this achievement, local upgrading would be shallow and limited. Meanwhile, upgrading in the above studies is mainly measured by official statistics. The qualitative nature of upgrading, such as functional upgrading, is also unclear.

6.2.2 Potential of Upgrading in the Apparel Industry

In the apparel industry, the primary imperatives of global lead firms are to provide clothing products at a lower price, in a more flexible manner, and within a shorter time. Global lead firms premise their bargaining power not only from financial risk-taken during ordering and selling products, but also from expertise and lavish expenditures in advertising, building market channels, renting retail shops, and other operations as well (Sturgeon and Lester 2004b). These competences enable global lead firms to have dominant power (normally buying power) over their suppliers. Due to the very substitutable nature, suppliers suffer pressures and have to improve their performance through upgrading, because other lower-cost producers keep entering global markets and intensifying competition.

During the process of global industrial shift, developing regions are chosen as sites for industrial relocation from industrialized regions. As technologies in the apparel industry are less sophisticated, local firms can gradually upgrade through learning by doing (Hudson 1989; Ozawa 1991; Kim 1993; Gereffi and Korzeniewicz 1994). In order to maintain precise product definition and to avoid supplier failures, global lead firms have incentives to help local technological improvement. This effort nurtures substantial product and process upgrading in local suppliers, such as the rise of East Asian apparel firms (Gereffi 1999; Humphrey and Schmitz 2002b; van Grunsven and Smakman 2005). These latecomer firms were upgraded from simple subcontractors into OEM suppliers as the strategic partners of global lead firms, such as the Pou Chen Group and the Feng Tay Group from Taiwan in the sport wear industry. Some of them also grew up as intermediary trading firms coordinating subcontractors located in multiple developing regions, such as Itochu from Japan and the Li and Fung Group from Hong Kong (Gereffi 1999; Lüthje 2004; Hobday and Perini 2005; Yeung 2007b).

While product and process upgrading is possible during the global industrial shift, functional upgrading in latecomer economies is rather limited according to the GVC literature. This is because local functional upgrading will challenge the position of global lead firms. Hence, it tends to be restricted, constrained, and even deliberately blocked by global lead firms which have strong governance power over their suppliers (Humphrey and Schmitz 2002b; Bair and Gereffi 2003; Humphrey and Schmitz 2004). In the view of Gereffi (2001b: 1620), 'the main leverage in buyer-driven industries is exercised by marketers and merchandisers at the design and retail ends of the chain.' The changing trend of modern consumption, the alleged 'consumer fetishism,' also reinforces this asymmetry of power relations between buyers and suppliers. This trend increases the difficulty of latecomer firms in mastering core knowledge (e.g., fashion design and branding). Such knowledge is intensively contextualized in an immense variety of consumer demands which are subject to complex social and cultural preferences, including consumers' desire to express their tastes, identity, and lifestyles through their choices of clothing (Appadurai 1990; Aspers 2010; Tokatli and Omur 2010). Global lead firms reinforce their governance power through taking advantage of this industrial feature, such as the strategies of specializing in marketing and logistics, creating socialized values of brands, and spending lavishing budgets in advertising to make 'brand bully' over branded latecomers and so on (Klein 2002; Arvidsson 2005, 2007).

Following the logic of the above studies, local functional upgrading would be extremely difficult. However, these studies have been too deterministic and neglected the potential of local upgrading grounded in broader institutional–spatial contexts. There are two critical points needed to be recognized.

First, core knowledge in the apparel industry may not necessarily be confined within global buyers. Compared with the electronics industry, production technologies in the apparel industry are technologically less sophisticated and more standardized. Latecomer firms would not have great difficulties to approach production technologies. Global buyers have no intent to confine the diffusion of production technologies because they do not rely on manufacturing capabilities to sharpen their competitive edges. Global buyers have strong expertise in the skills of marketing and branding, but it is hard for them to block the diffusion of this knowledge. Latecomer firms can approach these skills through various learning channels, such as public research institutes, associational economies, educational training programs, professional service providers, and trans-regional communities of designers or talents (see my review in Chap. 2). Therefore, latecomer firms do not necessarily depend on global buyers for absorbing market knowledge from them. The problem is that latecomer firms need a critical mass (market and time) to accumulate profits, practice skills, and train designers so that they can internalize the skills of understanding, capturing and commercializing rapid changing fashion trends, and consumer preferences.

Second, markets are not a universally globalized field that is fully occupied by global lead firms. Previous studies tend to oversimplify markets as a uniform place controlled by global buyers which play as a gatekeeper. In fact, there are diverse market niches for latecomer firms to explore, particularly to those firms are located in a country with a huge domestic market. By identifying new market niches, especially the domestic market which may be less demanding and less regulated, latecomer firms may reduce dependence on global buyers and conduct functional upgrading. Indian and Turkish apparel firms have provided some positive cases in which local firms realized functional upgrading through exploring domestic and Russian markets (Tokatli 2003; Tokatli and Kizilgun 2004; Tokatli 2007; Tewari 2008). Specific to local firms in the PRD, regarding the market size of China and the liberalizing domestic environment, they do have an opportunity to practice functional upgrading. Moreover, local firms may improve their production capabilities and develop some non-cost-based advantages, such as competent supply networks, regional learning networks, and domestic distribution channels. The combination of these conditions may incentivize international buyers/traders to cooperative with local firms.

By recognizing these points, power relations between global buyers and local suppliers are possible to be reshaped. Local firms would have some alternative strategies to leverage the power of global buyers. They can diversify learning channels to reduce dependence on global lead firms. They also can nurture more synergy by venturing new market niches with international buyers. The next two sections draw on the case of the PRD's apparel industry to demonstrate this potential.

6.3 Development and Upgrading

This section starts by reviewing the national context and the formation of captive coupling in the PRD. I then trace the progress and features of industrial upgrading. The main analysis focus rests at the evolution of coupling on the basis of the relational framework proposed in Chap. 3.

6.3.1 National Contexts of the Apparel and Textile Industries

Before the opening reform in 1978, SOEs and COEs had dominated the apparel industry through nationalization. But the apparel industry achieved little progress in upgrading due to limited usage of modern machines and other production technologies (Hua 2008). After the reform, export-oriented development in the industry was highly encouraged by the central government in order to provide mass employment and accumulate foreign currency reserves (Jiang 2009). Key strategies were marketization, promotion of FDI, and structural adjustment in which SOEs withdrew from the apparel industry and created space for private and foreign firms. The central government turned to focus on coordinating two issues: rationing export quotas according to the regulation of MFA and leveraging export rebate rate.[4] The export rebate rate was frequently adjusted as an infant industrial policy to offset negative impacts from global markets (Jiang 2009). It was raised to 16% for helping domestic firms overcome the negative consequences of the global financial crisis in 2008.

The reform of marketization was expanded further in 1992. The disallowance of vertical integration in fiber-textile-apparel-retail chains was removed and various market regulations were set up for providing a competitive domestic market environment (Gu and Yang 1999; Hua 2008). For the first time, international branded-name retailers were allowed to enter into China.[5] These foreign branded firms spurred the growth of the domestic market and also provided a benchmark for local firms to learn.

While SOEs withdrew from the apparel industry, they consolidated in the textile industry. They received tremendous state investments in upgrading machines and equipment. From 1985 to 1997, Chinese SOEs invested over $1 billion annually in importing advanced textile-processing equipment (Chandra 1998). During the 2000s, China was the largest global recipient of circular knitting machinery (both single and double jersey), electronic flatbed knitting machines, shuttle-less looms, open-end rotors, and short-staple spinning machines (Frederick and Gereffi 2011: 84). Although these SOEs largely do not locate in the PRD, the technological upgrading of these textile SOEs does help domestic apparel firms reduce dependence on foreign firms in raw material procurement.

6.3.2 Formation of Captive Coupling

As the above elaboration has indicated, the apparel industry in the PRD was sharing a similar context with the electronics industry at the beginning of the reform. The difference is that local authorities were the key actors in promoting foreign investments in the apparel industry (Chen and Pu 1999). Prefectural and provincial governments preferred constructing industrial parks for higher-value-added industries such as the

---

[4]China set up the infant policy for the textile and apparel industries based on a floating rebate rate based on export values.

[5]The early pioneers were Giordano (Hong Kong), Nike (US), Stefanell (Italy), and Esprit (Hong Kong) in 1992; Adidas (German), Mexx (Holland), and Jeanswest (Hong Kong) in 1993; and Liz Claiborne (US) and Benetton (Italy) in 1994 (Gu and Yang 1999: 14).

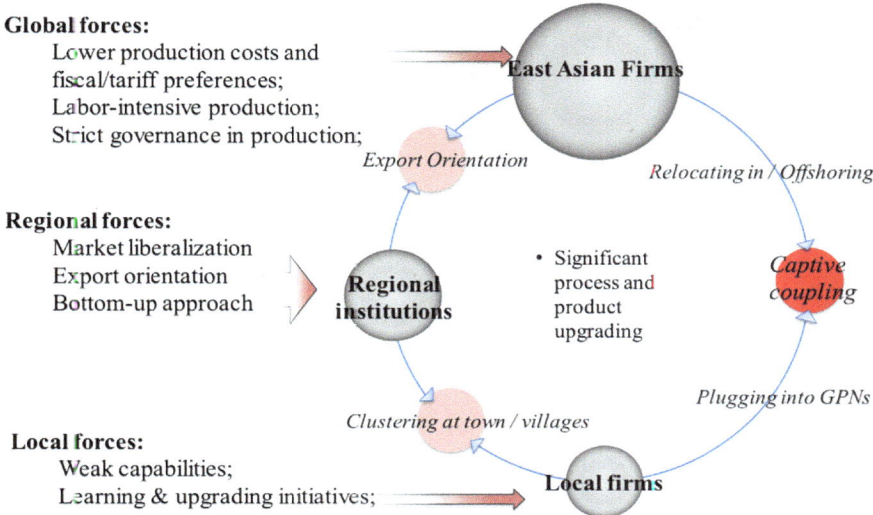

Global forces:
  Lower production costs and
  fiscal/tariff preferences;
  Labor-intensive production;
  Strict governance in production;

Regional forces:
  Market liberalization
  Export orientation
  Bottom-up approach

Local forces:
  Weak capabilities;
  Learning & upgrading initiatives;

Fig. 6.1 Captive coupling in the PRD's apparel industry in the 1980s. Compiled by author

electronics and chemical industries. Due to huge technology and market gaps, captive coupling was formed in the apparel industry as shown in Fig. 6.1.

Synergy was fostered between the global imperative of industrial relocation and the local initiative of industrialization, whereby the 'front-shop-back-factory' pattern was developed and dominated by Hong Kong apparel firms (see Chap. 4). Substantial industrial growth has been achieved during the 1980s. In 1991, the total industrial output of the apparel industry reached 73 million *yuan* which was mainly contributed by EPEs. During the 2000s, most of the EPEs were restructured into FIEs or local private enterprises. By 2008, EPEs only accounted for less than 1% of both industrial value added and export values in this industry (GDPBS 2009). In 2009, the total output value of the apparel industry had reached 125 billion *yuan*. Meanwhile, its export value reached $13.5 billion which accounted for 4.8% of the world total exports. This amount exceeded the total exports of many latecomer economies such as Bangladesh, Turkey, or India, respectively (see Fig. 6.2).

6.3.3 Characteristics of Upgrading and the Catching-up of Local Firms

After decades of rapid industrialization, upgrading in the apparel industry has been significantly achieved in the PRD (see my summary in Table 6.1). In terms of functional upgrading, many local firms have been upgraded from export-processing firms into OEM suppliers and then further into ODM and OBM suppliers. According

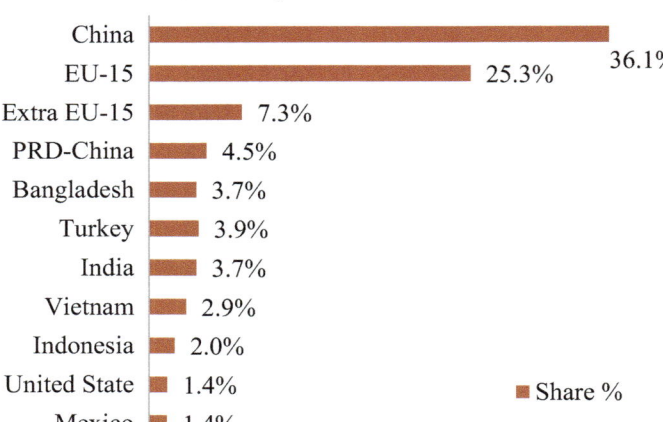

Fig. 6.2 Global top exporters of clothing products in 2009. *Source* World Trade Organization, International Trade Statistics 2009, at: http://www.wto.org/english/res_e/statis_e/its2009_e/its09_toc_e.htm

Table 6.1 Upgrading in the apparel industry in the PRD (author's fieldwork.)

Types of upgrading	Contents
Function	• Processing and assembly (1980s) → OEM (1990s) → ODM (2000s) → OBM (domestic → international)
Channel/network	• Truncated subcontracting base → global manufacturing center (4% of the world export in 2010) • Re-export through Hong Kong → world-class logistic infrastructure • Domestic wholesale hub → domestic fashion design center
Product	• Low value added → higher value added • Simple types → diverse, all product ranges, particularly, in sport wear, underwear, women wear, jeans, and leatherware
Process	• Hand-made, low-efficient machines → the most advanced production lines in domestic environment • Vertically integrated clusters • Mass production → more flexible and specialized

to records in Guangdong Apparel Industrial Association (GAIA) and Guangdong Apparel Designer Association (GADA), more than 60% of local firms which attended Canton Fair[6] have provided ODM business for global markets since 2007. There were over 2000 local firms which officially registered their own brands in GAIA by 2009.

---

[6]Canton Fair is held biannually in Guangzhou every spring and autumn, with a history of 53 years since 1957. The Fair is a comprehensive one with the longest history, the highest level, the largest scale, the most complete in exhibit variety, the broadest distribution of overseas buyers, and the greatest business turnover in China. see: http://www.cantonfair.org.cn/en/.

Table 6.2 Indicators of upgrading in the apparel industry in the PRD

Year	No. firms	IVA	IVA-E	IVA-L	NEE
	Unit	Billion	Million	Thousard	Person
1991	1138	5.2	4.6	16.9	269
2001	1513	12.3	8.2	21.3	382
2005	1992	20.7	10.4	30.1	360
2010	2527	55.51	21.97	68.23	322
2015	1924	63.86	33.19	98.99	335

Notes Currency is Chinese *yuan* at constant 2000 price. *IVA-E* industrial value-added per enterprise; *IVA-L* industrial value-added per employee; *NEE* number of employee per enterprises. All data refer to enterprises have an annual turnover over 5 million *yuan*
Guangdong statistic yearbook 1992, 1996, 2000, 2006, 2010

Most of them created more than one brand. By 2010, 18 local firms were entitled the National Famous Brands in China. Each of these 18 firms had an annual turnover over 1 billion *yuan* and at least owns 1000 retail stores in the China market.[7] As one of the largest local branded firms, Yishion has franchised 4000 stores and established 500 outlets in China and another 22 countries. The design capabilities of the apparel industry have also been upgraded. Hundreds of foreign firms have established design and brand-development centers in the PRD in collaboration with local partners. By 2010, there were 860 registered designers in GADA. About 100 of them have been awarded the Guangdong top designer, and 13 of them were entitled the China top designers. They regularly launch personal design shows in China and 6 of them have launched personal design shows in Paris, New York, and London in the past decade.[8]

Besides, function, product, and process upgrading are also achieved apparently which we can see through some concrete indicators of upgrading in Table 6.2. As shown in Table 6.2, from 1991 to 2009, the IVA of apparel firms increased dramatically from 5.2 billion *yuan* to 38.8 billion *yuan*. IVA per enterprise increased by sevenfold and IVA per employee also grew up with four times. In contrast, the number of employees per enterprise increased a bit firstly and then declined after 2005. This trend indicates that the production efficiency of firms and labor was both improved significantly and this achievement did not result from massive usage of labor. In 2009, the normal lead time of clothing-sample confirmation in the PRD has been improved to 20–30 days. This lead time was higher than the national average standard which was about 30–40 days (IARE 2010b).

While the electronics industry in the PRD has been led by FIEs, local (private) firms in the apparel industry have caught up and overtaken FIEs as the leader of the region. The watershed roughly appeared around 2000 (see Fig. 6.3). By 1999, FIEs still contributed to a major share with more than 67% IVA and 75% export value in

---

[7] *The competitiveness of Guangdong Apparel Industry in 2010,* at http://www.gdfz.org/?action-viewnews-itemid-4575.

[8] *Sources* interview with the vice chairman and an officer of GAIA on May 31, 2010, in Guangzhou; official Web site at: http://www.gdfz.org/.

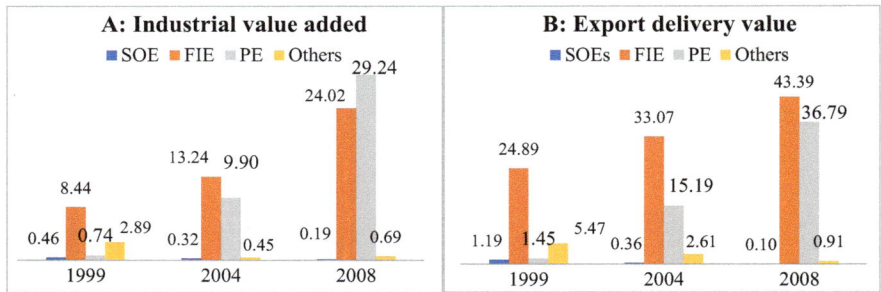

Fig. 6.3 Value creation of firms in PRD's apparel industry. *Notes* Currency is billion yuan at constant 1999 price. PE refers to private enterprises. Others refer to COEs and enterprises with annual turnover lower than 5 million. (The national economic census conducted in 2004 and 2008; Guangdong Industrial Census Yearbook 2000.)

the region. However, local firms subsequently reshaped the industrial profile. From 1999 to 2008, in terms of IVA, local firms increased by more than 40 times and exceeded FIEs in 2008. In terms of export value, local firms increased by 26 times and matched closely the contribution of FIEs in 2008. However, SOEs and other firms totally lost their influence within the same period.

A further comparison illustrates that local firms have developed their competitiveness with smaller sizes and more efficient performance (see Fig. 6.4). Between 1999 and 2008, the number of local firms mushroomed with a ten-time increase, but the labor intensity of local firms declined (see part A and B in Fig. 6.4). During the same period, FIEs had doubled their firm number and had a four-time increase of employees. This phenomenon led to a better performance of local firms in comparison with FIEs. From 1999 to 2008, the gap of IVA per enterprise between FIEs and local firms was almost bridged. Moreover, the IVA per employee of local firms remarkably increased from 26,000 *yuan* to 52,000 *yuan*, while the IVA per employee of FIEs decreased from 35,000 *yuan* to 30,000 *yuan*. This trend implies that local firms have been upgraded from a captive follower into a competent competitor.

6.3.4 From Captive to Cooperative Coupling

The above analyses show that local upgrading has been achieved to a substantial degree, particularly, during the 2000s. Examining changing multi-scalar forces and institutional–spatial contexts, this chapter argues that this local upgrading is produced by the formation of cooperative coupling between the PRD and the apparel GPNs. *Cooperative coupling* refers to a situation that local (latecomer) firms in a region develop a complementary relationship with foreign firms in GPNs (see details in Chap. 3).

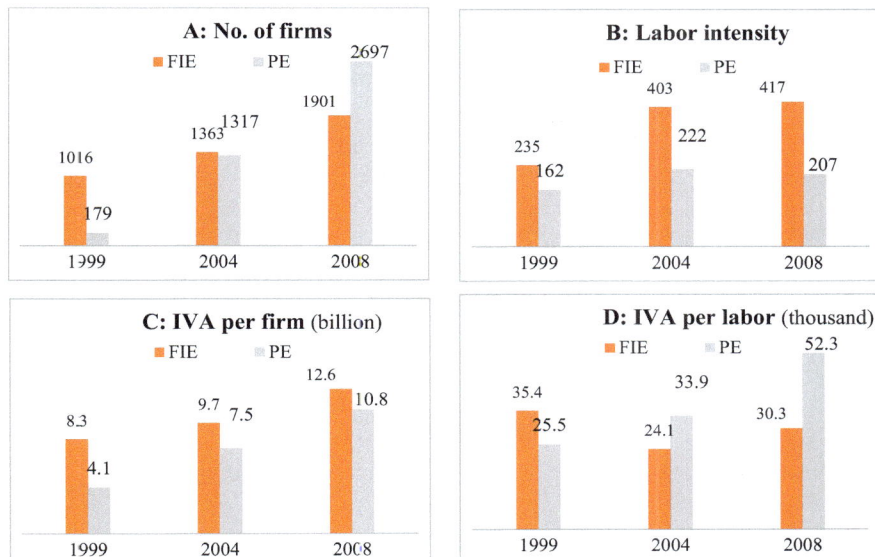

Fig. 6.4 Performance of firms in PRD's apparel industry. *Notes* Currency is billion yuan at constant 1999 price. PE refers to private enterprises. Others refer to COEs and enterprises with annual turnover lower than 5 million. Data at PRD level are unavailable. Regarding that the output of the apparel industry in the PRD accounted for more than 75% of the whole province throughout the 2000s, provincial level data were used to represent the PRD roughly. (The national economic census conducted in 2004 and 2008; Guangdong Industrial Census Yearbook 2000.)

The formation of cooperative coupling can be reflected by the changing configuration of firm types and number. By 1999, the majority of apparel firms comprised about 1000 FIEs. More than 60% of them were from Hong Kong, Taiwan, and Macao. More than half of them were wholly foreign-owned enterprises (GDPBS 2000a, 2000b). But this configuration was reshaped during the 2000s. Among 4700 apparel firms in 2008, there were about 3100 joint ventures comprising equity joint venture, contractual joint venture, and other forms of collaborative enterprises. 1755 of them were controlled by local private investors, while 1330 were controlled by foreign investors. This change meant that most of the firms had become cooperative forms of enterprises. This study has mapped the formation of cooperative coupling in the apparel industry as Fig. 6.5.

At the *global* scale, the imperative of global lead firms/buyers is shifting from offshoring into outsourcing. This change enables the PRD to transform into a global manufacturing hub rather than a subcontracting node which is controlled of East Asian CMs. The incentive of this changing imperative is derived from increasing competitive pressures and attraction from higher-value added in non-manufacturing segments (Gereffi 2001b; Bair and Gereffi 2003; Robinson 2010). In doing so, global buyers can concentrate their investments in fashion design, brandings, logistic, and

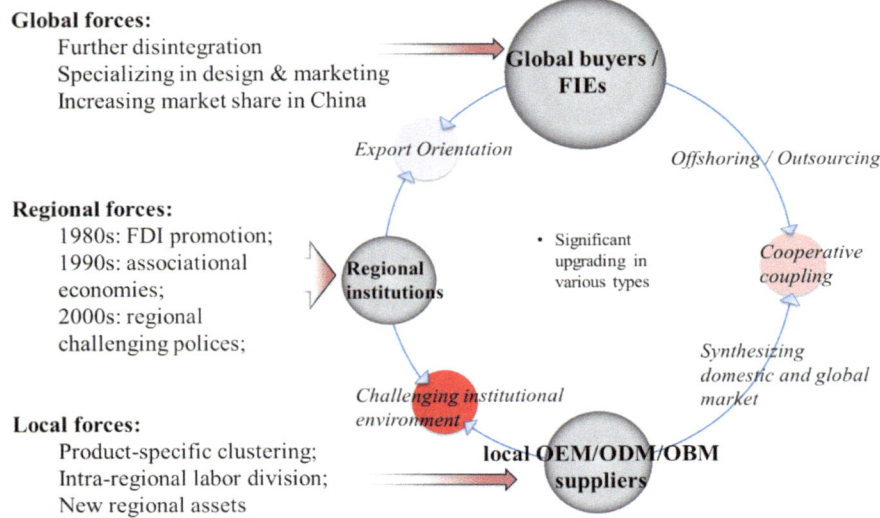

Global forces:
    Further disintegration
    Specializing in design & marketing
    Increasing market share in China

Regional forces:
    1980s: FDI promotion;
    1990s: associational
    economies;
    2000s: regional
    challenging polices;

Local forces:
    Product-specific clustering;
    Intra-regional labor division;
    New regional assets

Fig. 6.5 Cooperative coupling in the apparel industry in PRD in the 2000s. Compiled by author

marketing. The PRD has grasped this opportunity chiefly in three steps: (1) agglomerating East Asian CMs; (2) constructing regional supply networks and serving as the local suppliers of these CMs; (3) learning the capabilities of systematic integration and upgrading into CMs (OEM suppliers). For instance, the Hongying Apparel Group from Foshan has been serving a s a key supplier for two Taiwanese CMs (Pou Chen and Feng Tay) since the 1990s. By learning from them for years, Hongying mastered the capabilities of supply chain management and vertically integrated production. It then constructed its own supply networks and upgraded into a C M s a competitor of Pou Chen and Fend Tay. Hongying currently has been the strategic partner of many global brands such as Lee, Woolrich, Harley Davidson, Chicco, Energie, and so on.[9] With the growth of local CMs like Hongying, the PRD presently has become a global supply base for a wide range of global lead firms, like Nike, Adidas, Rebook, and Puma in the sport wear industry; Levis, Tommy Hilfiger, and Ralph Lauren in the leisurewear industry; as well as some luxury brands like Prada, Gucci, and Armani.

At the *regional* scale, associational economies have been developed since the 1990s through a bottom-up process. The first regional industrial association in the PRD was found by 25 local private firms and five industrial associations in towns in 1990. It was recognized by the provincial government as GAIA two years later. GADA was also established subsequently. After that more than 80 industrial associations have been established among all cities and industrial-specialized towns in the PRD by 2005. The key efforts of these industrial associations are to organize fashion festivals, trade fairs, and design competition within the PRD, such as Guangdong

---

[9]*Source* interview with an anonymous supplier of Hong Ying Apparel on June 25, 2010 in Foshan.

International Fashion Week and the Top-Ten Designer Competition of Guangdong.[10] Since 2000, these activities have attracted thousands of producers, global buyers, international designers, and traders to the PRD annually. Moreover, these associational economies actively built up collective learning networks by organizing various learning groups, public lectures, training programs, enterprise field trips international business trips, and so on. By devoting tremendous efforts, these associational economies helped local firms' bridge knowledge gaps in marketing and design. The CEO of Watermark Co. Ltd who is also one of the National Top-Ten Designers told me that:

> Normally it needs ten year to bring up a qualified fashion designer. A good designer needs a time to learn and a place to practice for years. In my view, the PRD should be one of the best locations for developing indigenous fashion designers in China. Obviously, we cannot compare the PRD with Paris, New York, Tokyo or Hong Kong. But at least, firms, industrial atmosphere and fashion events here provide us a chance. We can know the peers, present our works and learn from each other without going abroad necessarily (Interview, 100525, on 25th May 2010 in Guangzhou).

Her sentiment was echoed by the vice chairman of GAIA:

> It should be summarized that the most important contribution of our work is the construction of such an information-sharing and fashion-exhibition platform. It provides an opportunity for local entrepreneurs, designers and professionals to learn, cooperative and compete with each other. All these prosper the growth of the industry, particularly in the segments of design, exhibition and branding (Interview 100531, on 31 May 2010 in Guangzhou).

The above two quotations articulate the critical role of these associational economies in diversifying knowledge channels for local firms. A collective learning platform is gradually formed and helps local firms accumulate knowledge and practice what they have learned. Fashion events served as various types of temporary relational clusters that facilitated local learning processes and benefited the proliferation of local apparel firms, traders, suppliers, and designers at the regional scale.

At the *local* scale, domestic firms have managed to strengthen their capabilities and power on the basis of two important regional assets: dozens of product-specific clusters and a huge domestic market. Although these assets are not exclusive to foreign firms, local firms have socio-cultural advantages in utilizing these assets. Through an agglomeration effect, the PRD has developed 24 industrial-specialized towns by 2010. Different from the electronics industry, local firms are playing a dominant role in all these towns. Most of the towns are product-specific clusters, such as jeans in Xintan and Junan towns, woman wear in Chanshan and Humen towns, and underwear in Dali town (see Fig. 6.6). Serving as local integrated production networks, these clusters enable local firms to conduct flexible production or industrial specialization with certain collective efficiency. The owner of Xinyi Group is the

---

[10]*Source* the above data come from interviews with the vice chairman of the GAIA on May 31, 2010 in Guangzhou and the chairman of Humen Apparel Industrial Association on July 9, 2010 in Dongguan.

Fig. 6.6 Industrial clusters in the apparel industry in the Pearl River Delta. Compiled by author

chairman of Yanbu Underwear Industrial Association. He exemplified this point by telling me that:

> Yanbu now is called the 'China Sexy Town' according to our scale of production volume and good reputation in the lady underwear products. This industry was developed initially by a Hong Kong firm. Now the town becomes led by six local [private] spinoff firms from that Hong Kong firm. We got at least 150 competent local firms which have created owned brands for domestic markets. About ten of them have explored international markets… My firm almost can source all materials without going out of the town. There are also professional companies helping me to sort out some technological or design problems. More interestingly, we [the six key enterprises] often subcontract to each other for casting the time limit of orders (Interview 100530, on 30th May 2010 in Foshan).

6.3.5   New Assets and Challenges to Local Upgrading

Apart from regional supply networks and associational economies, the domestic market is another crucial emerging asset that facilitates the formation of cooperative coupling. This asset enables firms to sell own branded products in a more flexible and lower-cost manner (see case studies in Sect. 6.4). Today, China has become an arena of global competition rather than simply a global factory in the global apparel

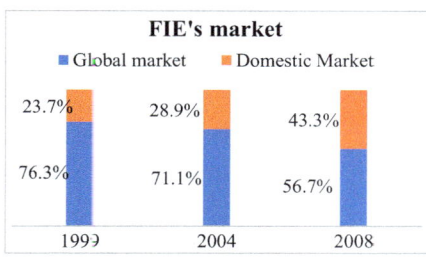
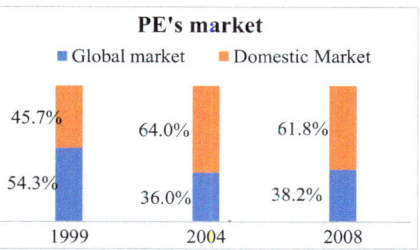

Fig. 6.7 Changing market structure in the apparel industry in the PRD. *Notes* Currency is Chinese yuan at constant 1999 prices. All enterprises have an annual turnover over 5 million yuan. (The national economic census conducted in 2004 and 2008; Guangdong Industrial Census Yearbook 2000.)

industry (Yu 2008; Ghosh and Rao 2010; Ma 2010). In 2010, 44 billion pieces of clothing products were produced by firms within China. Meanwhile, the domestic market sale reached 1.4 trillion *yuan* (not include import values).[11] Figure 6.7 shows that the important influence of the domestic market on firms in the PRD. Since 2004, the domestic market has accounted for more than 60% of local private firms' output. FIEs were also attracted to increase the share of the domestic market from 24% in 1999 to 43% in 2008.

Although there are emerging regional assets, there are also new challenges to the PRD's apparel industry. Since the mid-2000s, regional policy makers in the PRD attempted to spur local upgrading by proposing the dual-transformation policy (see Chap. 1). In Schmitz (2007) language, the regional institutional environment was shifting from supportive into challenging in the apparel industry. This industry was deemed as low value added and suggested to be relocated from the PRD. This challenging policy has generated tension between local authorities and firms in which local firms had to find a way to show that they had promising performance. Otherwise, they would be required to move to designated industrial parks without competent supply networks and less geographical accessibility (Yang 2012). The owner of Xinyi Group reflected this tension and the local responsive in his comments:

> Even though I am the chairman of the local industrial association and the owner of four local brands, my factories have been suggested to move to Shaoguan which is more than hundred miles away from Here [Yanbu town]. Moving to there will be a nightmare to my business. I even cannot find enough skilled workers to operate my machines, let alone the logistic problem of material procurement. I did try to argue but my voice was ignored. Hence I did a calculation carefully in front of local cadres. I showed them that I was producing more value added than many electronics firms here and contributed more taxation and wages to local economies. Only in so doing, they agreed to let me stay. It looked funny, but that was the true story. Eventually, some of my suppliers were still relocated (Interview 100530, on 30th May 2010 in Yanbu).

---

[11]Data from China National Apparel Association, http://www.cnga.org.cn/news/View.asp?NewsID=29607.

According to the policy, environmental-sensitive segments like dyeing and printing must be compulsorily relocated. Simply manufacturing firms without own brands, design functions or strategic partnership with global buyers were also suggested to relocate. As estimated by the vice chairman of GAIA, about eight to ten hundreds apparel firms were moved in the PRD within the past two years. Many local firms rushed to create their own brands and develop marketing partnerships with global buyers in order to fulfill the 'upgrading' requirement set by regional policy makers (see more details in Sect. 6.4).

In the formation of cooperative coupling, local firms caught up with FIEs and moved away from captive coupling. The channels of knowledge diffusion were proliferating, and more importantly, synergy between local firms foreign firms may be developed in more possibilities. However, the achievement of upgrading should not be overestimated. As told by the vice chairman of GAIA, local firms were mostly concentrated in low- and middle-end markets. Only a few of them were able to articulate their own brands in international markets, such as Yishion. Meanwhile, local firms are still significantly lagging behind global lead firms in marketing, branding, and logistics.

6.4 Upgrading Dynamics: Changing Rules of the Game

On the basis of cooperative coupling, power relations between local and foreign firms are changing in the PRD's apparel industry. On the one hand, local firms reduce dependency on global buyers in terms of technologies and markets. On the other hand, they have certain autonomous power in selecting partners and partnerships. Sustained by the improvement of indigenous capabilities and the emergence of new regional assets, local firms are able to develop more synergy with foreign partners and achieved functional upgrading eventually. This section exemplifies this change based on two cases of industrial towns: Humen town in Dongguan City and Xintang town in Guangzhou City.

The common thread of these two cases is that local firms tend to adopt a synthesized strategy through developing domestic and global markets simultaneously. In global markets, local firms strengthened their OEM/ODM business for learning state-of-art fashion trends and accumulating sufficient profits. Local firms used the domestic market as a low-cost experimental field and practice design and marketing skills. In doing so, they realized functional upgrading in the form of brand creation. It went through a step-by-step marketing process: wholesaling—dealership leasing—franchising—systematic marketing and branding. Meanwhile, global buyers were further attracted to the PRD because of the growing-up local supply capabilities and the large market size of China. More synergy was thus developed within cooperative coupling.

Institutional conditions between the cases are a bit different. Local firms in Humen more relied on domestic markets in the beginning and were backed up by proactive local authorities. In contrast, Xintang firms more depended on international markets and received limited supports from associational economies. More recently, they suffered pressures from the new industrial policy. To overcome this problem, Xintang firms deepened their embeddedness in GPNs and strengthened their bargaining power. Specifically, they adopted a multi-tasking strategy that performed multiple functions and certain technological cutting edges for global buyers. The case in Humen reflects the influence of regional assets on upgrading, while the case in Xintang articulates the importance of local entrepreneurship and upgrading opportunities embedded in GPNs.

6.4.1 Humen Town: Creating Fashion China

Located at the West Bay area of Dongguan city, Humen was merely a small fishing-based town before 1978. Based on the effort of proactive local authorities, the first EPE in China, Taiping Handbag Factory, was established in Humen. The demonstration effect of this factory-made Humen industrialized quickly. By the end of the 1980s, Humen had established about 600 EPEs in the apparel industry. In 2007, Humen agglomerated 350,000 workers employed by 2,000 apparel firms (Yu 2008: 6). By 2010, its total sale value of the apparel industry reached $2200 million and its export value grew to $600 million.[12] There were over 2000 local brands registered in Humen in which four were entitled as National Famous Brand and 22 were entitled as Provincial Famous Brand.[13] In fact, 1/3 of them were newly created due to the pressure of the 'dual-transformation' strategy. This problem is reflected by a chief officer of the Foreign Economy and Trading Office of Humen.

> As Humen has been a National Industrial Town, we did not have serious pressures under the new challenging policy. However, the apparel industry was still deemed as a low-value-added industry. So we must do something. We thus shut down all EPEs if they did not covert into a FIE or a normal enterprise in due call. We also encouraged local firms to establish an owned brand so that we could argue with the governments with some good reasons at least. Nevertheless, we still got about 50 sound brands in domestic markets and a couple of them in international markets. That earns the industrial reputation for Humen (Interview 100709, on 9 July 2010 in Humen).

The essence of Humen's accomplishments is a combination of a vertically integrated cluster, a proactive local state, and a domestic wholesale center. The vertically integrated production network comprises about 2000 manufacturers, 400 local suppliers, and 50 professional service providers (Yu 2008; Li 2011). This kind of agglomeration economies also exists among other clusters within the PRD.

Besides establishing the first EPE in China, local authorities (Humeng township governments) have devoted tremendous efforts in fostering a supportive institutional environment within the town, such as providing fiscal incentives, organizing business

---

[12]http://www.humen.gov.cn/hmnewsread.asp?newid=32910.

[13]The listed data of Humen in this subsection are sourced from the official Web site of local authority, at http://humen.gov.cn/.

Table 6.3 Organization of the Fumin Group (author's fieldwork and Fumin Group official Web site at http://en.fumin.com/index.asp.)

Subordinates	Contents
Fumin International Trade Town	Currently, 1000 shops, 6000 shops in maxima
Fumin Fashion Town	1500 shops
Fumin Underwear Market	About 500 shops
Fumin Business Pedestrian Street	
Fumin Drapery Market	600 shops
Fumin Footwear and Leatherwear Market	About 500 shops
Fumin Accessory Wholesale Center	About 800 shops
New Fumin Accessory Wholesale Center	Currently 200 shops, 1000 shops in maxima
Fumin Agricultural Product Wholesale Market	About 200 shops
Fumin Fashion News	Magazine, monthly
Fumin Commercial Center	Professional consultancy
Fumin Fashion Net	Official Internet Web site

trips and trade fairs, constructing educational systems and a knowledge-sharing platform, and so on. These efforts helped local firms in bridging knowledge gaps with global buyers particularly in supply chain management, production, and design. The most important effort was the development of local wholesale economies. Originally, Humen had merely several street bazaars selling smuggled electronics and clothing products from Hong Kong. In 1986, funded by local authorities, Humen commercial committee established the first apparel wholesale market in the PRD named as Fumin.[14] It soon attracted hundreds of retailers and became a famous domestic trading center. In the mid-1990s, the committee aggressively privatized the Fumin market into a business group which still had a close relationship with local authorities for receiving financial and institutional supports. By 2010, the Fumin Group has restructured into a modernized share-holding corporation owning 9 commercial buildings which accommodate 5000 shops in Humen (see Table 6.3). Encouraged by Fumin, 31 textile/apparel wholesale markets were established so far accommodating 12,000 shops.

By attracting thousands of traders and buyers, Humen's wholesale economies benefited local firms with two advantages. First, the arrival of international buyers allowed local firms to connect to international markets without the necessity of relying on Hong Kong traders. Second, local firms could explore the domestic market at a low cost. In the wholesale markets, Humen's local firms sold copycat products, imperfect products, and the surplus products from their OEM orders by putting a different trademark (Yu 2008). Overtime, some local firms accumulated sufficient profits and some skills in design and marketing. They started to invest in brand creation and hired professional designers to develop their own fashion styles. Eventually, some local firms realized functional upgrading and established their brands in the

---

[14]It means making people rich.

domestic market. This process can be reflected by a former vice CEO of Huedy. As he told me that:

> In those days [the 1980s], domestic demands exceeded supply totally. Once you could make clothes, people would buy them. After years, some foreign buyers appeared in Fumin markets and delivered order to us. Their orders were large and more profitable. Hence we quitted from the EPE partnership and worked for global buyers. By copying the designs from OEM orders, we made clothes quickly and sold them in Fumin. But soon, we were told that we could not do so anymore since it was illegal. We did some changes. We still copied the designs but made some revision on our own efforts. Since our products were partly designed by our own already, we decided to brand them. After years, we have learned a lot from buyers and our name also became famous in Humen. We then formally set up marketing and branding departments (Interview 100824, on 24 Aug 2010 in Dongguan).

The development of Yishion, the largest local OBM enterprise in Humen, demonstrates a step-by-step process of functional upgrading in brand creation. Yishion was derived from an EPE in the early 1990s. It was upgraded into an OEM firm and sold their own branded products in local wholesale markets before 1997. In 1999, Yishion withdrew from the wholesale market and articulated into domestic retail markets by leasing out the brand to dealers in hundreds of towns and counties. This strategy aimed to avoid direct competition with global lead firms in the main cities of China. Based on the dealership, Yishion sold their products in a large number of areas in China, though marginal profits were low. After years of profit accumulation, Yishion increased investments in branding and marketing by employing Pop stars in their new advertisements. Meanwhile, Yishion ceased dealership and started to construct retail networks (franchised stores). Around 2003, Yishion ventured into prefectural and capital cities to compete with branded lead firms. After accumulating enough profits, Yishion begun establishing owned outlets for sharpening its corporate image. This low-cost strategy helped Yishion earn a critical time for implementing functional upgrading. In 2005, Yishion ventured into international markets in Middle East by replicating the same strategy in China: wholesale market—dealership—franchised stores.

Based on the efforts of local authorities, the formation of clusters and the prosperity of wholesale economies, cooperative coupling has been developed in Humen. In production governance, most of the local private firms currently are providing OEM and ODM services simultaneously. They are able to manage international supply chains and their products are qualified according to international industrial standards.

In design and branding, Humen has not been only a manufacturing node within the apparel GPNs, but also been upgraded into a design and branding center in China. The registered number of designers in the Designer Association of Humen increased from 400 in 2004 to more than 1000 in 2010 (Yu 2008: 51). Many of them are former designers working in global lead firms. For instance, Yishion hired a chief design from H&M as well as two top designers in China. Another example comes from Suosha. This local firm has specialized in middle-end women dress. It has established four retail stores in Paris and hundreds of franchised stores in the central cities of China. The owner of Suosha is one of the top designers in Humen. In order to explore international markets, she hired a designer from a French sound brand during a business trip organized by local authorities in 2004. The designer was attracted by the industrial and market potential in the PRD. These designers actively attend various business events and training sessions organized by local authorities. New and young designers are keen in participating in the Humen International Fashion Design Competition every year. Once they win the competition, they will be sought and hired by local firms.

To summarize the Humen case, market opportunities, local supply capabilities, proactive authorities, and wholesale economies have helped local firms move away from captive coupling. It is the combination of these institutional–spatial conditions that sustains the functional upgrading of local firms in Humen.

6.4.2 Xintang Town: Deepening Embeddedness

Located 50 km away from the North of Humen, Xintang town is hosting about 3 thousand firms specialized in jeans products in which 1/3 are FIEs, comprising about 200,000 workers. In 2009, its apparel industrial outputs reached $3.2 billion in which $1.5 billion came from export value. These amounts accounted for 30% the total exports of jeans products in China (Guo and Wang 2010:12).[15] There are 1200 brands registered in Xintang, including one National Famous Brands and four Provincial Famous Brands. An integrated local production network has been developed covering the segments of textile cutting, dyeing, sewing, washing, and patterning. In the past five years, about 60 thousand sets of machines were installed in Xintang, such as high-speed tow dyeing machines, multi-wefts rapier weaving machines, and automatic jeans washing lines.[16]

Different from Humen, proactive local authorities were interested in the electronics and automotive industries and provided rare supports for Xintang's jeans industry. Local wholesale economies did not come to exist in Xintang until 2006. Therefore, local jeans firms focused on utilizing social ethnic ties, local entrepreneurship, and opportunities embedded in GPNs in their pursuit of upgrading.

The economic takeoff of the Xintang town was initiated by a local entrepreneur who introduced his Hong Kong relative to establish the first EPE in the town in 1986. The relative relocated 40 sewing machines from Hong Kong to the EPE. Cooperating with another 11 countrymen, the entrepreneur loaned from local village committees, and recruited rural workers for extending the production scale of the EPE. Through this example effect, more and more Hong Kong relatives and businessmen were introduced to Xintang. Local entrepreneurs also mushroomed simultaneously. Xintang was gradually specialized in jeans products and led by Hong Kong firms (Zhu and Li, 2004). Since the 1990s, local entrepreneurs directly established trading agencies in Hong Kong for receiving orders from global buyers. This effort enabled local

---

[15]*Source* interview with the vice mayor of Xintang town on 21 May 2010 in Guangzhou.
[16]http://www.xintang.gov.cn/Item/1551.aspx.

firms to bypass the market control of Hong Kong firms which had little power to block this local effort. The owner of Changjiang Clothing and Wash Ltd has told the vulnerability of Hong Kong firms' power:

> After a couple of years, we figured out that making jeans was not so difficult. So why we still needed to work for Hong Kong men. We [the 11 entrepreneurs] soon decided to set up a trade office in Hong Kong directly. We mobilized our villagers to tell their relatives overseas that they did not need to go to Hong Kong anymore. They just came to Xintang to deliver orders directly. We could provide competent goods with a lower price already (Interview 100427, on 27 April 2010 in Xintang).

Local entrepreneurs are the key drivers in developing cooperative coupling. All of the eleven entrepreneurs have provided OEM services for global buyers since the 1990s. They gradually specialized in different segments or products for avoiding internal competition. Some of the entrepreneurs chose to specialize in dyeing, printing and washing segment for strengthening the supply base of Xintang. Some of them consolidated cooperative partnership in a few group of global buyers and strengthened their production capabilities. Hence, they got more learning opportunities from global buyers on the basis of mutual trusts and industrial reputations. Some of them collaborated with global buyers to venture into the domestic market. Particularly, some local firms adopted a strategy of multi-tasking by shaping technological edges and cooperating with a wide range of buyers. This strategy helped local firms develop design and marketing capabilities in functional upgrading. These local enterprises have become the mainstay of Xintang's apparel industry, such as Conshing, Zengzhi, and Golden Rhino. Their patterns were imitated by many other local firms. This chapter uses the case of Conshing to illustrate the local trajectory of upgrading.

Conshing has been upgraded into an ODM/OBM company integrated with some textile-processing segments in the jeans industry.[17] In its pursuit of upgrading, it adopted two strategies to leverage the power of global buyers and bargain for more upgrading opportunities. First, it developed technological cutting edges in jeans washing technics and green production. Conshing built up the largest jeans washing center in the PRD with about 150 sets of automatic machines and 100 skilled washing talents. In order to improve production environment, Conshing certificated with the ISO 9001 in 2002, the ISO 14001 in 2003, and the GOTS[18] in 2005. It heavily invested 30 million *yuan* in constructing an internal sewage disposal system which recycled 99% wastewater. Conshing further invited Novozymes, a famous Danish biochemical corporation, to set up a collaborative laboratory for developing some high-end solutions in jeans washing and wastewater processing. In doing so, Conshing's jeans products were qualified in a wide range of environment criteria and international industrial standards. This advantage enabled Conshing to have certain

---

[17] Source: interview with a vice CEO of Conshing on July 2, 2010 in Xintang, Guangzhou.

[18] The Global Organic Textile Standard (GOTS) is recognized as the leading processing standard for textiles made from organic fibers worldwide. It defines high-level environmental criteria along the entire supply chain of organic textiles and requires compliance with social criteria as well.

bargaining power in selecting partners, rather than be passively selected and controlled by global buyers. For instance, Conshing frequently bargained for using its own components, materials, and designs, instead of procuring designated materials provided by the buyers. In other words, Conshing has better control over its production/supply chain management, comparing with many other local apparel firms in the PRD.

The second strategy was to cooperate with partners in different positions within GPNs for developing ODM/OBM capabilities. Since the 2000s, Conshing has actively worked for first-tier global buyers which have well-known branded names such as Polo, LEE, Abercrombie and Fitch, Hollister, GUESS and Express. These buyers tended to enforce stricter governance in supply chain management with fixed profit margins. Under this control, Conshing earned less than supplying some unknown branded firms or international traders. But Chonshin insisted on this partnership for learning state-of-art fashion trends and improving industrial reputation. Meanwhile, Conshing strategically worked with second-tier global buyers which were developing both China and international markets, such as Vera Moda, Only, Jack & Jones, Texwood and Clride. N. Empowered by strong technological competence, Conshing bargained with these second-tier buyers for increasing ODM content and providing joint-learning programs, such as organizing field trips in China or attending international fashion salons. Mutual interests were thus developed because these buyers were also interested in China markets and would like to know more.

After years of accumulation, Conshing established its own brand 'Conshing Jeans' in China after 2000. The new brand did not create much tension to Chonshing's customers. Conshing provided detail assessment reports about the market positioning of its new brand. It also invited customers to visit factories regularly for securing their copyrights. This effort earned a good reputation for Conshing and lowered tension within the partnership. In 2006, a Hong Kong-based customer of Conshing invited a France design institute and actively cooperated with Conshing for venturing the domestic market. A new brand (Hitwon) was created and positioned in a specific market niche in Chonshing's product range. In sum, Conshing fostered much synergy with global buyers through synthesizing various resources within GPNs. This effort has helped it realize functional upgrading (from OEM to ODM and brand creation) without creating much tension in cooperative coupling.

6.5 Evolutionary Nature of Strategic Coupling

While previous studies hold a pessimistic view of local functional upgrading in the apparel industry, the PRD case offers an alternative reading. Local firms in the region have managed to move away from captive coupling, overtake FIEs, and eventually achieved functional upgrading to a certain degree. But this progress should not be overemphasized, since most of the branded local firms were relatively small in comparison with incumbent global lead firms. Most of them had not articulated into global markets with their own brands yet.

Associational economies, product-specific clusters, and the huge domestic market were all important institutional–spatial conditions that sustained the formation of cooperative coupling. The combination of these conditions enables the PRD to become a powerful player at the lower end of the apparel GPNs. Cooperative coupling mattered because it endows local firms more autonomy in selecting partners and upgrading strategies. It also allowed local firms to foster more synergy with their foreign partners; and eventually reduces the asymmetry of power relations. These power relations were different from the ones in captive coupling. Local firms were coupling to foreign firms for advanced knowledge and co-development, rather than just for profits to survive. Foreign firms gradually treated local firms as strategic partners, while not subcontractors/suppliers.

The apparel industry in the PRD showed the variety of local upgrading strategies beyond the limited options offered in the GVC literature and development studies (e.g., collective action and innovation). The cases of Humen and Xitnang towns exemplify that the more capable are local firms in channeling knowledge or synthesizing assets, the more possibly will they achieve upgrading. They demonstrate the potential upgrading opportunities embedded within GPNs, which sheds light on alternative pathways of achieving industrial upgrading and regional development.

References

Appadurai, A. (1990). Disjuncture and difference in the global cultural economy. *Public Culture*, 2, 1–24.

Arvidsson, A. (2005). Brands: A critical perspective *Journal of Consumer Culture, 5*, 235–258.

Arvidsson, A. (2007). The logic of the brand. *European Journal of Economic and Social Systems, 20*, 99–115.

Aspers, P. (2010). Using design for upgrading in the fashion industry. *Journal of Economic Geography, 10*, 189–207.

Bair, J., & Gereffi, G. (2001). Local clusters in global chains: The causes and consequences of export dynamism in Torreon's blue jeans industry. *World Development, 29*(11), 1885–1903.

Bair, J., & Gereffi, G. (2003). Upgrading, uneven development, and jobs in the North American apparel industry. *Global Networks-a Journal of Transnational Affairs, 3*(2), 143–169.

Chandra, P. (1998). Competing through Capabilities. Strategies for Global Competitiveness of Indian Textile Industry. *Economic and Political Weekly, 34*, 17–24.

Chen, J, & Pu, X. (Eds.). (1999). *The fifty years of Guangdong- official statistics report of Guangdong provincial government*. Beijing: China Statistics Press. (in Chinese).

Dicken, P. (2007). *Global shift: Mapping the changing contours of the world economy* (5th ed.). London: Sage.

Frederick, S., & Gereffi, G. (2011). Upgrading and restructuring in the global apparel value chain: why China and Asia are outperforming Mexico and Central America. *International Journal of Technological Learning, Innovation and Development, 4*(1/2/3), 67–95.

GDPBS. (2000a). Guangdong statistic year book of industry 1999. Beijing: Guangdong Provincial Bureru of Statistics. (in Chinese).

GDPBS. (2000b). Guangdong statistic yearbook 1999. Beijing: Guangdong Provincial Burenu of Statistics. (in Chinese).

GDPBS. (2009). Guangdong economic census in 2008. Beijing: Guangdong Provincial Burean of Statistic. (in Chinese).

GDSY. (2000). Guangdong statistic yearbook. Beijing: Guangdong Provincial Burenu of Statistics. (in Chinese).

GDSY. (2010). *Guangdong Statistic Yearbook.* Beijing: Guangdong Provincial Burenu of Statistics. (in Chinese).

Gereffi, G. (1999). International trade and industrial upgrading in the apparel commodity chain. *Journal of International Economics, 48,* 37–70.

Gereffi, G. (2001). Shifting governance structures in global commodity chains, with special reference to the internet. *American Behavioral Scientist, 44*(10), 1616–1637.

Gereffi, G., & Korzeniewicz, M. (1994). *Commodity chains and global capitalism.* USA: Greenwood.

Ghosh, M., & Rao, S. (2010). Chinese accession to the WTO: Economic implications for China, other Asian and north American economies. *Journal of Policy Modeling, 32*(3), 389–398.

Gu, Q.-L., & Yang, Y.-X. (1999). The development of the china apparel industry. Beijing: China Textile University and Harvard Center of Textile and Apparel Research.

Guo, S.-K., & Wang, H. (2010). Suggestions for building a innovation system of jeans industrial cluster in Xintang Town. *Enterprise Vitality, 6*(2), 12–16. (in Chinese).

Hill, R. C., & Fujita, K. (1996). Flying geese, swarming sparrows or preying hawks? Perspectives on east Asian industrialization. *Competition and Change, 1*(3), 285–298.

Hobday, M., & Perini, F. A. d. B. (2005). *Latecomer entrepreneurship: A Policy Perspective.* Paper presented at the IPD Task Force Meeting, Rio de Janeiro, Brazil, 17–19, 2005.

Hua, M. (2008). *The modern history of China apparel industry.* Beijing: China Textile Press.

Hudson, R. (1989). *Wrecking a region: State policies, party politics and regional change in north east England.* London: Pion.

Humphrey, J., & Schmitz, H. (2002b). How does insertion in global value chains affect upgrading in industrial clusters? *Regional Studies, 36,* 1017–1027, https://doi.org/10.1080/0034340022000022198.

Humphrey, J., & Schmitz, H. (2004). Chain governance and upgrading: taking stock. In H. Schmitz (Block), *Local Enterprises in the Global Economy* (pp. 349–381). UK: Edward Elgar.

IARE (2010b). *Industrial Analysis Report—The Apparel Industry in Guangdong.* Guangzhou: Industrial Research Club, www.industrybbs.com.

Jiang, X. (1999). Industrial restructuring and industrial policies: Reflection after the shortage economy (in Chinese). *Review of Economic Research (Jing Ji Can Kao Yan Jiu), Z1,* 16–26.

Kim, W. B. (1993). Industrial restructuring and regional adjustment in asian NIEs. *Environment and Planning A, 25,* 27–46.

Klein, N. (2002). *No logo: Taking aim at the brand bullies.* Knopf Canada: Picador.

Li, J.-H. (2011). A study on the interactive mechanisms of industrial clusters and regional industrial upgrading—Case in humen apparel industrial clusters (In Chinese). *Journal of Guangdong University of Business Studies, 1,* 70–76.

Li, L., Dunford, M., & Yeung, G. (2012). International trade and industrial dynamics: Geographical and structural dimensions of Chinese and Sino-EU merchandise trade. *Applied Geography, 32,* 130–142.

Lüthje, B. (2004). Global production network and industrial upgrading in China: The case of electronics contract manufacturing.

Ma, H.-H. (2010). *International competitiveness of China's apparel industry: A global value chain perspective (in Chinese).* Beijing: China Geology University Press.

Ozawa, T. (1991). Japan in a new phase of multinationalism and industrial upgrading: Functional integration of trade, growth and FDI. *Journal of World Trade, 25,* 43–60.

Ozawa, T. (2005). *Institutions, industrial upgrading, and economic performance in Japan- the 'Flying-Geese' paradigm of catch-up growth.* Northampton, Massachusetts: Edward Elgar.

Robinson, I. (2010). The China road: Why China is beating Mexico in the Competition for U.S. Markets. *New Labor Forum, 19*(3), 51–56.

Schmitz, H. (2004). *Local enterprises in the global economy.* UK: Edward Elgar.

Schmitz, H. (2007). Reducing complexity in the industrial policy debate. *Development Policy Review, 25*(4), 417–428.

Sturgeon, T., & Lester, R. (2004b). The new global supply-base: New challenges for local suppliers in east Asia. In S. Yusuf, A. M. Anjum., & K. Nabeshima (Eds.), *Global production networking and technological change in east Asia*. Oxford UK: Oxford University Press.

Tewari, M. (2006). Is price and cost competitiveness enough for apparel firms to gain market share in the world after quotas? *Global Economy Journal, 6*(4), 1–46.

Tewari, M. (2008). Varieties of global integration: Navigating institutional legacies and global networks in india's garment industry. *Competition & Change, 12*, 49–67.

Tokatli, N. (2003). Globalization and the changing clothing industry in Turkey. *Environment and Planning A, 35*, 1877–1894.

Tokatli, N. (2007). Asymmetrical power relations and upgrading among suppliers of global clothing brands: Hugo Boss in Turkey *Journal of Economic Geography, 7*, 67–92.

Tokatli, N., & Kizilgun, O. (2004). Upgrading in the global clothing industry: Mavi jeans and the transformation of a Turkish firm from full-package to brand-name manufacturing and retailing. *Economic Geography, 80*(3), 221–240.

Tokatli, N., & Omur, K. (2010). Coping with the changing rules of the game in the global textiles and apparel industries: evidence from Turkey and Morocco. *Journal of Economic Geography, 10*(2), 209–229. https://doi.org/10.1093/jeg/lbp033.

van Grunsven, L., & Smakman, F. (2005). Industrial restructuring and early industry pathways in the Asian first-generation NICs: the Singapore garment industry. *Environment and Planning A, 37*(4), 657–680.

Yang, C. (2012). Restructuring the export-oriented industrialization in the Pearl River Delta, China: Institutional evolution and emerging tension. *Applied Geogrpahy, 32*, 143–157.

Yeung, H. W.-C. (2007). Remaking economic geography: Insights from East Asia. *Economic Geography, 83*(4), 339–348.

Yu, Y.-H. (2008). *Road to the fashion: Transformation of apparel industrial cluster in humen*. Guangzhou: Guangdong People Press. (in Chinese) (Development of Guangdong Industrial Specialized Towns).

Zhu, C.-S., & Li, X.-N. (2004). Status quo of jeans industrial clusters in China. *Shandong Textile Science and Technology, 121*(3), 29–32. (in Chinese).

Chapter 7
Reciprocal Coupling and Industrial Upgrading in the Automotive Industry: The Balance of Interplay

7.1 Situating the Automotive Industry in the PRD

Scholars in the literature of industrial governance have argued that the automotive industry is subject to both captive and modular governance. Automakers play a dominant role due to high asset specificity and the complexity of inter-firm knowledge transactions. Auto part suppliers are required to provide competent manufacturing works so as to comply with a wide range of parameters and criteria set by automakers (Gereffi and Korzeniewicz 1994; Schmitz 2004; Gereffi et al. 2005; Sturgeon et al. 2009; Sturgeon and Biesebroeck 2011). This pattern of governance posts great challenges to latecomer firms who have to be constantly qualified as suppliers. It would be extremely difficult for latecomer firms to catch up and upgrade into an automaker, particularly when the global automotive is currently dominated by a few giant automotive groups such as General Moto, Ford, Toyota, Volkswagen, Daimler-Chrysler, and Nissan-Renault. Scholars in this camp tend to believe that the market and technology gaps between latecomer firms and lead firms are rather large and almost unbridgeable. But what if the primary markets are domestic rather than foreign?

Different with the governance literature, some geographical studies have argued that strong national interventions can serve as a source of crucial power to counteract the control of global lead firms and then foster domestic upgrading (Harwit 1995; Sit and Liu 2000; Hudson 2002; Pavlínek 2003; Liu and Dicken 2006; Barnes and Kaplinsky 2007). The logic is that proactive states may alter the pattern of knowledge diffusion by exchanging their possessed territorialized assets with advanced technologies possessed by lead firms (automakers). The development of China's automotive industry has provided such a case in which this latecomer country utilizes its huge domestic market to bargain with lead firms for more knowledge sharing and technological co-development. This process was termed as 'obligated embeddedness' in Liu and Dicken (2006)'s study which revealed the importance of firm–state relations in fostering domestic industrial development. However, interactions in such a firm–state relation and its consequences to local upgrading are still unclear. How

© Springer Nature Singapore Pte Ltd. 2020
Y. Liu, *Local Dynamics of Industrial Upgrading*, Economic Geography,
https://doi.org/10.1007/978-981-15-4297-8_7

will lead firms strategically react to strong national intervention? What if the upgrading of local firms proposes new challenges to lead firms? This chapter attempts to provide an answer to this point.

Specific to the China's contexts, the appearance of proactive states a crucial factor that reshapes the pattern of integration between domestic firms and global automakers. According to my conceptualization in Chap. 3, this integration represents a form of *reciprocal coupling* through which actors develop partnerships for exchanging technology and market resources possessed by each actor. In the case of the PRD, it specifically refers to a circumstance in which automakers are complied with specific criteria from the central government so as to get access to the China market. Situated in such a context, this chapter focuses on two issues: (1) the interplay between SOEs, local suppliers, and lead firms within the coupling; (2) the mechanism of upgrading, power dynamics, and strategic responses result from this interplay. The overall attempt is to show that local upgrading in the PRD's automotive industry is contingent on the balance of power relations between the coupled firms, rather than on the sole governance power in either lead firms or proactive states.

7.2   Global Governance Imperatives or National Initiatives in the Automotive Industry

The global automotive industry is predominantly 'an industry of very large corporations, which has increasingly organized their activities on transnationally integrated lines. In so doing, they engage very closely—sometimes collaboratively, sometimes conflictually—with national governments' (Dicken 2007: 278). The significance of this industry rests in its scale in terms of input/output, employment, revenue, and its linkages to many other manufacturing industries and services. This section begins with an overview of ongoing global tendencies and the organizational pattern of the automotive industry. The implications for industrial upgrading are analyzed in relation to the governance pattern and the political economy within GPNs. This effort helps us understand why reciprocal coupling is possible to be developed in the automotive industry.

7.2.1   Industrial Governance in the Automotive Industry

The automobile industry is an industry in which assemblers and suppliers construct complex production networks at a global scale. The automotive industry stands in stark contrast to the apparel and electronics industries which are high-volume and consumer-orientated manufacturing. In the contemporary process of global industrial shifts, the global organization of vehicle production has three general tendencies which have important geographical implications for upgrading.

First, the automotive industry is characterized by an enduring organizational convergence of automakers. Through waves of mergers, acquisitions, and equity-based alliances in the 1990s and the 2000s, global markets were dominated by twelve lead firms from six countries: the USA, Germany, France, Italy, Japan, and South Korea (Sturgeon et al. 2009). By 2010, the top 10 automakers accounted for 72% of the world sales of motor vehicles.[1] This trend reinforces the governance power of automakers which have developed strong capabilities to orchestrate GPNs that span multiple production regions. It further spurs the innovation of vehicle platforms which enable a single series of vehicle model to be globally produced among differentiated markets. Moreover, leading automakers have blunted efforts to establish the sort of industry-level technical and business process standards. This standardization benefits automakers by raising technological entry barriers and imposing more asset specificity on their suppliers. But the available platform solution also provides a shortcut for latecomer firms to adopt a vehicle platform without investing in its prototype development.

The second tendency is that the political economy of this industry is increasingly influential and gradually develops the global fragmentation and variegation of production systems among different regions and countries. Each locality feeds a few assembly plants that manufacture certain vehicle models for a regional or national market This tendency of 'build where they sell' is caused by market saturation in developed countries, the sensitivity to logics costs, and more importantly by political pressuring in both host and home countries (Freyssenet and Lung 2000; Jurgens and Krzywdzinski 2009; Sturgeon and Biesebroeck 2011). Due to the large scale of industrial organization and economic multiplier effects in jobs and revenues, the automotive industry is often treated as a 'must develop and retain industry'. In both developed or developing countries, substantial state interventions are devoted for avoiding the risk of political backlash when the value of imported vehicles becomes too large and threatens the survival of domestic producers (EIU 1997; Liu and Deng 2003; Sturgeon and Florida 2004). This tendency explains why automakers in North America do not concentrate all their production plants in Mexico, despite lower operation costs.

The third tendency is the imperative of regionalization of production networks at a global scale. The inter-firm transactions of technologies in automotive industry are diverse, complicated, and hard to be codified. Automakers require intensive interactions and co-development with their suppliers within a manageable geographical distance (Gereffi et al. 2005; Frigant and Layan 2009). The prevalence of technology modularization helps automaker reduce geographical dependency, but a strong partnership between assemblers and first-tier suppliers is still developed in this industry. Since the mid-1980s, global suppliers have emerged through the acquisition of firms with complementary assets and geographies so as to resonate with the globalization of assembly plants. As automakers set up final assembly plants in new locations and try to leverage common platforms over multiple products and in different markets, they request suppliers (normally first-tier ones) to offshore with them. This strategy causes

---

[1] http://auto.gasgoo.com//News/2011/03/020839233923298157278.shtml.

a process known as the 'follow sourcing' of global suppliers (Humphrey and Schmitz 2000; Humphrey 2003; Sturgeon et al. 2008). The prevalence of just-in-time system and lean production systems reinforces the imperative of follow sourcing because these systems require closer cooperation between assemblers and suppliers to main a quick production beat with the least inventory (Imai 1997; Hudson 2002; Lung et al. 2004; Sturgeon and Lester 2004a). Therefore, an imperative of the regionalization of production networks is developed which gives rise to opportunities for local firms (in latecomer regions) to participate in. The formation of regional production networks provides a large number of channels for knowledge spillover whereby local firms can learn knowledge about entire production systems instead of a single processing segment.

7.2.2 Knowledge Sharing: When Automakers Meet State Intervention

The tendencies above constitute the complex economic geographies of the automotive industry. The automotive GPNs tend to be organized regionally and nationally with bulky final assembly plants. Lead firms in these GPNs are often surrounded by a large number of part/model-specific suppliers to ensure timely delivery (e.g., engines, transmission and seats). Lighter/generic parts are produced at a distance to take advantage of scale economies and lower production costs (e.g., batteries and tiers). These regionalized production networks are not isolating within the region, but interconnected through various global pipelines in a nested and nonlinear structure (see Fig. 7.1).

Technologies of assembly and auto part manufacturing tend to be entrenched within these regionalized networks, but are exclusive to outsiders particularly among the networks constructed by Japanese automakers (Cusumano 1985; Ahmadjian and Lincoln 2001). Although local firms have been plugged into GPNs, they are often marginalized outside the core of the networks and only achieve some trivial upgrading in processing less-sophisticated components (Freyssenet and Lung 2000; Kotabe et al. 2003; Sturgeon and Florida 2004). How can local firms identify a better position within these networks? According to the industrial governance literature, opportunities are limited due to the overwhelming governance power of lead firms (automaker and their key suppliers). The governance power of automakers mainly derives from three sources: (1) technological capabilities in parameter setting with high asset specificity; (2) capabilities in systematic integration and coordination; and (3) regulatory advantages based on industrial standardization (Humphrey and Schmitz 2000; Schmitz 2007; Sturgeon et al. 2008; Frigant and Layan 2009; Sturgeon and Biesebroeck 2011). Local firms would meet extremely hard difficulties in bridging technological gaps if they do not heavily invest in improving technological competence. Moreover, technological lock-in will be developed due to high asset specificity. Local

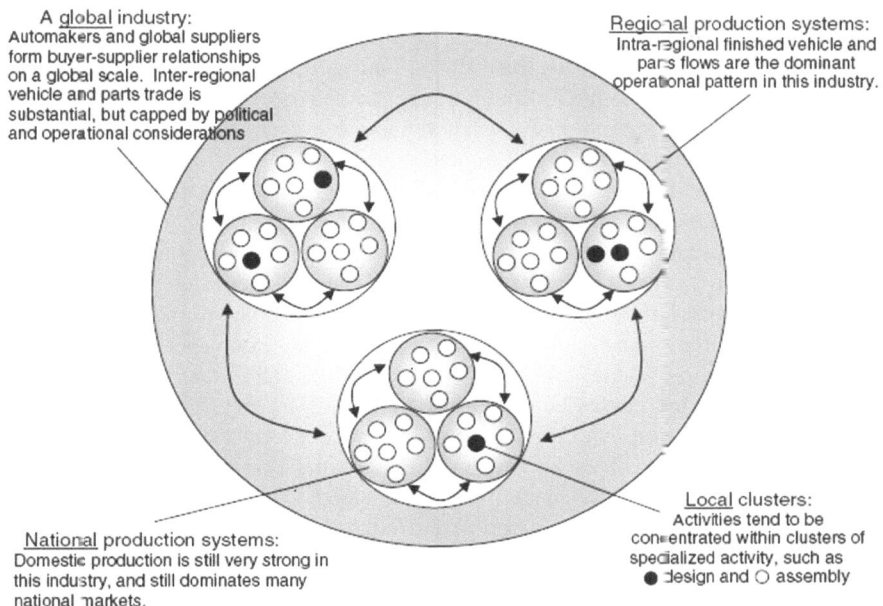

A global industry:
Automakers and global suppliers
form buyer-supplier relationships
on a global scale. Inter-regional
vehicle and parts trade is
substantial, but capped by political
and operational considerations

Regional production systems:
Intra-regional finished vehicle and
parts flows are the dominant
operational pattern in this industry.

National production systems:
Domestic production is still very strong in
this industry, and still dominates many
national markets.

Local clusters:
Activities tend to be
concentrated within clusters of
specialized activity, such as
● design and ○ assembly

Fig. 7.1 Structure of the automotive global production network (Fig. 1 in Sturgeon et al. (2008: 304))

firms face heavy transaction costs if they switch over the partnership. This problem hinders them to look for new upgrading opportunities.

In this predicament of local upgrading, recent geographical studies have offered an alternative view that state intervention can serve as a crucial political force in leveraging the governance power of automakers. Supported by this state intervention, many latecomer firms are able to plug into the automotive GPNs without the necessity of fully developing their technological capabilities (Pavlínek 2003; Liu and Dicken 2006; Barnes and Kaplinsky 2007). Specific to the automotive industry, latecomer economies may raise the barriers of market access and tariffs and bargain with lead firms for a better partnership, such as more knowledge sharing or additional technological assistances. To achieve this partnership, latecomer economies must possess sufficient scare assets that attract the interests of lead firms to accept the deal. The more scare assets do latecomer firms possess, the more bargaining power will they have (see Chap. 3).

While the importance and effectiveness of state intervention is a key to understand contemporary dynamics in the automotive industry, there are two unclear issues needed to be examined. First, how will lead firms respond to these state interventions? This question is critical because their response will determine the content and extent of knowledge sharing which have a strong influence on local upgrading. Second, how can local firms implement functional upgrading without raising tension to their foreign partners? This issue is crucial because it ensures the stability of coupling partnership. It should be noted that there are dark sides of state interventions, such as protectionism, industrial discriminations, and inefficient investment (Lin 1999; Huang 2002; Pack and Saggi 2006). There are failures cases of state interventions in promoting the automotive industry, such as Indonesia and Malaysia (Harwit 1995; Humphrey and Memodovic 2003; Liu and Yeung 2008).

Taking these two issues into account, this study argues that local upgrading in the automotive industry is subject to the balance of power relations between latecomer economies (firms and states) and lead firms in reciprocal coupling, rather than merely a matter of state power or firm power. With a balanced power relation, synergy will be developed to foster knowledge diffusion and reproduction within the partnership. Synergy within reciprocal coupling is more than mutual interests (such as synergy mentioned in Chaps. 5 and 7), but is also related to the committed benefits between actors who exchange possessed assets, respectively. However, if state power over-rides lead firms' power, lead firms would adopt a short-term strategy as a response. They may deliberately block knowledge diffusion and become resistant to further cooperation. If local upgrading incurs tension and local firms fail to lower the tension, lead-firm partners would also constrain knowledge sharing to defend their positions. If tension lasts overtime and local upgrading fails, decoupling will happen. The concept of 'obligated embeddedness' is insufficient to explain this tension because the literal meaning of it tends to privilege the influence of state power at the expense of lead firms. This study thus prefers the concept of *reciprocal coupling* to describe the pattern of integration, as it emphasizes the balance of interactions between firms and non-firms actors.

7.2.3   Formation o f Reciprocal Coupling in China's Automotive Industry

In China, reciprocal coupling happens in the way that automakers comply with specific regulatory criteria set by China's central government as an exchange to get access to domestic market. The criteria include ownership structures, local contents, and technological agreements. Meanwhile, Chinese partners accept the requirements of corporate governance, supply chain management proposed by automakers. The formation of reciprocal coupling in China reflects how domestic firms are assisted by state institutions to avoid being captive to global automakers.

From 1958 to 1984, China pursued indigenous innovation for developing domestic automotive industry due to political reasons. But technological gaps between China and the global automotive industry were enlarged during this period. Japan and Korea had grown up sharply through coupling with global lead firms since 1960s (Kim 1998; Dyer and Chu 2003; Liu and Deng 2003; Liang et al. 2010). China's domestic automotive industry was seriously lagging behind.

Reciprocal coupling was developed around 1984 when China decided to restructure the domestic automotive industry and cooperated with global automakers.

Table 7.1 Key criteria of the automotive industrial policy in 1994 (NDRCSC 1994)

Criteria	Contents
Market entry requirement	• FIEs are allowed to develop set up maximally two joint ventures with a designated Chinese partner • With a few exceptions, Chinese partners will be one of the pillar enterprises in the 'Three Big & Three Small' group* and will own no less than 50% of equity share
Localization requirement	• Minimal local content of production is 40%, while tariff rates on components are subject to the level of local content (ranging from 50 to 20%) • Introducing a new car model or an engine project must meet the minimal volume of vehicle production (ranging from 10,000 to 200,000); car models invented before 1990 are not allowed to be introduced • the SKD or CKD patterns of component production are disallowed
Local R&D requirement	• R&D activities are encouraged with preferential financing policies in bank loan, treasury capitalization, and stock funding; minimal R&D expenditure is required when applying national subsidizes for upgrading; all joint venture must establish at least one R&D center in due call

Notes The group of pillar enterprises was subsequently extended into a three-layer system comprising 2–3 core auto groups, 6–7 second-tier auto assemblers and 8–10 motorbike makers. *SKD* Semi-completely knock-down; *CKD* Completely knock-down

Preparing for the coupling, the central government merged SOEs among different provinces into a pillar group[2] for increasing the capability of a single SOE. A directive of the *State Guidance of Car Price and Product* was then established in 1984. Under the directive, joint ventures were encouraged between SOEs and global automakers. All product ranges and vehicle prices were governed and allocated by the central government (Jiang 1999). The directive was revised into an industrial policy in 1994 (NDRCSC 1994; see Table 7.1). Three specific criteria were consolidated for fostering knowledge transfer and local upgrading. First, to avoid monopoly and ensure competition, all automakers had to establish joint ventures with Chinese SOEs, but were only allowed to couple with two SOEs maximally. Second, all SOEs must have an equity share not less than 50% in joint ventures. Minimal local content of production was 40% with a tariff rate of 30% on components. Third, all joint ventures were encouraged to establish R&D centers funded by the central government.

The overall strategy of the 1994 policy was to 'exchange domestic market with foreign technologies' in which the domestic automotive industry was protected as an infant industry (Wang 2003; Lu and Feng 2005). As a response, foreign automakers invested 50% of equity stake which was the same as Chinese partners so as to ensure

---

[2]In 1988, the central government designated six SOEs as the 'Three Big & Three Small' group. Projects beyond these groups generally would not be approved. They are FAW, Second Auto Work (renamed as Dongfeng in 1990) and Shanghai Auto Work; the three small are: Beijing Auto Work, Tianjin Xiali Corporation; and Guangzhou-Peugeot joint venture.

full access to managerial rights in the joint ventures. Meanwhile, as requested, foreign firms were allowed to establish wholly own suppliers. A reciprocal partnership was thus generated, as commented by a director of Guangzhou Automotive Research Institute:

> The policy was welcomed at that time. In the beginning of 1990s, key automakers have noticed the potential of China markets due to its significant growth, and particularly, the previous succeed of the Shanghai-VW joint venture. Moreover, China also had abundant cheap labor. That was crucial to all big automakers when North America and Europe markets were increasingly saturated... On the issue of technological transfers, automakers were not worried about so much because localized production systems were fully under their control (Interview 100519, on 19th May 2010 in Guangzhou).

Reciprocal coupling was reinforced through further liberalization after the accession of China into the WTO in 2001. The state guidance of price and product control was abolished. The restriction of tariffs and import quota was tapping off gradually. In 2004, the 1994 industrial policy was revised for spurring more domestic upgrading with three key adjustments (NDRCSC 2004). First, the joint ventures were required to develop new car models specific for the China market with a proprietary brand. SOEs in the pillar group must develop at least one proprietary-branded car model before 2010. This requirement directly spurred local functional upgrading in brand creation and model development (local R&D for developing new models). Second, after-sale and service markets were open to foreign firms. This strategy was meant for indirectly upgrading the marketing capabilities of SOEs by intensifying domestic competition. Third, to all firms, the average fuel consumption of vehicle must reduce 15% before 2010, and new car models with energy-saving or new-energy technologies were encouraged with less restriction. This requirement was for stimulating technological upgrading. These changes indicated that the strategy of coupling was gradually shifted from: 'exchanging domestic markets with foreign technologies' into 'co-developing new technologies for domestic markets'.

This form of reciprocal coupling was proved to be effective in booming China's industrial growth. Figure 7.2 shows that the growth of Chinese automotive industry has accelerated since 1984, speeded up after 1994, and significantly soared after 2001. By 2010, 26 joint ventures were established which involved most of the global leading

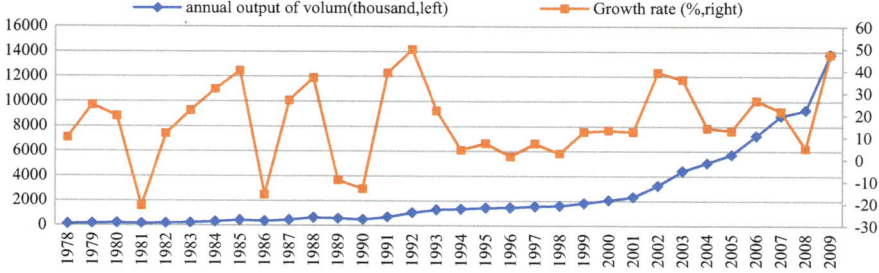

Fig. 7.2 Annual output of volume and growth rate in China's automotive industry (Li and Zhu 2008, 2010; NDRCSC 2008)

automakers (see Table 7.2). Meanwhile, due to market liberalization, automakers in China have increasingly faced fierce domestic competition. The existing provincial federalism intensified market competition because each SOE was embedded in their respective regional/provincial markets under certain local protection (Liu and Yeung 2008; Brandt and Thun 2010; Li and Zhu 2010). The fierce competition is shown in Table 7.3 which presents that the China market was regionally fragmented in 2009. In terms of production volume, none of the joint ventures had a share of more than 5%. None of the TNCs (owning more than one joint venture) accounted for more than 10%. This competitive pressure spurred the joint ventures to upgrade their product ranges and production efficiency so as to make more vehicles at a

Table 7.2 Automotive joint ventures in China (Li and Zhu 2008 and author's fieldwork)

Year of entry	Name	Register capital ($ million)	Shares of Chinese partner (%)	Location
1983	Beijing Jeep (Daimler-Chrysler)	605.21	50	Beijing
1984	SAIC-VW	335.4	50	Shanghai
1985	GAIG-PSA (Peugeot)	156	74	Guangzhou
1991	FAW-VW	1857	60	Changchun
1991	Jinbei-GM	230	50	Shenyang
1992	Dongfeng-PSA (Citroen)	1202	73	Wuhan
1992	Hainan-Mazda	80	75	Hainan
1993	Chang'an-Suzuki	190.85	51	Chongqing
1998	GAIG-Honda	139.76	50	Guangzhou
1998	Sichuan-Toyota	67	50	Chengdu
1999	Nanjing-Fiat	362	50	Nanjing
1999	Shanghai-GM	1521	50	Shanghai
2000	Dongfeng-Nissan	2000	50	Wuhan and Guangzhou
2000	Tianjin-Toyota	100	50	Tianjin
2001	Chang'an-Ford	98	50	Chongqing
2001	Dongfeng-PSA (Peugeot)	152	50	Wuhan
2002	Beijing-Hyundai	400	50	Beijing
2002	Huachen-BMW	110	50	Shenyang
2002	Dongfeng-Yueda-Kia (Hyundai)	90	50	Yancheng
2003	Dongfeng-Honda	98	50	Wuhan

(continued)

Table 7.2 (continued)

Year of entry	Name	Register capital ($ million)	Shares of Chinese partner (%)	Location
2004	GAIG-Toyota	560	50	Guangzhou
2004	Jianghuai-Hyundai	780	50	Hefei
2006	Chang'an and Ford-Mazda	60	50	Chongqing
2009	Chery-Fiat-GAIG	182	50	Wuhu
2010	BYD-Daimler	100	50	Shenzhen
2011	Changan-PSA	80	50	Shenzhen

Note The joint ventures only refer to passenger car

Table 7.3 China's vehicle sales in 2009 (CAAM 2010)

Ranking	Name	Sale volume	Location	Region
1	Shanghai-VW	728	Shanghai	East
2	Shanghai-GM	708.4	Shanghai	East
3	FAW-VW	669.2	Changchun	Northeast
4	Beijing-Hyundai	570.3	Beijing	North
5	Dongfeng-Nissan	519	Guangdong	South
6	Chery	466.5	Tianjin	North
7	BYD	445.1	Guangdong	South
8	FAW-Toyota	417.3	Sichuan	West
9	Guangzhou-Honda	365.6	Guangdong	South
10	Geely	329.1	Anhui	East
11	Chang'an-Ford-Mazda	316.1	Hainan	South
12	Shenlong-PSA	270	Hubei	Center
13	Dengfeng-Kia	241.4	Hubei	Center
14	Tianjin FAW	212.2	Tianjin	North
15	Dongfeng-Honda	210.6	Hubei	Center
16	Guangzhou-Toyota	209.6	Guangdong	South
17	Changcheng	155.2	Hebei	North
18	Chang'an-Suzuki	150.1	Chongqing	West
19	Huachen	134.7	Liaoning	Northeast
20	Jianghuai	123	Anhui	East

Unit Thousand vehicles; passenger vehicles only

cheaper price and better quality. However, regional protectionism constrained SOEs to launch large-scale projects in vehicle model and platform innovation. In the PRD, Guangzhou Auto Industrial Group (GAIG) hardly received funds and investments from the central government and could only rely on limited supports from provincial and municipal governments (Li and Zhu 2010; Liang et al. 2010).

7.3 Industrial Upgrading Through Reciprocal Coupling: The Changing Fortunes of GAIG

The development of China's automotive industry has presented an upgrading trajectory in which the domestic market and industrial policies were used for developing reciprocal cooperation with global lead firms. The automotive industry in the PRD was involved because GAIG was selected in the national pillar group in 1984. The industry was initially developed in the mid-1980s based on the establishment of Guangzhou-Peugeot joint venture. Currently, the PRD has become one of the largest manufacturing hubs of China comprising three joint ventures located in Guangzhou: Dongfeng-Nissan, Guangqi-Honda, Guangqi-Toyota, plus a private enterprise—BDY in Shenzhen (see Fig. 7.3).

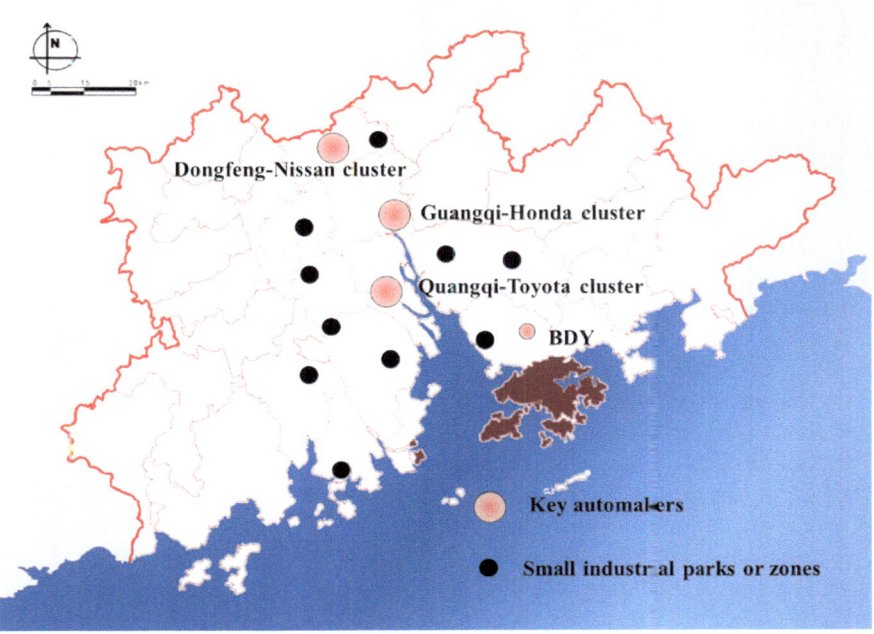

Fig. 7.3 Location of the automotive industrial clusters in the Pearl River Delta (drawn by author)

As the analytical framework proposed in Chap. 3, the relative bargaining power of actors involved mainly depends on the extent to which each possesses assets sought by the other party and the extent to which either party can control that access (Appleyard 1996; Liu and Dicken 2006). When local firms possess more assets, they tend to have more bargaining power. Within the joint ventures, the balance of power relations is reflected by a set of operational variables ranging from technological capabilities, equity participation, ownership structures, managerial structures, decision making, profit sharing and risk sharing, and so on (Killing 1982; Lecraw 1984). This section does not go into analyzing these operational variables in great detail, but focuses on the general pattern of collaboration between Guangzhou SOEs and Japanese automakers. The common thread of the cases is that reciprocal coupling leads to substantial industrial growth, while not necessarily leads to significant upgrading subsequently. In the case of Guangzhou-Peugeot, the coupling firstly spurred the growth of the joint venture, but failed to achieve the balance of interplay due to unequal equity structure, mismatched interests, and unwelcome responsive strategies. This problem constrained upgrading and led to the failure. By learning from it, Guangqi-Honda devoted a great deal of efforts in maintaining the balance of power relations, such as keeping an equal equity/managerial structure, fostering mutual interests in product development, and reducing tension during functional upgrading. These efforts lead to significant upgrading at both local and regional scales.

7.3.1 Rise and Fall of Guangzhou-Peugeot

Similar to the electronics industry, the automotive industry in the PRD hardly had any industrial base in the early 1980s. After the opening reform in 1978, China's central government allowed Guangdong Province to establish a joint venture project with foreign firms. The motivation of the central government was to balance domestic regional inequality and improved industrial development in Southern China. As the provincial capital, Guangzhou government grasped this opportunity and developed partnership between GAIG and Peugeot from the French PSA Group. Originally, the central government only allowed Guangzhou-Peugeot to manufacture light trucks for preventing direct competition with other key SOEs (e.g., First Auto Work, Dongfeng Group, and Shanghai Auto Work). But provincial and municipal governments strongly requested the permission to manufacture passenger vehicles. This central-local mismatched interest was finally reconciled at the expense that Guangzhou-Peugeot needed to rely on self-finance without any additional support from the central government.

Strategic coupling between GAIG and PSA was formed with the establishment of a joint venture in 1984 (see Fig. 7.4). At that time, the *State Guidance of Car Price and Product* only set up national criteria in ownership structure, the type of vehicle model, and the volume of production. It had no criteria for technological sharing. The coupling of Guangzhou-Peugeot did not reach a reciprocal stage due to mismatched interests and imbalanced power relations. In terms of capital investment, GAIG bore

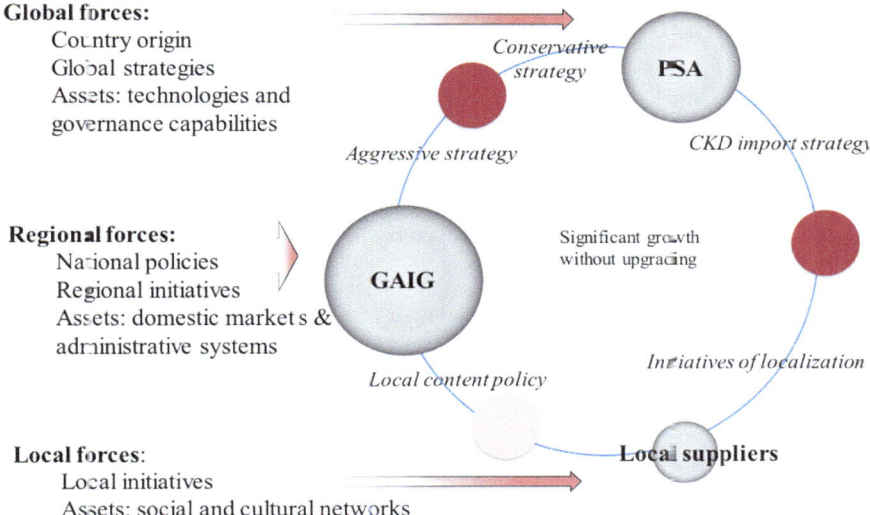

Global forces:
    Country origin
    Global strategies
    Assets: technologies and
    governance capabilities

Regional forces:
    National policies
    Regional initiatives
    Assets: domestic markets &
    administrative systems

Local forces:
    Local initiatives
    Assets: social and cultural networks

Fig. 7.4 Reciprocal coupling of Guangzhou-Peugeot joint venture (drawn by author)

more responsibilities and risks. GAIG had to provide full investments in capital, infrastructures, and facilities, while Peugeot invested in the forms of technological licensing and training. In terms of technologies, the gap between two partners was quite huge. GAIG had a little industrial base and there were no regional supply networks. Local SOEs in the automotive industry hardly had experience in organizing modern production systems. Concerning these conditions, Peugeot decided to install two manual production lines in the joint venture, though automation production lines had been prevalent in Peugeot's production networks. Moreover Peugeot insisted on introducing the 505 car model which was going to exit the Euro market at that time. Base on Peugeot's strategy, GAIG was situated in a disadvantaged position with limited power in production management and product development. Under the pressure of self-finance, GAIG insisted on holding a major share so as to defend its governance power. As a result, Chinese partners occupied a larger equity share of 74%,[3] while the share of French partners was just 26%.

The highly asymmetrical ownership structure disappointed Peugeot which in turn took a conservative and short-term strategy as a response. Instead of constructing regional supply networks, Peugeot implemented the CKD (complete knock-down) strategy in component procurement to offset the disadvantage position in equity structure. All components were then purchased from and distributed by a designated trader which was virtually a subsidiary of the PSA Group. This strategy made PSA able to reap huge profits from the component procurement of the joint venture. Apart

---

[3] In equity share, Chinese partners held 46% from the GAIG, 20% from the Citic Auto China, and 8% from China International Finance Ltd. French partners held 22% from PSA-Peugeot and 4% from Paris Banque Nationale.

from the CKD strategy, Peugeot postponed introducing new car model, the 405 series, as a reservation for further renegotiation with GAIG. This responsive strategy disappointed GAIG as well. But GAIG had little power to change the situation due to its weak indigenous capabilities. Tension was generated within the partnership under asymmetrical power relations and mismatched interests. This problem was told by the chief of technology division of Guangqi-Honda:

> GAIG looked like a provider of capital and Peugeot was a technology provider. This kind of cooperation was not good, because there was a lack of harmony. Whatever Guangzhou-Peugeot was profitable or not, they [Peugeot] were earning profits [from the components]. I may exaggerate the situation, but they did seem to get nothing to lose in the joint venture…-Surely there were other reasons that led to our failures, but I think this problem [synergy] was one of the keys. We were both too short-sight (Interview 100526, on 26 May 2011 in Guangzhou).

Due to the tension, reciprocal coupling was not truly developed in Guangzhou-Peugeot. Coupling did lead to the significant industrial growth of Guangzhou-Peugeot, but industrial upgrading did not occur. From 1985 to 1994, the annual production volume of Guangzhou-Peugeot increased from 5000 to 25,000. Before 1990, the Peugeot 505 model was highly welcomed by Chinese consumers due to increasing domestic demands and lacking of competitors in the domestic passenger vehicle market. But after that, the 505 model gradually lost market shares and was beaten by Santana from VW. In 1995, Guangzhou-Peugeot suffered from over-inventory with an amount over 8000 vehicles in warehouses. This problem put the joint venture in debt seriously.[4]

The 505 model was losing competitiveness due to two reasons. First, without product upgrading, VW's Santana series turned out to be a better option for Chinese consumers because it had better performance at a lower price. Second, without upgrading production systems, the 505 model met a bottleneck of cost reduction. The CKD strategy and manual production lines put the 505 model at bay. Tariffs imposing on components made the 505 model had a much higher production cost than Santana. The later one was using locally manufactured components and assembled by automated production lines.

When the market share of the 505 model declined sharply, after rounds of renegotiation, PSA decided to introduce the 405 series to take back the market lost. However, Guangzhou-Peugeot had missed the window of industrial opportunity. According to the new industrial policy in 1994, the 405 series could only be introduced by satisfying two requirements: (1) the production volume of the 505 model must reach 30,000; and (2) the local content of the 505 model must reach 40%. Regarding to the problem of over-inventory and the CKD strategy, it was an impossible mission for Guangzhou-Peugeot to achieve these requirements within a short time. In 1997, Guangzhou-Peugeot collapsed with the divestment of the French PSA Group. The entire joint venture was sold to Honda at a price of one *franc*.

---

[4] Source: Interview with the former vice president of Guangzhou Seat Factory of GAIG, on July 19, 2010, in Guangzhou.

Although there were many problems leading to the failure of Guangzhou-Peugeot, such as the wrong market strategy of PSA or the weak capability of GAIG, the lack of synergy within Guangzhou-Peugeot should be the key. PSA held a conservative and short-term strategy due to its disadvantaged position in the equity share, while GAIA did not have sufficient competence to conduct product and functional upgrading. Therefore, when market and institutional environment changed, the joint venture failed.

7.3.2 Resurgence Through the Success of Guangqi-Honda

Guangqi-Honda was established between GAIG and Honda in 1997 to replace Peugeot. In 2004, GAIG established another joint venture with Toyota in 2004 as Guangqi-Toyota. These two joint ventures are both manufacturing passenger vehicles. In 2005, GAIG was restructured into Guangzhou Auto Ltd. Co. (GAC).[5] By learning from Guangzhou-Peugeot, GAC devoted a great deal of efforts in fostering the balance of the interplay for nurturing synergy. Guangci-Honda currently has grown into one of the best joint ventures in China's automotive industry (Li and Zhu 2010).

7.3.2.1 Fostering Synergy

The reciprocal coupling of Guangqi-Honda is shown in Fig. 7.5 in which more balanced power relations are formed compared with the ones in Guangzhou-Peugeot. Grounded in the new national industrial policy and the imperative of upgrading from provincial governments, GAC strongly demanded three elements of the new partner that was selected to replace Peugeot. First, the new joint venture must develop local supply networks to meet the national criteria of local content (40%). Second, the new partner must gradually introduce new vehicle models that were synchronizing with global markets (particularly Europe and the US markets). Third, co-development and innovation were compulsory in the new joint venture. These strong initiatives were reflected by comments from the division chief of the production department of Guangqi-Honda:

> The most important lesson of Guangzhou-Peugeot was that we must construct local supply networks to take advantage of low production cost here. Otherwise, we cannot reduce production costs as much as our competitors do in China. Meanwhile, we need to introduce the best models, because other competitors in China market were doing so. Moreover, co-development was very important because it was a foundation of long-term prosperity and we never want to repeat our failure with Peugeot again (Interview 100526, on 26 May 2010 in Guangzhou).

---

[5]GAC also established another two joint ventures: Guangqi-Hino in 2007 in Guangzhou making commercial vehicles; Guangqi-Fiat in 2009 located in Changsha (Hunan Province) manufacturing passenger vehicles and engines.

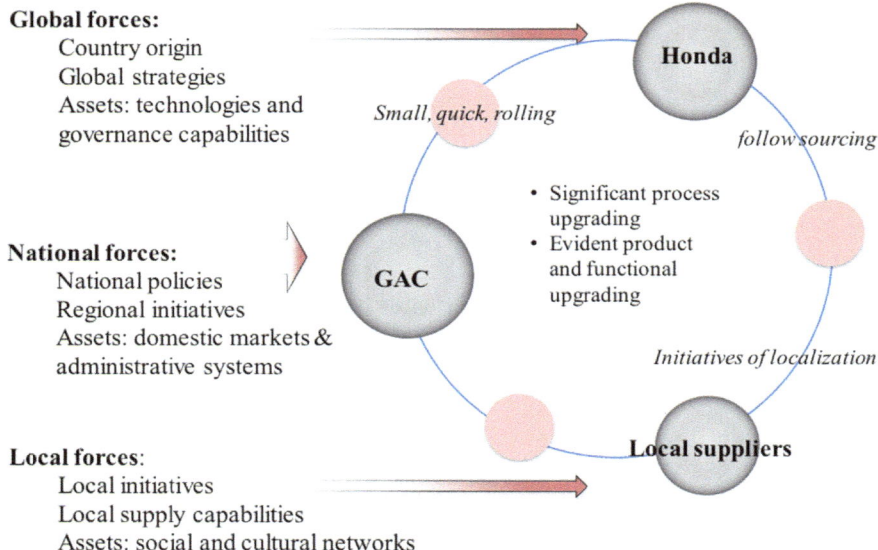

Global forces:
Country origin
Global strategies
Assets: technologies and
governance capabilities

Small, quick, rolling

Honda

follow sourcing

- Significant process
  upgrading
- Evident product
  and functional
  upgrading

National forces:
National policies
Regional initiatives
Assets: domestic markets &
administrative systems

GAC

Initiatives of localization

Local forces:
Local initiatives
Local supply capabilities
Assets: social and cultural networks

Local suppliers

Fig. 7.5   Reciprocal coupling of Guangqi-Honda joint venture (compiled by author)

GAC was able to bargain for these requirements by possessing two regional assets: (1) the national industrial policy in 1994 (see Table 7.1); (2) a huge regional market in South China that had not been saturated and the only assembly plant (Guangzhou-Peugeot) had just quitted. There was a niche in the scale of GAC. It was just a new SOE with several subsidiaries without heavy institutional and labor burden. These reasons made GAC an interesting partner to 11 global lead firms such as BMW, Mercedes-Benz, Opel, Fiat, Hyundai, Toyota, and Honda. Honda was finally selected because it had the strongest initiative to cooperate with GAC and was willing to meet the demands of GAC. Compared with Honda, Toyota did not have such a strong initiative to cooperate with GAC because it was simultaneously negotiating with First Auto Work (FAW). Toyota considered FAW as a much more promising partner than GAC at that time.

The initiatives of GAC were satisfied by the Japanese style of management in organizing GPNs. The 'just-in-time' system has a strong imperative of localization and regionalization in constructing in situ supply networks (Cusumano 1985). Honda's lean production system is famous for its incremental upgrading on the basis of on-spot technological improvement known as *Gemba Kaizen* (Imai 1987, 1997). More importantly, in contrast to PSA, Honda regarded China as an extremely important market. This attitude was embedded in Honda global marketing strategy. While Honda's global market shares were relatively small compared with other Japanese automakers at that time, Honda decided to use China market as a strategic resource to sustain its long-term competitiveness in the global market. The motivation of Honda was revealed by a Chinese director of Guangqi-Honda:

Comparing with other global lead firms, Honda is a relatively late-comer in the global market. It was hard for Honda to compete in the U.S. or Europe markets which have been largely occupied by giant automakers like GM, VW, Ford and even Toyota. But in the China market around 1997, there were a lot of opportunities for Honda to grasp, particular in South China market. Honda had ambition to win the China market against other gain automakers. Therefore, Honda took a very pro-active and friendly attitude during the negotiation with GAC and made it count (interview 21th May 2010 in Guangzhou).

7.3.2.2 Balancing Power Relations and the SFR Strategy

The above-matched interests serve as a fundamental force in nurturing a cooperative and reciprocal relationship between GAC and Honda. Based on this relationship, GAC and Honda tried various efforts to ensure a balanced power relation so as to foster product and process upgrading within the joint venture—Guangqi-Honda.

In order to avoid creating tension in ownership structure, GAC and Honda took up 50% of equity share, respectively, and invested the same amount of capital ($140 million) in Guangqi-Honda. In managerial structure, the managerial team was made of Chinese and Japanese evenly with certain labor division. At the top level, they were two general managers representing two sides of the partnership. At the department level, Chinese directors were mainly in charge of marketing, human resource, administration, and procurement. Japanese directors were in charge of production management and technical supports. In knowledge sharing, Honda's lean production system was fully replicated into the joint venture. Japanese engineering took up several key positions in operating the system, while Chinese workers were fully trained and constituted the majority of workforce.

In product development, Guangqi Honda Automobile Research Institute (GHARI) was set up in which Honda was responsible for basic R&D and engineering designs and GAC was in charge of product localization and body designs. The distinctive feature of GHARI was that it was wholly owned by Guangqi-Honda, whereas all other R&D institutes with Honda' GPNs were wholly owned by Honda itself. GHARI was also the first R&D institute set up by joint ventures in China at that time. Intensive knowledge sharing was dominated by Honda for reducing technological gaps between GAC and Honda. But in marketing, the situation was reversed. GAC played an active role and Honda worked closely with GAC's experts for understanding the China market, collecting information, and constructing distribution channels. Based on this collective endeavor, Guangqi-Honda managed to introduce competitive vehicle models to China almost every year from 2002 to 2010 (see Table 7.4). These models were quite welcomed and Guangqi-Honda's market share increased from 5% in 2000 to 14% in 2009. Guangqi-Honda sold about 3.5 million units of vehicles in 2009 (Li and Zhu 2010: 86).

Honda enforced a specific strategy to ensure sustainable market and product development. The strategy comprised three principals: *small input, fast output, and rolling development* (SFR strategy). *Small input* meant that the development of Guangqi-Honda fully depended on the initial investment. No additional loan was allowed.

Table 7.4 Product introduction of Guangqi-Honda (author's survey and the official Web site of GAC, at: http://www.ghac.cn/)

Years	Products	Type	Prices (thousand *yuan*)
1998	Accord 6	Middle	250–350
2002	Odyssey 2	MPV	230–290
2003	Accord 7	Middle	230–350
2004	Fit	Economic	90–130
2005	Odyssey 3	MPV	230–290
2006	City	Economic	100–150
2007	Accord 8	Middle	200–330
2008	Everus	SUV concept car	
2009	Odyssey 4	MPV	230–290
2010	Crosstour	High	400–430
2011	Everus	Economic	70–100

Note Honda's SUV series is allocated in Dongfeng-Honda in Wuhan, the geographical center of China

Fast output was meant for making investment cycles as short as possible. Starting with a small volume (10 thousand vehicles) of production with one production line, Guangqi-Honda was able to recover the initial investments and then further invested in new production lines and facilities with the accumulated profits. In doing so, *rolling development* was accomplished in the sense that all accumulated profits were invested for follow-up development.

The underlined motivation of the SFR strategy was to prevent the joint venture being driven by ambitious local authorities which tended to focus on extending the scale of production. Guangzhou and Guangdong governments did try to offer more investments and persuaded Guangqi-Honda to speed up the extension of its production scale more quickly. But all attempts were declined according to the SFR strategy. In 2010, GZ-Honda extended its annual production volume from 360,000 to 480,000. All the current assets (0.9 billion *yuan*) came from self-accumulation.[6] In short, this SFR strategy ensured the independence of the joint venture which reinforced synergy and maintained the stability of reciprocal coupling.

Within such reciprocal coupling, Guangqi-Honda has achieved product, process, and functional upgrading to a significant degree. In *product upgrading*, Guangqi-Honda totally introduced 11 vehicles models to the China market (see Table 7.4). Although most of these models were innovated and transferred from Honda's GPNs elsewhere, the arrival of them significantly helped GAC absorb Honda's advanced skills including product designs, model development, and the processing technologies of the introduced models. These technologies were also transferred to GHARI for conducting product localization and developing new models. Moreover, the introduction of these vehicle models fostered regional supply networks in which Chinese

---

[6]http://auto.ifeng.com/roll/20100601/328185.shtml.

suppliers were trained to manufacture more sophisticated auto parts, thus achieving product upgrading regularly.

The progress of *process upgrading* is indicated by the improvement of the lean production system, PPM rate,[7] just-in-time delivery, and cycle time. These efforts made Guangqi-Honda as one of the best assembly plants in Honda's GPNs. On the basis of *Gemba Kaizen*, Honda paid a lot of efforts in training Chinese workers in the ways of regular training courses, annual study groups, and overseas specialized training sections, and so on. Hundreds of Chinese workers were trained every year for manipulating the lean production system. In this way, Guangqi-Honda kept having high performance in PPM rate among its peers. In 1999, when the normal PPM rate in China was about 1500–3000, Guangqi-Honda had managed to keep a three-digit PPM rate. By 2003, when introducing the Accord 7 to China, Guangqi-Honda had maintained the PPM rate within a two-digit level which was the average level in Honda's GPNs. In 2010 when introducing the first luxury vehicle model (Crosstour) to China, Guangqi-Honda amazingly reached a top-level record in its GPNs by maintaining the PPM rate at 12. This standard was also enforced among regional supply networks in the PRD, while suppliers were allowed to have a lower criterion of PPM rate (12–20).

Apart from improvement in the PPM rate, the just-in-time system was also gradually upgraded. Guangqi-Honda initially set up its standard inventory at 15 days. The standard was subsequently reduced into 10 days around 2001, 5 days in 2006, and recently 1.5 days in 2010. Meanwhile, the cycle time of assembling a single vehicle was reduced from about 65 s in 1998 to 53 s in 2005. In 2010, the cycle time was improved to 49.3 s, hitting the top record among all assembly plants of Honda.[8] From 1998 to 2010, production lines in Guangqi-Honda were significantly renovated at least four times and upgraded from single-line production to mixed-line production.[9]

Functional upgrading was also implemented through the efforts of GHARI in developing a new vehicle model. In 2008, GHARI innovated with the Everus series which was specific for the China markets with an appropriate brand under Guangqi-Honda (see Table 7.4). The Everus series had three indigenously developed models by 2010. Combined with Japanese and Chinese technologies, the creation of the Everus is a win-win deal of functional upgrading for both GAC and Honda. To GAC, it identified a new market niche and released the economic and political pressures of GZ-Honda. This point is reflected as the quotation below:

> GZ-Honda was getting near to a bottleneck of cost reduction, since the average of local content of GZ-Honda's product was about 85% now. We also faced the task of creating new proprietary brands. Therefore, innovating new product was the best solution for both of

---

[7]It refers to the number of disqualified part per million. For instance, 100 ppm means there are 100 disqualified products among 1 million manufactured products.

[8]Data are from interview with the director of sourcing department of Guangqi-Honda on May 21, 2010, in Guangzhou.

[9]Mixed-line production: manufacturing different vehicles in the same production line.

us. That was why we convinced Honda to innovate new vehicles with us. (Zhang Fangyou, President of GAC, interview by the magazine of *Automan* on 20th, May, 2008[10])

To Honda, it was the 'best solution' because the joint venture could adopt more local-made auto parts without necessity of revising or complying with Honda's global standards. The brand creation of Everus was a way of lowering tension between GAC and Honda. Putting Everus within Honda's brand range would take a long and complicated procedure to get approval from the Honda Group. GAC was also unwilling to do so because it had great contributions in the innovation of Everus. Similarly, Honda did not allow Everus to be wholly owned by GAC.

In order to prevent technological leak out in developing Everus, Japanese partners took charge of platform development, modularization, and systematic engineering, while Chinese partners were responsible for marketing research, body design, and external trimming. Although GAC did not play a dominant role in this process, GAC's engineers benefited from participation observation, learning by doing, and knowledge spillover from Honda. GAC finally developed a sufficient group of talents for establishing a proprietary brand two years later (see Sect. 7.3.3). Guangqi-Toyota was established in 2004 and generally went through a similar trajectory with Guangqi-Honda.

7.3.3 Industrial Upgrading in Regional Supply Networks and GAC

The above elaborations show the importance of synergy and balanced power relations in maintaining reciprocal coupling and fostering industrial upgrading in the joint ventures. A further question is whether local Chinese suppliers and GAC have also achieved upgrading. Drawing on my interviews with 14 automotive firms in Guangqi-Honda regional production network, this study finds that industrial upgrading among the supply network has been occurring. As shown in Fig. 7.6, process upgrading was the most significant among all types of upgrading, which achieved a value of 2.36. Product upgrading was following with a value of 2.21. The extent of functional upgrading was moderate with a value of 1.71. The evident product and process upgrading is driven by the supply network management conducted by Guangqi-Honda which is known as the 'single-point supply' (SPS) strategy. Because local R&D activities are encouraged, functional upgrading is achieved to a certain degree. Sectoral upgrading is rather insignificant because these suppliers are specialized in manufacturing certain components and hardly intend to move to a new sector.

---

[10]http://www.cb-h.com/news/qcr/2008/520/0852010584C006K71C200JK7993FCC.html.

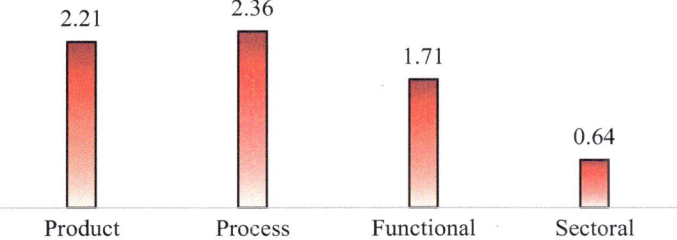

Fig. 7.6 Upgrading in regional supply networks of Guangqi-Honda. *Notes* Informants were requested to evaluate the extent of upgrading in four types. A value ranged from absent (0) to very high (3) was attributed. The result was averaged. *Source* author's survey on 14 suppliers of Guangqi-Honda

7.3.3.1 Upgrading in Regional Production Networks

On the basis of the SPS strategy, Honda subcontracts one single component to one supplier for one specific vehicle model. Unless any serious financial or trust failure of the supplier happens, Honda will not change the supplier. Toyota has a similar strategy in its supply networks, but Dongfeng-Nissan tends to maintain 2–3 regular suppliers for one single component. Qualified local firms which become first-tier suppliers will receive continuous technological assistance from Honda. Following Honda's standards, the first-tier suppliers will assist the second-tier suppliers in a similar way.

This SPS strategy works as a crucial impetus that nurturing synergy and upgrading among Guangqi-Honda's regional supply networks. This strategy not only comes from Honda's imperative of cost reduction, but also derives from the necessity of maintaining the 'just-in-time' system and the lean production system. When Guangqi-Honda reduces the delivery days of inventory or the cycle time of vehicle assembly, it will have stronger demand for the stability and punctuality of suppliers. Hence, Guangqi-Honda has incentives to help suppliers upgrade their technological capabilities. Since 1998, about 40 local firms have been assisted and 'upgraded' into the first-tier suppliers of Guangqi-Honda and Guangqi-Toyota.[11] At least 3–4 hundreds of local firms were upgraded into the second- or third-tier suppliers of the joint ventures. As a result, the joint ventures managed to achieve a high level of local content which helped them reduce production costs continuously. As shown in Fig. 7.7, the level of local content of the joint ventures was much higher than the national criteria of 40%.

---

[11] Interviewee in Guangqi-Toyota declined to offer this information.

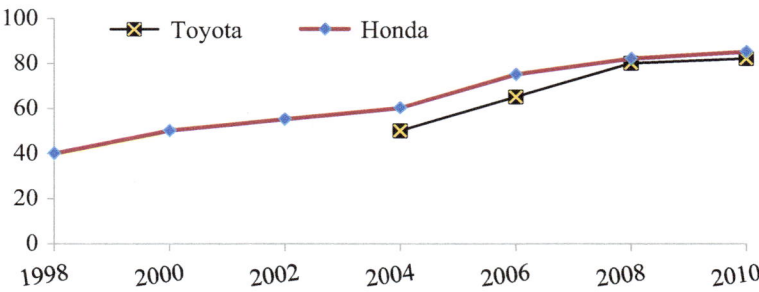

Fig. 7.7 Local content of Guangqi-Honda and Guangqi-Toyota (%) (author's fieldwork)

The high level of local content implies that Honda and Toyota did not build up technological enclaves and isolate knowledge diffusion, but have devoted significant efforts in fostering a regional production network in the PRD. The increasing domestic competition has reinforced this localization tendency. This point can be reflected by the division chief of procurement department of Guangzhou-Toyota:

> Today [in China markets], the national requirement of 40% local content is meaningless, because if your local content is less than 60%, your cars cannot be sold out due to higher production costs. Though tariffs and import quotas are liberalizing, the tendency of localization is unstoppable since we have so many global leaders competing with us in China. The more localization of production, the cheaper the car will be (Interview 100601, on 1 June 2010 in Guangzhou).

When Honda and Toyota transplanted their suppliers to Guangzhou, GAC took advantage of the SPS strategy and established dozens of joint ventures with these transplanted suppliers, such as Guangzhou-JFE (auto body sheet), Guangqi-Toyota Engine, Guangzhou-Chuo Seik (wheeler), Guangzhou-Showa (damper), Weigao-Stanley (electronic parts), Guangzhou-Mitsuba (magnetic motor), Guangzhou-TSK (car seat), and Guangzhou-NHK-UNI (spring), and so on. Meanwhile, some local firms quickly caught up and been upgraded into the first-tier supplier of Guangqi-Honda and Guangqi-Toyota, such as Haifeng Machinery and Zhongxin Plastic.

7.3.3.2   Functional Upgrading of GAC: Integrated Innovation

While upgrading occurred in regional supply network, GAC has achieved product and functional upgrading. GAC has constructed various linkages to absorb and transfer knowledge from the joint ventures to itself. In a formal manner, GAC sent a large number of study groups to the joint ventures annually for learning the operation of Honda's lead production system and the TPS (Toyota production system). Comprising about 10–15 technicians, each group was sent to different production segments for two weeks or one month. The groups were requested to develop at least one upgrading proposal for improving the efficiency of production system.[12] Informally, GAC rotated Chinese engineers between the two joint ventures and the subsidiaries of GAC. When GAC set up Guangzhou Automotive Engineering Research Institute (GAERI) in 2006, 80% of its technicians (about 300 people) originally worked in GZ-Honda and GZ-Toyota.[13] By absorbing knowledge for a decade, GAC implemented functional upgrading in 2010 by launching a proprietary brand termed as Trumpchi.

There was a critical challenge to GAC: how to achieve functional upgrading without creating tension in the joint ventures.[14] GAC had to resolve two problems for securing the synergy with Honda and Toyota. GAC must avoid any disputes about intellectual property rights involved in the product development of Trumpchi. GAC also had to avoid direct market competition between Trumpchi and Honda and Toyota's incumbent product ranges in the China market. In order to resolve these problems, GAC adopted a strategy of *integrated innovation*. The new model of Trumpchi resulted from a combination of multiple sources of technologies which were intensively revised through indigenous efforts. GAC licensed the platform technologies (e.g., decking and engine) of Alfa Romeo 166 from Fiat Group and purchased gearbox technologies from Aisin. Nevertheless, GAC revised suspension system and engine so as to transfer the executive car (Alfa Romeo 166) into a family sedan. Apart from these core technologies, GAC devoted great efforts in developing electronic systems, internal trim, external appearance, and a new body design. All these efforts helped GAC avoid the potential disputes of intellectual property rights. In terms of market positioning, the price of Trumpchi was set between 120,000 and 190,000 *yuan*, while the major market segments of the joint ventures' products were either lower than 150,000 *yuan* or higher than 200,000 *yuan*. Hence, the market segment of Trumpchi bypassed the key markets of the joint ventures.

The integrated innovation strategy did help GAC create the first own brand without harming reciprocal coupling in the joint ventures. But it should be noticed that the functional upgrading of GAC is a bit shallow because there is not much innovation in the new model. Most of the key components and technologies were purchased or licensed from other firms. It means that GAC has not been innovative yet. In 2011, Trumpchi sold 18,000 vehicles merely accounting for about 0.1% of the domestic market sales.[15] The future of this brand is yet to be told.

To sum up this section, the comparative analysis between Guangzhou-Peugeot and Guangqi-Honda has demonstrated how important a balanced interplay in reciprocal coupling is. It nurtures synergy, ensures the sustainability of reciprocal coupling, and leads to various outcomes of industrial upgrading. The upgrading is not confined

---

[12]Sources: two interviews with the vice directors of production department in the joint ventures in Guangzhou on May 21, 2010, and June 1, 2010.

[13]From a public interview with the director of GAERI: http://auto.xinmin.cn/rollnews/2010/09/04/6649866.html.

[14]There are various difficulties to approach to relevant data to this issue. Most of the information about the appropriate brand of GAC was kept as confidential.

[15]http://news.21cn.com/caiji/roll1/2012/01/14/10495276_4.shtml.

within the joint ventures, but is diffused in a broader regional production network in which local firms benefited indifferent ways.

7.4 The Balance of Interplay

Local upgrading in the automotive industry in the PRD was driven by reciprocal coupling between automaker and SOEs. The reciprocal coupling tended to occur under four conditions: strong national interventions, strong global governance imperatives, small market gap while large technological gap. In the case of Guangzhou, either corporate governance power or state power alone is insufficient to explain the outcomes of upgrading. Instead, the balance of interplay between actors coupled is a crucial factor that produces synergy and nurtures industrial upgrading subsequently. This formation of reciprocal coupling sheds light on an alternative pathway of local upgrading which receive substantial helps from global lead firms.

The Guangzhou case shows that possessing huge domestic markets is a crucial precondition of developing reciprocal coupling. It serves as a crucial regional asset for local firms to increase their bargaining power under state interventions. In this way, local firms would be able to leverage the governance power of lead firms, but better not to override the power. Investigating two important joint ventures in the PRD's automotive industry, this chapter has verified that reciprocal coupling leads to substantial industrial growth, but not necessarily leads to subsequent upgrading. If upgrading is not achieved, reciprocal coupling may fail when institutional and spatial conditions changed over time.

The case of Guangzhou-Peugeot has demonstrated a negative example of reciprocal coupling in which industrial upgrading was hindered due to the lack of synergy, mismatched interests and unwelcome responsive strategies. In contrast, the case of Guangqi-Honda has illustrated a positive example in which reciprocal coupling is sustainable on the basis of balanced power relations and various efforts in maintaining the balance. The efforts of lowering tension within the joint ventures are proved to be crucial in maintain reciprocal coupling and nurturing the functional upgrading of GAC. All these efforts lead to significant upgrading at both local and regional levels. However, the achievements of upgrading should not be overstated. The functional upgrading of GAC is virtually a corner-cut strategy with limited content of indigenous innovation. The technological and marketing capabilities of local firms are still lagging behind global automakers seriously.

References

Ahmadjian, C. L., & Lincoln, J. R. (2001). Keiretsu, governance, and learning: Case studies in change from the japanese automotive industry. *Organization Science, 12*(1), 683–701. https://doi.org/10.1287/orsc.12.6.683.10086.

Appleyard, M. M. (1996). How does knowledge flow? Interfirm patterns in the semiconductor industry. *Strategic Management Journal, 17*(2), 137–154.

Barnes, J., & Kaplinsky, R. (2007). Globalization and the death of the local firm? The automobile components sector in South Africa. *Regional Studies, 34*(1), 797–812.

Brandt, L., & Thun, E. (2010). The fight for the middle: upgrading, competition, and industrial development in China. *World Development, 38*(11), 1555–1574.

CAAM. (2010). China automotive industry yearbook. China Automotive Technology and Research Center, China Association of Automobile Manufactures.

Cusumano, M. A. (1985). *The Japanese automobile industry: technology and management at Nissan and Toyota.* Boston: Harvard University Press.

Dicken, P. (2007). *Global shift: Mapping the changing contours of the world economy* (5th ed.). London Sage.

Dyer, J. H., & Chu, W. (2003). The role of trustworthiness in reducing transaction costs and improving performance: Empirical evidence from the United States, Japan, and Korea. *Organization Science, 14*(1), 57–68.

EIU. (1997). *Multinational companies in China: Winners and losers.* Hong Kong: The Economist Intelligence Unit Limited.

Freyssenet, M., & Lung, Y. (2000). Between globalization and regionalization: What is the future of the automobile industry? In J. Humphrey, Y. Lecler, & M. Salerno (Eds.), *Global strategies and local realities: The auto industry in emerging markets.* GERPISA. Macmillan.

Frigant, V., & Layan, J.-B. (2009). Modular production and the new division of labour within Europe: The perspective of French automotive parts suppliers. *European Urban and Regional Studies, 16*(1), 11–25. https://doi.org/10.1177/0969776408098930.

Gereffi, G, Humphrey, J., & Sturgeon, T. (2005). The governance of global value chains. *Review of International Political Economy, 12*(1), 78–104. https://doi.org/10.1080/09692290500049805.

Gereffi, G., & Korzeniewicz, M. (Eds.). (1994). *Commodity chains and global capitalism.* Westport: Greenwood Press.

Harwit, E. (1995). *China's automobile industry: policies, problems, and prospects.* Armonk, NY: M.E. Sharpe.

Huang, Y. (2002). *Selling china: Foreign direct investment during the reform era* (Cambridge Modern China Series). Cambridge University Press.

Hudson, R. (2002). Changing industrial production systems and regional development in the New Europe. *Transactions of the Institute of British Geographers, 27*(3), 261–281.

Humphrey, J. (2003). Globalization and supply chain networks: The auto industry in Brazil and India. *Global Networks, 3*(2), 121–141.

Humphrey, J., & Memodovic, O. (2003). The global automotive industry value chain: what prospects for upgrading by developing countries? In *Sectoral studies series.* Vienna: United Nations Industrial Development Organization.

Humphrey, J., & Schmitz, H. (2000). *Governance and upgrading: Linking industrial cluster and global value chain research.* Brighton: IDS Working Paper, 120, Institute of Development Studies, University of Sussex.

Imai, M. (1987). *Kaizen: The key to Japan's competitive success.* Irwin: McGraw-Hill.

Imai, M. (1997). *Gemba Kaizen: A commonsense low-cost approach to management.* McGraw-Hill.

Jiang, X. (1999). Industrial restructuring and industrial policies: Reflection after the shortage economy (in Chinese). *Review of Economic Research (Jing Ji Can Kao Yan Jiu), Z1*(1), 16–26.

Jurgens, U., & Krzywdzinski, M. (2009). Changing east-west division of labour in the European automotive industry. *European Urban and Regional Studies, 16*(1), 27–42. https://doi.org/10.1177/0969776408098931.

Killing, P (1982). How to make a global joint venture work. *Harvard Business Review, 24*(3), 120–127.

Kim, L. (1998). Crisis construction and organizational learning: Capability building in catching-up at Hyundai motor. *Organization Science, 9*(4), 506–521. https://doi.org/10.1287/orsc.9.4.506.

Kotabe, M., Martin, X., & Domoto, H. (2003). Gaining from vertical partnerships: Knowledge transfer, relationship duration, and supplier performance improvement in the US and Japanese automotive industries. *Strategic Management Journal, 24*(4), 293–316. https://doi.org/10.1002/smj.297.

Lecraw, D. (1984). Bargaining power, ownership, and profitability of transnational corporations in developing countries. *Journal of International Business Studies, 15*(1), 27–43.

Li, J. T., & Zhu, M. H. (2008). Guangzhou automobile industry development report (in Chinese). In *Guangzhou Blueprint*. Guangzhou: Social Science Literature Press.

Li, J. T., & Zhu, M. H. (2010). Guangzhou automobile industry development report (in Chinese). In *Guangzhou blueprint*. Guangzhou: Social Science Literature Press.

Liang, Q., Zhang, G., Gui., & Zhang, C., Ye. (2010). *From agricultural to industrialized civilization—Automobile industrial cluster in Huadu*. Research Series on Guangdong Industrial Specialized Towns during the 30 year Opening Reform (Vol. 2). Guangzhou: Guangdong People Press.

Lin, G. C. S. (1999). State policy and spatial restructuring in post-reform China, 1978–95. *International Journal of Urban and Regional Research, 23*(4), 670–695.

Liu, R. W., & Deng, M. (2003). *Fifty years of China automobile industry (1953–2003)*. Shanghai: Shanghai Huabao Press.

Liu, W. D., & Dicken, P. (2006). Transnational corporations and 'obligated embeddedness': Foreign direct investment in China's automobile industry. *Environment and Planning A, 38*(1), 1229–1247. https://doi.org/10.1068/a37206.

Liu, W. D., & Yeung, H. W. C. (2008). China's dynamic industrial sector: The automobile industry. *Eurasian Geography and Economics, 49*(5), 523–548. https://doi.org/10.2747/1539-7216.49.5.523.

Lu, F., & Feng, D. K. (2005). *Policy selection for developing domestic auto mobile industry with proprietary intellectual property rights (in Chinese)*. Beijing: Peking University Press.

Lung, Y., Van Tulder, R., & Carillo, J. (Eds.). (2004). *Cars, carriers of regionalism?*. New York: Palgrave Macmillan.

NDRCSC. (1994). *Chinese automobile industry policy*. Beijing: The National Development and Reform Commission of State Council.

NDRCSC. (2004). *Chinese automobile industry development policy*. Beijing: the National Development and Reform Commission of State Council.

NDRCSC. (2008). *Chinese automobile industry development policy*. Beijing: The National Development and Reform Commission of State Council.

Pack, H., & Saggi, K. (2006). Is there a case for industrial policy? A critical survey. *World Bank Research Observer, 21*(2), 267–297.

Pavlínek, P. (2003). Transformation of the Czech automotive components industry through foreign direct investment. *Eurasian Geography and Economics, 44*(3), 184–209.

Schmitz, H. (2004). *Local enterprises in the global economy*. UK: Edward Elgar.

Schmitz, H. (2007). Reducing complexity in the industrial policy debate. *Development Policy Review, 25*(4), 417–428.

Sit, V. F. S., & Liu, W. (2000). Restructuring and spatial change of China's auto industry under institutional reform and globalization. *Annals of the Association of American Geographers, 90*(4), 653–673.

Sturgeon, T., & Biesebroeck, J. V. (2011). Global value chains in the automotive industry: an enhanced role for developing countries? *International Journal of Technological Learning, Innovation and Development, 4*(1/2/3), 118–205.

Sturgeon, T., & Florida, R. (2004). Globalization, deverticalization, and employment in the motor vehicle industry. In M. Kenny & R. Florida (Eds.), *Locating global advantage; industry dynamics in a globalizing economy*. Palo Alto, CA: Stanford University Press.

Sturgeon, T., & Lester, R. (2004). The new global supply-base: New challenges for local suppliers in East Asia. In S. Yusuf, M. A. Altaf, & K. Nabeshima (Eds.), *Global production networking and technological change in East Asia* (pp. 35–88). Washington, D.C.: The World Bank/Oxford University Press.

Sturgeon, T., Memodovic, O., Biesebroeck, J. V., & Gereffi, G. (2009). Globalisation of the automotive industry: Main features and trends. *International Journal of Technological Learning, Trade and Development, 2*(1), 7–24.

Sturgeon, T., Van Biesebroeck, J., & Gereffi, G. (2008). Value chains, networks and clusters: reframing the global automotive industry. *Journal of Economic Geography, 8*(3), 297–321. https://doi.org/10.1093/jeg/lbn007.

Wang, H. (2003). Policy reforms and foreign direct investment: The case of the chinese automobile industry. *Journal of Economics and Business, 4*(1), 287–314.

Chapter 8
The Geographies of Industrial Upgrading

To many developing regions, export-oriented industrialization has become a well-known strategy for promoting industrial growth. But whether local firms in these regions can catch up with TNCs is still in question. What is the scope for local strategies so that a latecomer region can be upgraded and improve its competitiveness? This book has probed into industrial changes and dynamics in the PRD from three different industries to look for the answer. This final chapter summarizes the main findings in the beginning and then articulates key contributions which response to the GVC/GPN literature and development studies, respectively.

8.1 How Strategic Coupling Influences Industrial Upgrading

The central focus of this book is how strategic coupling between latecomer regions and the global economy affects local industrial upgrading. There is a theoretical gap in the contemporary literature of GVC and regional development in explaining industrial upgrading in the PRD. This gap can be reflected by two critical questions: how do different ways of strategic coupling between local firms in the PRD and foreign firms in GPNs affect local upgrading? What do institutional and spatial conditions matter during the process of local upgrading?

In order to fill in the theoretical gap, this book has conceptualized the relational features of industrial upgrading and developed a fourfold typology of strategic coupling as an explanatory variable to the dynamic outcomes of local upgrading. It includes *captive, cooperative, reciprocal,* and *absorptive* coupling, referring to different patterns of the global integration of the PRD. The formation of strategic coupling is contingent on knowledge gaps and power relations between local firms and foreign firms. Local firms are critical actors in this nexus of firm–state–territory relations. They take advantage of institutional and spatial contexts by mobilizing various resources (assets) embedded in those contexts. In doing so, they manage to leverage

© Springer Nature Singapore Pte Ltd. 2020
Y. Liu, *Local Dynamics of Industrial Upgrading*, Economic Geography,
https://doi.org/10.1007/978-981-15-4297-8_8

the governance power of foreign firms and implement upgrading without harming the partnership of coupling.

Having addressed the research questions and conceptualization in Chaps. 2 and 3, this book has examined the achievement of industrial upgrading and the evolution of strategic coupling in the PRD from 1978 to 2010. Table 8.1 summarizes the main findings of this study at a regional level (Chap. 4). Table 8.2 summarizes the variety of coupling and its consequences to upgrading in three industries (Chaps. 5, 6, and 7). The overall findings exemplify the causal relationship between strategic coupling and the dynamics of upgrading.

The post-reform industrial development in the PRD showed that the upgrading trajectory of the PRD was not explained by the developmental state literature, because a developmental state did not come to exist. Instead, the region was merely mediated by China's central government under the strategies of market liberalization and export-oriented industrialization (Chap. 4). After three decades of rapid industrial

Table 8.1 Characteristics of industrial upgrading in the PRD: a summary (author's fieldwork)

Category	Features and main findings
Before 1978	• Agricultural backwater • Limited industrial base
Formation of captive coupling in the 1980s	• Export-oriented industrialization • Prevalence of export-processing enterprises • Liberalization of institutional environment • Captive to Hong Kong firms
Evolution of captive coupling during the 1990s and 2000s	• Articulating into global markets and directly trading with developed economies • Reducing dependency on Hong Kong • Reducing dependency on export-process trades • Disintegration of the front-shop-back-factory model • Rapid catching up of local private firms
Regional upgrading	• From component processing into full-package manufacturing/OEM • From a truncated processing base to a leading global manufacturing center supported by thousands of firms which form regional supply networks • Intensive upgrading in product ranges • Significant improvement in manufacturing capabilities, production efficiency, and international competitiveness • Regional sectoral upgrading: moving into more value-added sectors • The rise of the automotive industry
Limitations of regional upgrading	• FIEs made up major contributions to the regional prosperity • FIEs have been playing a dominant role in both value creation and distribution • SOEs had the best efficiency, but totally lost influence in the regional economy • About 50% of foreign trades were still export-processing trades
Changing institutional and spatial conditions	• Local: increasing indigenous capabilities and inter-firm cooperation • Regional: growing body of regional supply networks and associational economies • National: the emergence of huge domestic markets • Global: increasing competitive dynamics in global production networks

Table 8.2 Variety of strategic coupling and the dynamics of local upgrading: a summary (author's fieldwork)

Industries	• Features and mechanisms	Local strategies
Captive coupling in the electronics industry	• Upgrading from a truncated processing base into a global manufacturing and assemble center • Evident product and process upgrading, while functional upgrading was limited • High asymmetrical power relations with certain synergy • Absent of strong state supports and less significant associational economies • Intensive localization of FIEs • FIE dominated industrial clusters/parks/districts • Local firms upgraded through being captive to FIEs	• Synthesizing the assets of domestic markets and supply networks: the case of Shunde • Identifying opportunities in GPNs: the case of CZC • Deepening captive coupling with more synergy: the case of Jingtuo
Cooperative coupling in the apparel industry	• Significant functional upgrading • Evident product and process upgrading • Upgrading into a global manufacturing hub and a domestic design and fashion center • Moderate power relations with various mutual interests • Absent of state supports • Helpful associational economies • Increasing outsourcing of foreign firms • Local firms took over the dominant role of FIEs	• Synthesizing domestic and global markets • Constructing local supply networks, embedded into regional learning platforms • Based on proactive local states and wholesale economies: the case of Humen • Based on ethnic networks and local entrepreneurship: the case of Xintang
Reciprocal coupling in the automotive industry	• Significant product and process upgrading • Evident functional upgrading • A growing-up domestic auto assembling center • Strong state intervention and proactive regional governments: exchanging markets with technologies • Joint ventures played a dominant role • Balanced power relations enhanced the reciprocity in the partnership	• Maintaining the balance of power relations and lowering tension within the joint ventures: the case of Guangqi-Honda • Integrated innovation as a corner-cut strategy: the case of GAC • Being quick followers: local suppliers

growth, the PRD achieved substantial upgrading in terms of corporate performance, international competitiveness, regional industrial structure, and functional improvement. The PRD has transformed from a truncated processing base into one of the leading global manufacturing centers composed of a large number of competitive firms located in dozens of industrial clusters/districts/parks (see Figs. 5.2, 6.6 and 7.3).

Although some studies have praised the accomplishments of industrial growth in the PRD (Enright et al. 2005; Yeh et al. 2006; Yu and Zhang 2009), the achievement of local upgrading should not be overstated. FIEs were still playing a dominant role in the output of IVA and exports throughout the past three decades, particularly in the electronics industry (Chap. 5). In a word, local upgrading was not as significant as regional upgrading (see Table 8.1).

The initial upgrading of the PRD was led by the pattern of captive coupling in which rapid product and process upgrading was realized by foreign investors (Chap. 4). Local firms were captive to foreign investors as low-end processors with littler power and space to achieve functional upgrading. This observation resonated with previous studies that advocated the important role of Hong Kong firms and the influence of market liberalization in the PRD (Xu and Li 1990; Yang and Sit 1995; Li 1997; Lin 1997; Sit and Yang 1997).

Further investigations have revealed that the captive coupling has been evolving since the 1990s (see Table 8.1). A large amount of EPEs was replaced b y HEs and the front-shop-back-factory model was disintegrated. Meanwhile, the PRD was directly articulated into global markets by trading with many developed countries. Patterns of foreign trades were changed in which the portion of ordinary trade increased from 20% in 1990 to near 50% in 2009. In statistical terms, the key drivers of the regional economy had delineated a divergent trajectory. While FIEs still played a dominant role, local private firms were catching up with them quickly, particularly in the apparel industry (Chap. 6). SOEs totally lost the influence at the regional scale, but highly consolidated in a few industries, such as the automotive industry which was strongly supported by the central government (Chap. 7). In the meantime, local (private) firms have already performed better than FIEs from Hong Kong and Taiwan after 2005. This critical finding articulates a different view in contrast to previous studies that keep emphasizing the powerful roles of Hong Kong and Taiwanese firms in the PRD (Yeh and Xu 2006; Liao and Chan 2009; Yang and Liao 2009). All these trends imply that the PRD has been moving away from captive coupling formed since the 1990s. What types of coupling is the PRD evolving into? This study has found that the situation varied among different industries (see Table 8.2).

In Chap. 5, the electronics industry was the most important industry in the PRD in terms of industrial output and export value. It was too difficult for local firms to bridge technology and market gaps with FIEs. Hence, the PRD's local firms tended to be further captive to FIEs as local suppliers (see the cases of Shijie town, Shillong town, and the industrial parks of Flextronics and Foxconn). Captive coupling was thus developed, persisted, and reinforced. FIEs kept dominating industrial clusters and localizing their vertically integrated production systems in the PRD. This captive coupling yielded evident industrial upgrading but local firms lagged behind

FIEs to a significant degree (Tables 5.3 and 8.2). Local firms grew up into small firms with higher efficiency under the shadow of FIEs. This observation agrees with the governance literature which asserts that local upgrading tends to be defined by FIEs (Humphrey and Schmitz 2000, 2002; Bair and Gereffi 2003). However, local upgrading strategies in the PRD's electronics industry were not as the GVC studies predict (e.g., launching joint action) or the development state literature has advocated (e.g., close firm–state relations and indigenous innovation). In contrast, local firms managed to leverage the control of FIEs by taking advantage of emerging regional assets and competitive dynamics in GPNs. In so doing, local firms increased their bargaining power, such as the home appliance firms in Shunde; or bypassed the control of foreign firms, such as CZC in Shenzhen; and also fostered more mutual interests with foreign firms to reduce the asymmetry of power relations, such as the cooperation between Jingtuo and Flextronics (Zhuhai). All these local strategies pointed to the potential formation of cooperative coupling in the future. The overall findings in the electronics industry exemplify the first proposition of this book that: the deeper local firms become captive to TNCs, the faster will upgrading be facilitated (Chap. 3).

While local firms are still captive to foreign firms in the electronics industry, Chap. 6 has articulated how cooperative coupling has been developed in the apparel industry. Due to lower technological entry barriers, local firms in the apparel industry caught up with FIEs and eventually took over the role of FIEs (see Figs. 6.3 and 6.4). During this process, local firms moved away from captive coupling and developed cooperative coupling with foreign firms. In cooperative coupling, the PRD's apparel industry has upgraded into a global manufacturing hub and a domestic design and a fashion center, rather than just a 'world factory' full of sweatshops and low-skilled labor (see Tables 6.1 and 8.2). In Chap. 6, the growing body of the domestic market, product-specific clusters, and regional supply networks are important assets in local upgrading. The combination of these institutional–spatial contexts enabled the PRD to become a powerful player at the lower end of the apparel GPNs.

The overall findings of Chap. 6 exemplify the second proposition of this book that: in the cooperative coupling, the more complementarity and mutual interests are developed, the higher is the potential of local upgrading (Chap. 3). This proposition could revise the prediction of the GVC literature which argues that local functional upgrading is less possible in the apparel industry (Gereffi 1999, 2002; Gereffi and Memedovic 2003; Frederick and Gereffi 2011). The cases of industrial clusters in Humen and Xintang illustrate that local firms can synthesize various assets to achieve functional upgrading. Instead of challenging the power of global buyers, these local firms can develop further cooperation with global buyers for co-venturing the China market (see Table 8.2).

Drawing upon the automotive industry, Chap. 7 has addressed the question that how reciprocal coupling can be developed and retained overtime. In the PRD, the growth of this industry was highly related to the joint ventures between SOEs and global automakers which were established based on the national strategy of 'exchanging domestic markets with foreign technologies.' This chapter has verified that the reciprocal coupling can be developed in four conditions: strong national interventions, strong global governance imperatives, a small market gap, and a large technological gap. Previous studies have failed to explain the formation and mechanism of reciprocal coupling because they overlook the influence from state institutions and regional assets where the industry was embedded (Humphrey and Memodovic 2003; Sturgeon et al. 2008; Sturgeon and Biesebroeck 2011). Examining two important joint ventures in the PRD's automotive industry, this book has argued that reciprocal coupling does not necessarily lead to local upgrading which is contingent on a balanced power relationship in the coupling.

The case of Guangzhou-Peugeot presented a negative example of reciprocal coupling in which upgrading is hindered due to mismatched interests, lacking of synergy, and unwelcome responsive strategies. In contrast, the case of Guangqi-Honda illustrated a positive example in which reciprocal coupling is sustainable with continuous synergy with a balance power relationship. Guangqi-Honda devoted a great deal of efforts in maintaining the balance of interplay in terms of equity structure, management participation, labor training, and the interests of co-development. Specific strategies were adopted for lowering tension within the joint venture. These efforts helped Guangqi-Honda and its supply networks achieve substantial upgrading in the 2000s (see Table 8.2). This comparative case analysis verifies the third proposition of this book: the more balanced are power relations in reciprocal coupling, the more synergy is there for upgrading.

To conclude, local upgrading in the PRD does not result from the pre-determined patterns of industrial governance or merely a matter of state power or lead firm power in defining the content of upgrading as well. Instead, local upgrading is led by the evolutionary patterns of strategic coupling which are subject to specific configurations of knowledge gaps and dynamic power relations. Overtime, changing institutional–spatial conditions serve as a critical factor which enables local firms to leverage the governance power of foreign firms in different ways.

In the specific case of the PRD, the imperatives of foreign firms have changed at the global scale. Foreign firms are not only interested to outsource/offshore sophisticated-manufacturing works to the PRD, but are also attracted by the booming China market. At the regional scale, the developmental strategies of regional governments are evolving. Some strategies have further liberalized institutional environment (e.g., electronics); some have turned to provide direct supports (e.g., automobile), while some have raised industrial barriers so as to stimulate local upgrading in a radical manner (e.g., apparel). At the local scale, the capabilities of local firms increase based on the indigenous efforts of learning by doing and knowledge absorption from their foreign partners. Local firms are leveraging the control of their partners by frequently deploying three strategies: diversifying knowledge channels; utilizing new regional assets (domestic assets and indigenous supply networks); and identifying industrial opportunities embedded in GPN competitive dynamics. These are changing multi-scalar forces that reshape the outcomes of upgrading in the PRD.

8.2 Theoretical and Empirical Contributions

The key contribution of this book is the synthesis of insights in both geographical and non-geographical studies for reinterpreting local upgrading in the PRD. Indeed, economic geographers have tackled the issue of upgrading in an implicit way. Some recent efforts of the GPN studies have led us to appreciate the engagement of multi-scalar forces in producing regional industrial growth (Coe et al. 2008a; Yeung 2009a). But these studies have yet to articulate the influence of strategic coupling on local upgrading. Moreover, the typology of strategic coupling per se remains fuzzy. Non-geographical studies have elaborated on the mechanisms of industrial upgrading. Nonetheless, these studies, particularly, the GVC literature, tend to narrow the analytical scope within the pre-determined patterns of industrial governance (Bair 2005; Gereffi et al. 2005; Staritz et al. 2011). Hence, the geography of upgrading in these studies is ambiguous. They have ignored the institutional and spatial contexts where causal mechanisms, power relations, and the strategies of upgrading are enacted.

The theoretical effort of this book is to make a dialogue between these two strands of literature. Specifically, this book has reconnected the missing links by answering a question: how strategic coupling affects local upgrading under changing institutional–spatial conditions. This mechanism leads to variegated geographies of industrial upgrading in the contemporary global economy.

8.2.1 A Geographical Theorization Beyond the GVC Approach

This book has incorporated state actors and institutional influences which are generally absent in the GVC studies into central analyses. This attempt offers a geographical interpretation of knowledge diffusion and asymmetrical power relations within value chains. This effort is more capable of explaining the current dynamics of upgrading.

Scholars in the GVC literature believe that upgrading is driven by the patterns of industrial governance because the patterns define the ways of knowledge diffusion along value chains (Bair 2005; Gereffi et al. 2005; Pietrobelli and Rabellotti 2011). The variety of governance patterns is subject to the codification of knowledge, the complexity of inter-firm transactions and the supply-based capabilities. Because lead firms possess advanced knowledge and define industrial parameters, they have dominant power over their suppliers (local firms). According to my analyses, this conceptual causality is over determinant. It seems that the ways of knowledge diffusion are fixed and the power of lead firms is essential. This book has questioned this view by asking why firms share knowledge and what would be other possibilities.

Basically, knowledge is shared by firms which possess and have the ability to control the knowledge on the basis of anticipated costs and benefits. In other words, firms share knowledge for rent, such as technological licensing, setting industrial standards, or investing in credit and trust in business networks. This rent can be returns of profits in formal or informal forms, direct or indirect ways (Allen et al. 1983; von Hippel 1988; Schrader 1991; Arora 1995; Appleyard 1996). Therefore, when taking institutional–spatial conditions into account, the essential view of knowledge diffusion should be revised. First, if we situate local upgrading in a GPN while not a value chain, the channels of knowledge diffusion are far more diverse than inter-firm linkages (Bunnell and Coe 2001; Trippl et al. 2009). Second, by possessing certain scarce resources, local firms or regional institutions may offer non-cost or non-profit returns for TNCs and attract them to share more knowledge (Storper 1997a; Scott and Storper 2003; Liu and Dicken 2006). Third, local firms may take advantage of multi-tasking by serving different functions within the same GPNs. This effort helps them identify more upgrading opportunities, particularly, in the competition between global lead firms in the top hierarchy of value chains (Lüthje 2004; Yeung 2009a). In Table 8, three empirical chapters have shown that local firms may leverage the governance power of foreign firms through increasing indigenous bargaining power, bypassing the power, or develop more synergy with their foreign partners. In doing so, this book partly offers a geographical interpretation of the value-chain governance.

8.2.2 Whither a Typology of Strategic Coupling for the GPN Framework?

Another key contribution made by this book is the theorization of the typology of strategic coupling. This effort resonates with Yeung (2005: 37)'s avocation of 'theorizing sufficiently the nature of relationality and its manifestation through power relations and actor-specific practice.' It would be able to transcend previous works in the 'relational turn' of economic geography which tends to be restricted in interpreting various themes of social-spatial relations. As a preliminary attempt, this book has conceptualized the typology and causal effects of strategic coupling. This attempt is not novel but a reconceptualization of the earlier works in the GPN literature (Coe et al. 2004; Yang 2009; Yang et al. 2009; Yeung 2009a). The previous threefold typology of strategic coupling is a bit fuzzy and internally incoherent (Chap. 3). It is insufficient to develop an analysis on power dynamics in that typology. Therefore, this book further develops the typology of strategic coupling as a supplement to the GPN literature.

According to the GPN literature, the formation of coupling is subject to the changing configuration of knowledge gaps and power relations. When local firms in a region manage to reduce knowledge gaps or to reconfigure power relations with their foreign partners, the pattern of coupling will evolve. This evolution leads to the dynamics outcome of upgrading. This conceptual work adds critical and important values to the analytical framework of the GPNs. By consolidating analytical focuses on knowledge gaps and power relations, the GPN approach would be able to avoid the problem critiqued by Sunley (2008) that being trapped by involving immense network relations and related factors. This typology also can incorporate the analyses of value-chain governance into the GPN framework. By analyzing the evolution of strategic coupling, we are able to interpret how inter-firm governance power can be reshaped in a nexus of firm–state–territory relations in which each party mobilizes possessed resources to leverage the power of the other party. In the case of the PRD, my empirical examinations have exemplified the existing variety of strategic coupling (see Table 8.2). These results as well as the case studies have proved that the fourfold typology of strategic coupling is a feasible framework for explaining upgrading in latecomer regions.

8.2.3 Strategies of Local Upgrading Beyond Development Studies

Toward development studies, this book offers many alternative strategies of local upgrading. As reviewed in Chap. 2, previous studies have provided four important strategies for latecomer economies to catch up: being a quick follower of TNCs, seeking supports from a developmental state, investing in indigenous innovation, and launching joint actions (Clark and Kim 1995; Hobday 1995; Schmitz 1999; Schmitz 2004; Giuliani et al. 2005). Apart from the first strategy which was affirmed in the electronics industry, the rest three strategies were not pertinent in the case of the PRD. In fact, these advocated strategies in development studies might become stereotypes in some degree.

The role of development states in East Asia has been changing with some rise and fall (Beeson 2004). In recent dynamics, East Asian lead firms tend to deepen their articulation in GPNs rather than seeking for helps from developmental states, such as the rise of Huawei in the PRD (Fan 2011). Field investigation of this study has notified that a developmental state was absent in the PRD. Conversely, the RPD continuously underwent market liberalization throughout three decades of development. Statistic evidence in Chap. 4 has reported that innovation in the PRD was happening but not significant. This finding resonates with Viotti (2003)'s view that many latecomer economies actually adopt a strategy of learning rather than innovation. The field observation has informed that local firms in the PRD did not launch substantial joint actions or collective moments against foreign firms. There were merely some local collective initiatives in establishing industrial associations and seeking fiscal subsidies from local authorities. These findings critically imply the insufficiency of development studies in explaining the PRD's local upgrading.

Drawing upon three industrial-specific chapters, this book has articulated three alternative strategies: diversifying knowledge channels at the local scale (e.g., Jingtuo and Conshing); utilizing emerging assets at the regional or national scales (e.g., Yishion and GAC); and taking advantage of competitive dynamics at the global scale (e.g., CZC). The first and third strategies depend on local entrepreneurship in identifying opportunities and also require local firms to articulate deeply into GPNs.

The second strategy is critical, because these assets only become available in recent development. For instance, the huge China market did not exist in most of firms in the 1980s. It was originally small in size and regionally fragmented. Though there was a large population, the household incomes of domestic consumers were limited in the earlier stage of development. Under the export-oriented strategy, EPEs did not have the right to access the domestic market. Similarly, regional supply networks were unavailable initially. The growth of these supply networks has been largely attributed to the localization efforts of FIEs since 1990s. In short, these assets are emerging and increasingly valuable.

8.3 Policy Implications

Looking forward, this book provides regional policy options for latecomer upgrading and regional development. The most significant policy implication would be the emphasis that policy makers should choose a right way of global integration—an applicable pattern of strategic coupling. Policy makers shall appreciate multi-scalar forces, synergy, and the dynamics of power relations in shaping regional industrial upgrading. In a latecomer region, policy makers shall pay sufficient attention in assessing the features of GPNs both firms and structures with which the region would like to couple. They need to understand the position within GPNs where the region may be situated, rather than select an industry they would like to promote. Meanwhile, policy makers should also critically assess their possessed regional assets and the strategic needs of TNCs within GPNs. Without this positioning work, regional policy makers would not be able to designs suitable policies and build up corresponding regional capabilities for TNCs.

Suggesting to concern with synergy is a critical value added of this book. Dunning (1991: 315) has rightly observed that 'the world is continually throwing up new challenges and openings for multinational companies; and because of this, countries that wish to attract such institutions into their midst will have to abide by the rules of the game and provide them with the right kind of investment climate.' Nonetheless, few state institutions explicitly integrate their actions designed to affect the costs and benefits of TNCs' relocation activities into their general economic policies. Many host countries have yet to pay sufficient efforts to identify the balance between the ownership-specific advantages of TNCs as perceived by the host countries and the locational advantages of host countries as perceived by the TNCs (Dunning 1998; Dunning and Lundan 2008). The GVC studies have strongly suggested local firms in developing countries to insert into global value chains as a quick strategy of catching up. Many practical toolkits have been summarized such as the triple-C policy framework,[1] building local innovation system or encouraging collective private initiatives (Humphrey and Schmitz 1996; Schmitz 2004; Humphrey and Schmitz 2008). These

---

[1] In the triple-C of local industrial policy framework, customer-oriented, collective and cumulative are proposed as key features of effective approaches for fostering local development.

suggestions by and large are similar to the ones proposed in the new regionalism literature in economic geography (Chap. 2). However, these suggestions lack of a bilateral thinking about how mutual interests between the regions and foreign firms can be matched in a better way. To this point, this book suggests policy makers to pay attention in mediating and fostering the 'right' regional assets for developing better synergy within the coupling. There is no panacea or universal solution to this problem. But bearing the question in mind would help regional policy makers develop a more feasible policy framework.

By proposing a typology of coupling, this book provides some pragmatic options for regional policy makers to consider the trajectory of upgrading. In the East Asian contexts, regions have developed strategic coupling with GPNs in different ways. A few regions have more or less developed absorptive coupling with GPNs. Local firms in those regions either directly couple with global lead firms, like Taipei–Hsinchu region; or have developed into domestic/international lead firms in their own right, such as Seoul Metropolitan Area. There are many other regions like the PRD in which the majority of local firms have yet to develop strong organizational and technological capacities, such as the Yangzi River Delta and the Bohai Rim region in China, Bangkok region in Thailand or the Hanoi–Mekong Delta in Vietnam. These regions are still under tremendous pressures on cost-based competitions from themselves or other continents. What can regional policy makers do to help local firms develop absorptive coupling in the future? The book provides two optional pathways which can be pursued simultaneously in different industries.

The first option is to develop cooperative coupling with GPNs by helping local firms reduce technological gaps with foreign firms. To achieve this goal, governmental agencies can heavily invest in innovation to improve indigenous competence; or facilitate the formation of local supply networks for strengthening integrated-manufacturing capabilities; or focus on building a regional production platform to reap the economies of scale. The second option is to pursue reciprocal coupling. For this purpose, polices can be designed to identify or nurture a specific type of regional asset, such as domestic markets, associational economies, or infrastructures. These efforts increase the bargaining power of local firms which have locational advantages by possessing the assets. Apart from these strategies, governmental agencies can also devote some general efforts, such as encouraging inter-firm cooperation (not a specific collective moment), building up a public learning platform, or simply helping local firms find suppliers and customers. These help can create more linkages for local firms to diversify their knowledge channels. Last but not the least, governmental agencies can foster local entrepreneurship by providing more institutional supports rather than allocating all the supports for foreign firms. By then, local firms would be more capable of synthesizing regional assets and identifying industrial opportunities in GPNs.

8.4 Research Agenda in the Future

What are the future researches issues of after identifying the dynamics of local upgrading? By anchoring multi-scalar forces as the central analysis, the first issue should be further addressed is the examination of influence from international industrial standards, the home-country specificity of foreign-invested firms and macro-regional economic arrangements. Considering these influences is an increasing tendency in the GPN studies (Coe et al. 2008b). Scholars have emphasized to incorporate international regulatory regimes or organizations, as well as labor, into the GPN framework so as to realize its analytical potential in geo-political economic analyses (Fichter et al. 2011; Glassman 2011; Rainnie et al. 2011). For instance, case studies of this book can be extended by examining the impacts of country origin among global lead firms. The field survey of this study has noticed some differences among Foxconn, Flextronics, and Honda in constructing local supply networks and enforcing management. But empirical data so far cannot sustain this study to detail this issue. This nuance would be a niche for comparing the distinctive features among USA, Taiwanese, and Japanese firms. It can critically contribute to the literature of internationalization of TNCs, transnationalizing entrepreneurship or national business systems, and so on (Whitley 2000; Dunning and Lundan 2008; Yeung 2009b).

Concerning with the issue of labor, social upgrading can be the second important topic for further investigation. Social upgrading is a process of improvement in the rights and entitlements of workers as social actors, and the enhancement of their employment quality (Sen 1999, 2000). This topic is a common ignorance of the contemporary GPN and GVC studies. So far, neither of these approaches has well-incorporated workers into the upgrading studies (Barrientos et al. 2010; Frederick and Pickles 2010). One of the fundamental issues is the interrelation between the economic upgrading of firms and the social upgrading of labor. Judging by the empirical observation of this study, it would be fair to claim that firm upgrading does not necessarily lead to social upgrading. Sometimes, it may make the working conditions worse, such as pushing tougher working schedules for the upgrading of production system. The tragedy of suicides in Foxconn (Shenzhen) in 2010 has demonstrated the urgent need of examining social upgrading alongside with economic upgrading. More interestingly, the realm of social upgrading can be extended to a regional scale or even wider to a country or society. Issues of this boarder sense of social upgrading can be living standards, wage levels, work conditions, economic rights, gender equality, economic security, welfare systems, and so on. Contemporary studies have been able to provide many insights for this topic, such as the literature in labor geography, corporate social responsibility, or ethical trading in value-chain studies (Herod 1997; Collins 2003; Milberg 2004; Hughes et al. 2007; Cattaneo et al. 2010; Lund-Thomsen and Nadvi 2010).

Finally, this study only represents a single developing region—the PRD. To what extent are the findings generalizable to other developing regions? Will the regional trajectories of upgrading follow the same pattern? Will the propositions of this book be replicable to both developing and developed regions? Indeed, it is necessary to extend the empirical sample of this study to encompass other developing regions in China, East Asia, South East Asia, and other continents if possible. Comparing these regions among different countries or the same country will be quite valuable. For example, a comparative analysis between the PRD and the Yangzi River Delta would be insightful for examining the impacts of different national strategies (see Tang and Tian 2002). More interestingly, we can analyze a single lead firm's upgrading trajectory among different regions, such as Honda's two joint ventures in China (Guangqi-Honda in Guangzhou and FAW-Honda in Wuhan). This kind of research would open up a line of critical questions related to the responses of lead firm in coupling with local firms in different power and institutional contexts, such as firm sizes, the extent of state supports, investment climate, locational advantages, supply networks, and so on.

Looking forward again, what will be fate of the PRD? Will rapid industrial growth continue in the 2010s? On the prospect of such a national economic frontier, there are two different thoughts: the optimists (Yeh et al. 2006) and the pessimists (Steinfeld 2010). The critical issue here rests in the question that: whether local firms manage to find a way of upgrading. This study has identified the overwhelming economic power of FIEs in the PRD, particularly, in the electronics industry. If PRD's institutional environment does not go unrest, the further localization of FIEs may be reinforced unfortunately. Although the advantage of low labor wage is reducing, there are other emerging advantages, such as well-built infrastructures, the growing body of supply networks, booming domestic markets, and friendly business environment. These advantages would keep attracting more FDI to the PRD. If state supports are still not provided, local firms are more likely to be further captive to FIEs. A few of them maybe successfully leapfrog into new lead firms due to new industrial opportunities, right business strategies, or excellent entrepreneurship. Hong Kong firms may play a positive role in this process by providing professional technological, financial, and logistics services (Yeh and Xu 2006). But this outcome is not guaranteed.

It is also likely that local firms will prevail in some sectors, like the apparel industry, if the regional-upgrading policy will not further disfavor it. Sustained by the booming domestic market, most of the local firms would have a chance to achieve functional upgrading. Absorptive coupling is quite possible to be developed in this industry. But a bottom neck may emerge when these local apparel firms try to move up from low- and middle-end markets to high-end markets. Local firms will definitely encounter new knowledge gaps in branding and marketing, especially when they enter global markets. Hence, they may go back to captive coupling again. Overall, there is nothing fundamentally wrong with this trajectory of upgrading in the apparel industry. The trickiest part may come from the automobile industry. Any major policy change at the national or provincial governments may lead to recoupling among the joint ventures. Unexpected outcomes are also possible as the SOEs have yet to develop strong indigenous capabilities. The corner-cut strategy did enable GAC to achieve functional upgrading. But this accomplishment was shallow after all.

In the final comment, I have no aim to assert that the PRD is going to be bright or doom. Instead, it insists on arguing that the ongoing dynamics should be understood in relation to changing multi-scalar forces and institutional–spatial conditions. Local firms indeed have certain autonomy and space to find a way to upgrade, but the opportunity is contingent on interactions between the region and the global economy in the future.

References

Allen, T. J., Hyman, D. B., & Pinckney, D. L. (1983). Transferring technology to the small manufacturing firm: A study of technology transfer in three countries. *Research Policy, 12*(4), 199–211.

Appleyard, M. M. (1996). How does knowledge flow? Interfirm patterns in the semiconductor industry. *Strategic Management Journal, 17*(2), 137–154.

Arora, A. (1995). Licensing tacit knowledge: Intellectual property rights and the market for know-how. *Economics of Innovation and New Technology, 4*, 41–59.

Bair, J. (2005). Global capitalism and commodity chains: Looking back, going forward. *Competition and Change, 9*(2), 153–180.

Bair, J., & Gereffi, G. (2003). Upgrading, uneven development, and jobs in the North American apparel industry. *Global Networks-a Journal of Transnational Affairs, 3*(2), 143–169.

Barrientos, S., Gereffi, G., & Rossi, A. (2010). Economic and social upgrading in global production networks: Developing a framework for analysis. *Capturing the gains: Economics and social upgrading in global production networks*. Manchester, UK: Working Paper 2010/1.

Beeson, M. (2004). The rise and fall (?van Diermen) of the developmental state: The vicissitudes and implications of East Asian interventionism. In L. Low (Block) (Ed.), *Developmental states: Relevancy, redundancy or reconfiguration?* (pp. 29–40). New York: Nova Science Publishers.

Bunnell, T. G., & Coe, N. M. (2001). Spaces and scales of innovation. *Progress in Human Geography, 25*, 569–589.

Cattaneo, O., Gereffi, G., & Staritz, C. (Eds.). (2010). *Global Value Chains in a Postcrisis World*. Washington, DC.: World Bank.

Clark, G. L., & Kim, W. B. (1995). *Asian NIEs and the Global Economy: Industrial restructuring and corporate strategy in the 1990s*. The Johns Hopkins University Press.

Coe, N. M., Dicken, P., & Hess, M. (2008a). Global production networks—debates and challenges. *Journal of Economic Geography, 8*(3), 267–269. https://doi.org/10.1093/jeg/lbn006.

Coe, N. M., Dicken, P., & Hess, M. (2008b). Global production networks: Realizing the potential. *Journal of Economic Geography, 8*(3), 271–295. https://doi.org/10.1093/jeg/lbn002.

Coe, N., Hess, M., Yeung, H. W.-C., Dicken, P., & Henderson, J. (2004). 'Globalizing' regional development: A global production networks perspective. *Transactions of the Institute of British Geographers, 29*(4), 468–484.

Collins, J. (2003). *Threads: Gender, labor, and power in the global apparel industry*. London: The University of Chicago Press.

Dunning, J. H. (1991). *Multinational-entreprises in less-developed-countries-some concluding remarks*. New York: St Martins Press Inc.

Dunning, J. H. (1998). Location and the multinational enterprise: A neglected factor? *Journal of International Business Studies, 29*, 45–66.

Dunning, J. H., & Lundan, S. M. (2008). *Multinational enterprises and the global economy* (2nd ed.). Cheltenham: Edward Elgar.

Enright, M. J., Scott, E. E., & Chang, K. M. (2005). *Regional powerhouse: The greater Pearl River Delta and the rise of China*. Singpore: Wiley.

Fan, P. (2011). Innovation, globalization, and catch-up of latecomers: Cases of Chinese telecom firms. *Environment and Planning A, 43*(4), 830–849.

Fichter, M., Helfen, M., & Sydow, J. (2011). Employment relations in global production networks: Initiating transfer of practices via union involvement. *Human Relations, 64*(4), 599–622. https://doi.org/10.1177/0018726710396245.

Frederick, S., & Gereffi, G. (2011). Upgrading and restructuring in the global apparel value chain: Why China and Asia are outperforming Mexico and Central America. *International Journal of Technological Learning, Innovation and Development, 4*(1/2/3), 67–95.

Frederick, M., & Pickles, J. (2010). Re-embedding governance: Global apparel value. *Capturing the gains: Economics and social upgrading in global production networks*. Manchester, UK: Working Paper 2010/1.

Gereffi, G. (1999). International trade and industrial upgrading in the apparel commodity chain. *Journal of International Economics, 48*, 37–70.

Gereffi, G. (2002, April). Outsourcing and changing patterns of international competition in the apparel commodity chain. Paper presented at the Responding to Globalization: Societes, Groups, and Individuals. Boulder, Colorado: Hotel Boulderado, pp. 4–7.

Gereffi, G., Humphrey, J., & Sturgeon, T. (2005). The governance of global value chains. *Review of International Political Economy, 12*, 78–104. https://doi.org/10.1080/09692290500049805.

Gereffi, G., & Memedovic, O. (2003). *The global apparel value chain: What prospects for upgrading by developing countries? Sectoral Studies Series*. United Nations Industrial Development Organization (UNIDO).

Giuliani, E., Pietrobelli, C., & Rabellotti, R. (2005). Upgrading in global value chains: Lessons from Latin American clusters. *World Development, 26*(2), 549–573. https://doi.org/10.1016/j.worlddev.2005.01.002.

Glassman, J. (2011). The geo-political economy of global production networks. *Geography Compass, 5*(4), 154–164. https://doi.org/10.1111/j.1749-8198.2011.00416.x.

Herod, A. (1997). From a geography of labor to a labor geography: Labor's spatial fix and the geography of capitalism. *Antipode, 29*, 1–31.

Hobday, M. (1995). East-Asian latecomer firms—learning the technology of electronics. *World Development, 23*, 1171–1193.

Hughes, A., Buttle, M., & Wrigley, N. (2007). Organisational geographies of corporate responsibility: A UK-US comparison of retailers' ethical trading initiatives. *Journal of Economic Geography, 7*(4), 491–513. https://doi.org/10.1093/jeg/lbm011.

Humphrey, J., & Memodovic, O. (2003). *The global automotive industry value chain: What prospects for upgrading by developing countries? Sectoral studies series* Vienna: United Nations Industrial Development Organization.

Humphrey, J., & Schmitz, H. (1996). The triple C approach to local industrial policy. *World Development, 24*(12), 1859–1877.

Humphrey, J., & Schmitz, H. (2000). Governance and upgrading: Linking industrial cluster and global value chain research. Brighton: IDS Working Paper, 120, Institute of Development Studies, University of Sussex.

Humphrey, J., & Schmitz, H. (2002). How does insertion in global value chains affect upgrading in industrial clusters? *Regional Studies, 36*, 1017–1027, https://doi.org/10.1080/0034340022000022198.

Humphrey, J., & Schmitz, H. (2008). Inter-firm relationships in global value chains: Trends in Chain governance and their policy implications. *International Journal of Technological Learning, Innovation, and Development, 1*(3), 258–282.

Li, L.-X. (1997). Characteristics of township and village enterprises in Pearl River Delta (in Chinese). *Tropical Geography, 17*, 16–21.

Liao, H., & Chan, R. (2009). Industrial relocation of Hong Kong manufacturing firms: Towards an expanding industrial space beyond the Pearl River Delta. *GeoJournal*, 1–17, https://doi.org/10.1007/s10708-009-9316-3.

Lin, G. C. S. (1997). *The red capitalism in South China: Growth and development of the Pearl River Delta*. Vancouver: UBC Press.

Liu, W. D., & Dicken, P. (2006). Transnational corporations and 'obligated embeddedness': Foreign direct investment in China's automobile industry. *Environment and Planning A, 38,* 1229–1247, https://doi.org/10.1068/a37206.

Lund-Thomsen, P., & Nadvi, K. (2010). Global value chains, local collective action and corporate social responsibility: A review of empirical evidence. *Business Strategy and the Environment, 19,* 1–13. https://doi.org/10.1002/bse.670.

Lüthje, B. (2004). *Global production network and industrial upgrading in China: The case of electronics contract manufacturing.*

Milberg, W. (Block). (2004). *Labor and the globalization of production: Causes and consequences of industrial upgrading.* New York: Palgrave Macmillan.

Pietrobelli, C., & Rabellotti, R. (2011). Global Value Chains Meet Innovation Systems: Are there learning opportunities for developing countries? *World Development, 39,* 1261–1269.

Rainnie, A., Herod, A., & McGrath-Champ, S. (2011). Review and positions: Global production networks and labour. *Competition & Change, 15*(2), 155–169.

Schmitz, H. (1999). Collective efficiency and increasing returns. *Cambridge Journal of Economics, 23*(4), 465–483.

Schmitz, H. (2004). *Local Enterprises in the global economy.* UK: Edward Elgar.

Schrader, S. (1991). Informal technology transfer between firms: Cooperation through information trading. *Research Policy, 20*(2), 153–170.

Scott, A. J., & Storper, M. (2003). Regions, globalization, development. *Regional Studies, 37*(6–7), 579–593. https://doi.org/10.1080/0034340032000108697.

Sen, A. (1999). *Development as freedom.* Oxford: Oxford University Press.

Sen, A. (2000). Work and rights. *International Labour Review, 139*(2), 119–128.

Sit, V. F.-S., & Yang, C. (1997). Foreign-investment-induced exo-urbanisation in the Pearl River Delta. *China. Urban Studies, 34*(4), 647–677.

Staritz, C., Gereffi, G., & Cattaneo, O. (2011). Shifting end market and upgrading prospects in global value chains: Editorial. *International Journal of Technological Learning, Innovation and Development, 4*(1/2/3), 1–13.

Steinfeld, E. S. (2010). *Playing our game: Why China's rise doesn't threaten the West.* New York: Oxford University Press.

Storper, M. (1997). Regional Economies as Relational Assets. In R. Lee & J. Wills (Eds.), *Society, place, economy: States of the art in economic geography* (pp. 248–257). London: Edward Arnold.

Sturgeon, T., & Biesebroeck, J. V. (2011). Global value chains in the automotive industry: An enhanced role for developing countries? *International Journal of Technological Learning, Innovation and Development, 4*(1/2/3), 118–205.

Sturgeon, T., Van Biesebroeck, J., & Gereffi, G. (2008). Value chains, networks and clusters: Reframing the global automotive industry. *Journal of Economic Geography, 8*(3), 297–321. https://doi.org/10.1093/jeg/lbn007.

Sunley, P. (2008). Relational economic geography: A partial understanding or a new paradigm? *Economic Geography, 84,* 1–26.

Tang, W.-J., & Tian, B. (2002). Comparison of Institutional Evolution between Pearl River Delta and Yangzi River Delta (in Chinese). *Urban Economy and Special Zone Economy, 8*(2), 55–58.

Trippl, M., Todtling, F., & Lengauer, L. (2009). Knowledge sourcing beyond Buzz and Pipelines: Evidence from the Vienna software sector. *Economic Geography, 85*(4), 443–463.

Viotti, E. B. (2003). National Learning Systems: A new approach on technological change in late industrializing economies and evidences from the cases of Brazil and South Korea. *Technological Forecasting and Social Change, 69,* 653–680.

von Hippel, E. (1988). *The sources of innovation.* New York: Oxford University Press.

Whitley, R. (2000). The institutional structuring of innovation strategies: Business systems, firm types and patterns of technical change in different market economies. *Organization Studies, 21*(5), 855–886.

Xu, X. Q., & Li, S. M. (1990). China's open door policy and urbanization in the Pearl River Delta region. *International Journal of Urban and Regional Research, 14,* 49–69.

Yang, C. (2009). Strategic coupling of regional development in global production networks: Redistribution of taiwanese personal computer investment from the Pearl River Delta to the Yangtze River Delta, China. *Regional Studies, 43*(3), 385–407.

Yang, Y.-R., Hsu, J.-Y., & Ching, C.-H. (2009). Revisiting the Silicon Island? The geographically varied 'strategic coupling' in the development of high-technology parks in Taiwan. *Regional Studies, 43*(3), 369–384.

Yang, C., & Liao, H. (2009). Backward linkages of cross-border production networks of Taiwanese PC investment in the Pearl River Delta, China. *Tijdschrift Voor Economische En Sociale Geografie, 101*(2), 199–217.

Yang, C , & Sit, V. F. S. (1995). Integration of socialist market economy with the world market: Foreign investment in the Pearl River Delta, China. *Asia Profile, 23*, 1–16.

Yeh, A. G. A., Sit, V. F. S., Chen, G., & Zhou, Y. (Eds.). (2006). *Developing a competitive Pearl River Delta in South China under one country-two systems*. Hong Kong: Hong Kong University Press, 2006.

Yeh, A. G. O., & Xu, J. (2006). Turning of the dragon head: Changing role of Hong Kong in the regional development of the Pearl River Delta. In A. G.-O. Yeh, V. F. S. Sit, G. Chen, & Y. Zhou (Eds.), *Developing a competitive Pearl River Delta: In South China under one country-two system*. Hong Kong: Hong Kong University Press.

Yeung, H. W.-C. (2009). Regional development and the competitive dynamics of global production networks: An East Asian perspective. *Regional Studies, 43*(3), 325–351.

Yeung, H. W.-C. (2005). Rethinking relational economic geography. *Transactions of the Institute of British Geographers, 30*, 37–51.

Yeung, H. W.-c. (2009). Transnationalizing entrepreneurship: A critical agenda for economic geography. *Progress in Human Geography*, 1–26.

Yu, H., & Zhang, Y. (2009). New Initiatives for industrial upgrading in the Pearl River Delta. *EAI Background Brief*, p. 16.

Appendix
Methods and Data

This appendix is about methods and data applied in the research for this book. The difficulty of measuring empirically industrial upgrading comes from its multiple features. It has quantitative nature, like improvement in productivity and efficiency in relation to product and process upgrading. It also involves qualitative change, such as functional and inter-sectoral upgrading. This book applies quantitative and qualitative methods that are associated with each other and infused in analyses. Apart from reviewing Chinese literature, statistical yearbooks and reports in the PRD are important sources of secondary data. The collected statistical reports include three sets:

1. General statistical yearbooks in multiple years at national, provincial, and urban levels from 1990 to 2015 and some statistical reports about data before 1990s.
2. Specific statistical yearbooks: Industrial statistic yearbooks and scientific statistic yearbooks in 2000, 2005, and 2009.
3. Guangdong Economic Census in 2004 and 2008. They are currently most precise firm-level survey data in China. The 2004 census was provided by my collaborator, while a brief version of 2008 census was purchased from a local database company.

Building on insights in the previous studies, I used various indicators to measure industrial upgrading at a regional level on the basis of industrial value added. Industrial value added equals the difference between an industry's gross output (consisting of sales or receipts and other operating income, commodity taxes, and inventory change) and the cost of its intermediate inputs (including energy, raw materials, semi-finished goods, and services that are purchased from all sources). This indicator reflects the extent of value creation and captures more precisely than total industrial outputs.

Besides statistical reports, various urban planning reports were also collected (see Table A.1). These reports provide many firm-level economic data in different cities, towns, and industrial clusters, which support my elaborations on the pattern of strategic coupling throughout four empirical chapters. They also show the regional strategies and policies relevant to upgrading. Many representative firms presented in these reports were of top priority in my research interviews and visits.

© Springer Nature Singapore Pte Ltd. 2020
Y. Liu, *Local Dynamics of Industrial Upgrading*, Economic Geography,
https://doi.org/10.1007/978-981-15-4297-8

Table A.1 Referenced urban planning reports

In English	In Chinese
• DRCGP, 2009, 'Research Report of the High-Tech Renewal of Traditional Industries in Guangdong Province', (Development and Reform Commission of Guangdong Province, Guangzhou)	• 《广东省传统产业高新技术改造研究》,2009, 广东省发改委编制
• DRCGP, 2009, 'Research on the Development of High-Tech Industries in Guangdong Province in a New Era', (Development and Reform Commission of Guangdong Province and Sun Yet-sen University, Guangzhou)	• 《新时期广东省高科技产业发展研究》,2009, 广东省发改委、中山大学编制
• NDRC, 2003, 'Planning of the Coordination and Development of Megalopolis in Pearl River Delta', (National Development and Reform Commission, Guangzhou)	• 《珠三角城镇群协调发展规划》,2003,国务院 发改委编制
• NDRC, 2008, 'The Outline of the Plan for the Reform and Development of the Pearl River Delta 2008–2020', (The National Development and Reform Commission)	• 《珠三角改革规划发展纲要 2008–2020》,2008, 国务院发改委编制
• DRBBDGS, 2005, 'Research of Lessons from Industrial Upgrading from Taiwan, Hong Kong and Singapore (in Chinese)', (Development and Reform Bureau of Baoan District Government of Shenzhen)	• 《台湾香港新加坡产业升级经验借鉴研究 》,2005,深圳市宝安区发改局编制
• CDPRC, 2007, 'Industrial Planning Section in Urban Master Plan of Shenzhen 2006–2020 (in Chinese)', (Shenzhen Division of China Development and Planning Research Center, Tsinghua University)	• 《深圳市总体规划 2006–2020(产业规划专题) 》,2007,清华大学中国城市发展规划研究中心 深圳分院编制
• GDDRC, 2004, 'Development Planning of Night Key Industries in Guangdong Province 2005–2010 (in Chinese)', (Guangdong Development and Reform Commission, Guangzhou)	• 《广东省九大产业发展规划 2005–2010》,2004, 广东省发改委编制
• GDEIC, 2010, 'Development of the Strategic New Industries of the Guangdong Twelve Five-Year Plan', (Guangdong Economic and Informatization Commission)	• 《广东省战略新兴产业"十二五"规划》,2010, 广东省经济与信息化委员会编制

Source Author's fieldwork

Table A.2 Industrial specificity in the PRD

	Apparel	Automotive	Electronics
Types	• Traditional	• Complex products	• Specialized products
Product	• Simple products	• Complex products	• Specialized products
Production networks	• Simple • Short • Globalized	• Complex • Sophisticated • Regionalized	• Sophisticated • Globalized
Governance	• Buyer-driven	• Producer-driven	• Modularization
In PRD	• Traditional • Less important	• Newly • More important	• Traditionally strong • Remaining important
Dominant firms	• Local firms	• State-owned firms	• Foreign firms
Governmental supports	• Weak	• Strong	• Moderate

Sources Author's fieldwork

In-depth Interviews

While census data present the general characteristics of industrial upgrading, this book deploys in-depth interviews for identifying the mechanism of local upgrading and more critically, for linking different empirical findings together in order to explain the evolution of strategic coupling and the outcomes of upgrading. Three key industries (the automotive, electronics, and apparel industries) were selected to represent a variety of industrial specificity in terms of industrial governance and production organization (see Table A.2). These three industries have been playing a representative role in the transformation and upgrading of regional industrial structures. But, they went through different trajectories of industrial upgrading, respectively.

In-depth interviews constituted the main part of the fieldwork. They were conducted from February to September in 2010 during which site research and participation observation were accompanied. Informants were selected based on a non-probability sampling with two principles: (1) The sample enterprises were involved in upgrading activities or events no matter they failed or succeeded; (2) the sample enterprises were representative and not reflecting an *ad hoc* case. Ultimately, 110 interviews were accomplished in the field with a satisfactory sample pool (see Table A.3). Corporate informants made up the majority and senior-level informants accounted for a major share. About one-third of all informants came from governmental agencies and associations.

Table A.4 shows the profile of informants from another angle. Among corporate informants, 77 of them are manufactures, and 6 of them are from professional service providers and traders. The majority of manufactures are composed by three targeted industries. The informants are representative according to their positions. Table A.5 shows the economic profile of corporate informants. Among 83 interviewed companies, ten of them are top 50 companies in Guangdong Province in 2009 in terms of total industrial output. About 20% companies had a value of industrial output over

Table A.3 Types of informants and positions

Types of informants	Number	Percentage in total (%)
Corporate	83	75
Owner	9	8
Chairman	3	3
General manager	10	9
President	1	1
Vice president	14	13
Director	18	16
Manager	14	13
Section manager	11	10
Officer	3	3
Organization	27	25
Chairman	1	1
Chief party deputy	2	2
Vice mayor	1	1
Division deputy	3	3
Director	8	7
Officer	12	11
Total	**110**	**100**

Source Author's fieldwork

Table A.4 Industrial structure of informants

Types of informants	Number	Percentage in total (%)
Manufacturing	77	70
Apparel	21	19
Electronics	34	31
Automotive	16	15
Chemical	2	2
Ceramics	2	2
Steel	2	2
Other	33	30
Industrial association	11	10
Gov. agency	10	9
Research institute	6	5
Service company	4	4
Trader	2	2
Total	**110**	**100**

Source Author's fieldwork

Table A.5 Economic profile of corporate informants

Items	Number of enterprises	Percentage in total (%)
Decade established		
1980s	39	47
1990s	27	33
2000s	17	20
Start-up investment (million yuan)		
<1	10	12
1–5	27	33
5–10	23	28
>10	23	28
Revenue scale (in 2009, million yuan)		
<5	5	6
5–50	22	27
50–500	40	48
500–50,000	12	14
>50,000	4	5
Employment in 2010 (person)		
<100	10	12
100–1000	28	34
1,000–5,000	24	29
5,000–10,000	12	14
>10,000	9	11
Ownership types		
SOE	5	6
FIE	24	29
PE	54	65
Total	**83**	**100**

Source Author's fieldwork

500 million *yuan* in 2009. The total industrial output of the four largest interviewed companies was 363 billion *yuan* which accounted for 6% of the PRD's output value in 2009.

Questionnaire Survey

Only manufacturers were involved in the survey. The informants were asked to evaluate the progress of various types of upgrading of their companies and some

Table A.6 Sample profile of questionnaire survey

Industries	Number	Percentage in total (%)
Electronics	31	45
Apparel	20	29
Automotive	14	22
Steel	2	3
Ceramics	1	1
Chemical	1	1
Total	**69**	**100**

Source Author's fieldwork

influential factors during the process of upgrading. A pilot test was conducted with eight corporate informants and three professional researchers in March 2010. Two revisions were made accordingly: (1) The number of questions was reduced from 50 to 30; (2) the scale of value was reduced from 0–5 to 0–3.

The overall outcome of questionnaire survey was satisfactory. 77 sets of questionnaires were accepted by informants. About one-third of them were completed on the spot and the rest returned questionnaires through express delivery, fax, or email.[1] All returned questionnaires were checked to see whether informants had completed them and whether the answers were consistent with the interviews. Incomplete or unclear questionnaires were followed up accordingly. When the informants became unavailable, the questionnaires were deemed as unqualified samples. This effort ensured an effective returned rate (89%) of which 69 questionnaires were qualified eventually for my empirical analysis (see Table A.6).

In-site and Participation Observation

In-site and participation observation yielded data on knowledge diffusion during the process of local upgrading in the PRD. The observation allowed me to move beyond taking information from interviews as a matter of fact, and more significantly, developed a ground-level feeling of the on-going mechanisms and outcomes. I mainly engaged in three types of observation.

First of all, throughout the whole fieldwork, I travelled extensively through different cities, towns, and industrial districts in order to conduct interviews. Observation along the way was thus conducted. I observed in an impressionistic manner the outcomes of regional upgrading. During the interviews, many corporate informants also offered me a site visit to their factories, R&D centers, and production lines. I cognitively perceived the flow of knowledge diffusion from receiving orders to

---

[1] Many of them asked me to email the questionnaire to them later on instead of completing it on the spot.

delivering goods. Particularly, I was able to observe some in-house training sections and workshops for understanding better product and process upgrading. In some special occasions, the informants personally showed me around their factories and showcased their achievements of various kinds of upgrading.

Second, I managed to participate in various events to appreciate the process of collective learning and knowledge sharing. Since 2000, Guangdong Apparel Industrial Association (GAIA) has hosted various fashion festivals, trade fairs, and design competitions within the PRD annually. Invited by the vice chairman of GAIA, I participated in two events as a special guest in 2010: (1) Guangdong College-Student Fashion Week in June; (2) Guangdong International Fashion Week in September. Within these events, I got to understand the alleged 'collective learning platform' in the PRD's apparel industry. The platform is composed of these fashion events and has been hosting designers, entrepreneurs, and buyers from domestic and global markets.

All these above efforts ensure my study to have sufficient first and second-hand data for depicting the local dynamics of industrial upgrading in the Pearl River Delta. The major theoretical purpose is to theorize the typology of coupling and reveal the general mechanism between coupling and industrial upgrading. This mechanism is still blur and rough which cannot be directly measured by quantitative-based models. Hence, this study is eventually heavily relied on qualitative data from interviews and collected reports for better presenting the storyline which was supported by statistical evidences.

Bibliography

Breschi, S., & Lissoni, F. (2001). Knowledge spillovers and local innovation systems: A critical survey. *Industrial and Corporate Change, 10*(4), 975–1005. https://doi.org/10.1093/icc/10.4.975.

Dicken, P. (1976). The multiplant business enterprise and geographical space: Some issues in the study of external control and regional development. [Reprint]. *Regional Studies, 10*, 401–412. https://doi.org/10.1080/0034300701232173.

How the U.S. Lost Out on iPhone Work. (2012, January 21, 2012). New York Times.

Dunn, K. (2010). "Doing" qualitative research in human geography. In I. Hay (Block), *Qualitative research methods in human geography* (pp. 99–137). Ontario: Oxford University Press.

Gereffi, G. (2008). *The new offshoring of jobs and global development (ILO social policy lectures)*. Geneva International Institute for Labor Studies and International Labor Organization.

Jiang, Y.-S. (2009). *Problems of exportation in China textile and apparel industries (in Chinese)*. Beijing: Intellectual Property Right Press.

Kong, L. (1998). Refocussing on qualitative methods: Problems and prospects for research in a specific Asian context. *Area, 30*, 79–82.

MIIT. (2009). Import and export trading of electronics and information industries in China. Beijing: Ministry of Industry and Information Technology of the People's Republic of China. Available at http://www.miit.gov.cn/n11293472/n11293832/n11293907/n11368223/13007075.html.

Minichiello, V., Aroni, R., Timewell, E., & Alexander, L. (1995). *In-depth interviewing: Principles, techniques, analysis* (2nd ed.). Melbourne: Longman Cheshire.

Ning, Y. M. (1998). Mechanisms and features of urbanization in China during the 1990s (in Chinese). *Journal of Geography, 53*(5), 52–73.

Pavlínek, P., & Zenka, J. (2010). Upgrading in the automotive industry: Firm-level evidence from Central Europe. *Journal of Economic Geography, 12*(2), 1–28. https://doi.org/10.1093/jeg/lbq023.

PDFGD. (2009). *Regulations of new special fund for SMEs in 2009* (Vol. 16). Guangzhou: Provincial Department of Finance. in Guangdong.

Polenske, K. R. (Block). (2007). *The economic geography of innovation*. New York: Cambridge University Press.

Sayer, A. (1997). Critical realism and the limits to critical social science. *Journal for the Theory of Social Behaviour, 27*(4), 473–488.

Sayer, A. (2000). Social foundations of postindustrial economies. *Progress in Human Geography, 24*(3), 495–496.

Scott, A. J. (2008). Patterns of development in the furniture industry of Thailand: Organization, location and trade. *Regional Studies, 41*(1), 17–38.

Sturgeon, T., & Gereffi, G. (2009). Measuring success in the global economy: International trade, industrial upgrading, and business function outsourcing in global value chains. *Transnational Corporations, 18*(2), 1–36.

© Springer Nature Singapore Pte Ltd. 2020
Y. Liu, *Local Dynamics of Industrial Upgrading*, Economic Geography,
https://doi.org/10.1007/978-981-15-4297-8

Wheeler, S. (2009). Regions, megaregions, and sustainability. *Regional Studies, 43*(1), 863–876.

Foxconn ranks as the top exporter again in Shenzhen. (2011, 6, Jan, 2011). *Shenzhen special zone daily, 6 Jan, 2011.*

Wu, F. L. (2007). Developing a competitive Pearl River Delta in south China under one country-two systems. *China Journal, 57,* 160–162.

Yeung, H. W.-C. (2003). Practicing new economic geographies: a methodological examination. *Annals of the Association of American Geographers, 93*(2), 442–462.

Yeung, H. W. C. (1997). Business networks and transnational corporations: A study of Hong Kong firms in the ASEAN region. *Economic Geography, 73*(1), 1–25.

Yeung, G. (2001). *Foreign investment and socio-economic development in China: The case of Dongguan.* Palgrave: Basingstoke.